Innovation Reinvented:
Six Games That Drive Growth

ROGER MILLER AND MARCEL CÔTÉ

Innovation Reinvented

Six Games That Drive Growth

UNIVERSITY OF TORONTO PRESS
Toronto Buffalo London

© University of Toronto Press 2012
Rotman-UTP Publishing
University of Toronto Press
Toronto Buffalo London
www.utppublishing.com
Printed in Canada

ISBN 978-1-4426-4429-8

Printed on acid-free, 100% post-consumer recycled paper with
vegetable-based inks.

Library and Archives Canada Cataloguing in Publication

Miller, Roger, 1938–
Innovation reinvented : six games that drive growth / Roger Miller
and Marcel Côté.

Includes bibliographical references and index.
ISBN 978-1-4426-4429-8

1. Technological innovations – Economic aspects.   2. Competition.
3. Economic development.   4. Success in business.   I. Côté, Marcel,
1942–   II. Title.

HC79.T4M54 2012   338'.064   C2012-900028-0

The University of Toronto Press acknowledges the financial assistance to
its publishing program of the Canada Council for the Arts and the Ontario
Arts Council.

 Canada Council Conseil des Arts
for the Arts   du Canada

 ONTARIO ARTS COUNCIL
CONSEIL DES ARTS DE L'ONTARIO

University of Toronto Press acknowledges the financial support for its
publishing activities of the Government of Canada through the Book
Publishing Industry Development Program (BPIDP).

Contents

Preface

We have been studying innovation together for most of our professional lives. Our first book together, more than 25 years ago, analyzed how the harnessing of a technological wave by entrepreneurs could greatly enrich the economic fabric of a region. At the time, our view of innovation was built around the promise of technological discoveries that had the potential to generate exciting new products and support the development of great companies. It was a view inspired by the success of the great entrepreneurs that gave rise to the computer age, and before them, to the Henry Fords of this world who ushered in new industrial eras.

Over the years, however, consulting with businesses on innovation led us to change our views significantly. Our grandiose first conception, we discovered, was wrong: we found innovation to be much more mundane and ubiquitous throughout the economy, a basic mode of competition aiming at product differentiation through improvements and at a lowering of costs.

We also found the classic paradigm on innovation, structured around a linear path from the laboratory to the market place, to be of little use in understanding actual innovations. What matters most are customer interactions and marketing. It is not that technology is not important in many innovations, but its availability is not the main driver of most innovations, nor a determining factor of whether innovation occurs or not. Even in the sectors that embed the most effervescent technologies, innovation is mostly driven by competitive considerations. Moreover, most of the technological progress occurs over long periods after inventors' initial breakthroughs. How quickly innovation happens, where and why it happens, and who benefits from it are the questions that concerned us when we set out to write this book.

It may appear somewhat excessive to claim, as the title does, that we are reinventing the understanding of innovation. We are not the first ones to argue that innovation is a multi-form phenomenon that is best understood as a competitive game. Indeed, a new paradigm is slowly emerging, recognizing innovation as a fundamental characteristic of an evolutionary economy. It bears mainly on improvements to existing products, their costs, and their business models, as they evolve throughout their life cycle. Sporadically, inventions give birth to new products, which embark on a life of continuous improvements driven by the competitive process of innovation, and as a result most innovations are incremental. Our contribution to the development of this paradigm is to show that this process is structured around several distinct patterns, which are determined by the business environment, specifically the maturity of the market, and by the architecture of products. Each of the six patterns we have identified, which we called games of innovation, relates to a particular set of innovative activities that define a competitive strategy to create value and outclass competitors in a particular setting.

The concept of distinct patterns of innovation has been around for many years. In 2000 one of us, Roger Miller, came up with the idea of undertaking a global survey of innovative businesses to seek such patterns by documenting firms' approaches to innovation. The rich data base that resulted allowed us to formalize this new perspective on innovation built around the concept of competitive games, which is the original contribution of this book.

These views were developed under the influence of various sources, which we acknowledge in our bibliography. A few of them stand out. Roger Miller began to work with the Industrial Research Institute in Arlington, Virginia, around 2000, and it is in workshops at the Institute that the idea of games of innovation was born. The MINE project would not have been successful without the cooperation of many individuals, in particular Professor Xavier Olleros of Université du Québec à Montréal, who co-wrote with Roger Miller several of the scientific papers that came out of the MINE study. Over the years, Marcel Côté has had numerous discussions with Peter Nicholson on the nature and role of innovation in advanced economies. Peter also provided insightful commentary on the manuscript of this book, and many of his ideas undeniably seep through its pages.

We also want to express our gratitude to Secor, the management consulting firm we founded in 1975 and which, over the years, allowed us to immerse ourselves in the challenges of so many great businesses, where we were able to observe innovation from up close. The unique Secor culture made it a great place to develop and test ideas. Without that experience, this book would not exist.

We are indebted to Bruce McDonald and Terry Teskey, who both carefully revised the manuscript and suggested numerous improvements. Finally, we would like to thank the people at the University of Toronto Press, and in particular our editor, Jennifer DiDomenico. It was a pleasure to work together, and we had the assurance that we were guided by experienced hands.

PART ONE

Introducing the Games

1 The Diversity of Innovation

There is an aura of mystery surrounding innovation, the creation of something of value that did not exist before. This book aims to peel away some of the mystery from this economic phenomenon. We will start by relating three stories of innovation, showing its scope and diverse forms in today's economy.

Developing a Cure for Cancer

Terry Chow is a shy, unassuming Montreal biochemist who spent his whole life working on a little-known enzyme, endo-exonuclease. He has become one of the world's authorities on the enzyme, which is found in all living cells. For more than a decade, he has been on a quest to develop a cure for cancer, based on a treatment in which endo-exonuclease plays a central role.

There are more than a thousand different types of enzymes in a human cell. Endo-exonuclease is found in the nucleus of the cell. It is involved in the repair of DNA molecules, which often break when they divide. Each of the 23 pairs of chromosomes in a cell is a DNA molecule, a long double helix with more than 10 billion rungs linking each strand, each rung made of one of four nucleobases. When a cell divides, each DNA molecule is replicated with the nucleobases strung along exactly in the same order as the original. As one can expect, the replication of a 10-billion-rung helix in the nucleus of a cell is not always a smooth process. The strands often break, and rungs do not always connect. About 500 enzymes in the nucleus of a cell are specifically tasked to repair these breaks through complex mechanisms that we are just starting to understand.

In the seventies, endo-exonuclease was discovered in one of the simplest cells that exists, E.*coli*, as an enzyme playing a role in DNA repair. Building on this discovery while doing his PhD thesis at McGill University, Terry Chow identified it in more complex cells, playing the same role. A few years later, he located it in human cells and became convinced that it was one of the most important DNA repair enzymes.

Moving from that discovery to imagining a cure for cancer appeared at the time a simple step. Cancer cells divide and divide as their reproductive process runs amok. Most anti-cancer treatments focus on blocking the reproductive process of cancer cells. Chemotherapy, the most common one, obstructs the division of the DNA molecules of a cancer cell by binding some of its rungs with a chemical agent. This creates all kind of breaks that are fatal to the cell.

This is when the repair mechanism springs into action. Enzymes such as endo-exonuclease catch the strayed rungs and strands, line them up and reconnect them. Terry Chow wondered whether the DNA repair could be slowed down by preventing the endo-exonuclease from doing its work, thus increasing the efficiency of chemotherapy.

He first had to find a molecule that would inhibit the endo-exonuclease action. After pursuing many leads over several years, in 1998 he identified a 60-year-old generic drug called pentamidine that was used in the treatment of tropical diseases and of AIDS, and that was found to be associated with a bacterium containing a high level of endo-exonuclease enzyme.

Terry tested the hypothesis and had a *Eureka!* moment, confirming that pentamidine effectively blocked the enzyme. In 1998 he started Oncozyme with a colleague of ours, raised seed capital from friends and friends of friends (including one of the authors), and started his quest to find a new treatment for cancer.

Fourteen years later, Oncozyme is still searching for answers. It first conducted extensive test-tube experiments to document, in vitro, the interactions of pentamidine with endo-exonuclease, and then undertook trials on mice that showed promising results. Two small clinical trials conducted 10 years after the business began confirmed those results.

Unfortunately, neither pharmaceutical companies nor their surrogates, the venture capitalists, have shown any interest, uninspired by a 60-year-old off-patent drug. As we write this, the company has raised additional funds from angels, hired an experienced president, and is conducting more clinical studies. Definite results are expected around 2015, 17 years after Terry Chow's *Eureka!* moment.

Cancer research is one of the most heavily funded of all research areas, attracting as much as $40 billion a year worldwide.[1] Thousands of researchers are trying to improve current treatments. Several Nobel prizes in medicine have been awarded to researchers for advancing our understanding of cancer. Oncozyme illustrates a modest contribution in that global quest. Since 1978 Terry Chow and his colleagues at Oncozyme have accumulated a significant amount of know-how about one potential solution. Although it started with a *Eureka!* moment, their journey will not yield an innovation until it succeeds in developing an effective anti-cancer drug. If it ever does, it would demonstrate that the journey from serendipity to substantial innovation can sometimes take an unexpected path.

The Blackberry Saga

Success came somewhat more easily to Mike Lazaridis, although he also followed a long road through the desert before marketing a successful innovation. Mike Lazaridis was a computer nerd who enrolled in the early 1980s in the electrical engineering program at the University of Waterloo, one of Canada's premier technological universities, about a hundred miles west of Toronto. To make ends meet, Lazaridis moonlighted with two classmates as software developers. In their senior year they landed a $500,000 consulting contract with General Motors to develop a visual display package, triggering the launch of their company, which they appropriately called Research in Motion. Lazaridis became so engrossed in the assignment that he dropped out of school two months before his final exams to devote himself full time to the work. Research in Motion, or RIM for short, became one of a score of software-oriented service companies in the Waterloo area. For a while, the company survived from contract to contract, but neither Lazaridis nor his partners were getting rich.

One contract that RIM received was from a fledging Toronto-based pager company that was entering into mobile telephony. That led RIM into technologies for the mobile transmission of data, an area that fascinated Mike Lazaridis and that would become a critical competitive advantage for RIM in the future. The efficient processing of wireless signals enabled RIM to accommodate the Internet on a mobile phone and set the company on the path to becoming a global technological powerhouse.

Lazaridis noticed the growing infatuation of Waterloo engineering students with e-mails, and got the idea of using paging digital technology to transmit e-mails wirelessly. Pagers had been around since the early eighties, as well, but were quickly overshadowed by mobile phones for transmitting wireless information.

In 1992 a 30-year-old management consultant named Jim Balsillie joined RIM, then a 10-employees shop. As co-CEOs, Balsillie handled the business side while Lazaridis handled the technology. Under their joint leadership, RIM formed partnerships with several established players in the mobile phone industry and soon became a key player in the emerging market of wireless data technology.

RIM launched its first product in 1997, a pager that sent mail instead of phone numbers. The first messaging product on the market, it became a big hit with companies such as IBM, whose salespeople spent a lot of their time on the road. Buoyed by this success, RIM went public, collecting $115 million from its IPO just as the Internet bubble started to inflate. The Blackberry was introduced two years later, basically as a souped-up version of RIM's initial product. It allowed access to the Internet but did not include a telephone. Distributed initially on an exclusive basis through Rogers in Canada and Bell South in the United States and eventually on a non-exclusive basis through numerous telcos (telephone companies), the Blackberry became RIM's core brand.

Following accepted industry standards, RIM reinvested about 40% of its sales equally in R&D and marketing, regularly launching improved versions of the Blackberry. By applying its financial muscle equally to these two activities, RIM emphasized a somewhat misunderstood principle of innovation: success with a new product takes as much marketing as R&D. Competitors jumped into the market, and they included some well-established phone manufacturers. But RIM maintained its leadership on the strength of its superior technical performance. Mike Lazaridis's infatuation with signal processing was paying off.

In 2002 RIM became the first device manufacturer to merge voice and messaging on a single handset, an integration that required, among other things, an 'always-on' feature that had eluded developers of mobile telephone technology. The smart phone was born.

Initially, smart phone usage was confined mostly to the business market, and RIM dominated it. But the consumer market then took off, a much bigger market where established phone makers such as Nokia already had strong franchises and took the lead, while RIM struggled.

In 2007 Apple entered the market with the iPhone, profoundly changing the market. Building on the success of the iPod, which dominated the market for portable music players, the iPhone was an instant hit. In a new twist, Apple also invited developers to create special Web applications for the iPhone. In less than a year, iPhone users could download any of 100,000 applications from Apple's Apps Store. Google and Microsoft, also strongly connected to the developer community, entered the smart phone market. Despite the launching of consumer-oriented devices such as the Storm, the Bold, and the Pearl, RIM failed to significantly penetrate the fast-growing consumer market, whereas its competitors had more success in crossing into the business market.

The smart phone market continues to transform itself at the same stunning pace. Since the 2010 launch of Apple's iPad, tablets crowd the smart phone market, mainly because they offer superior performance in navigating the Web. The convergence of the two markets, stimulated by smaller tablets and voice recognition technology, is inevitable.

The industry will eventually consolidate, as the pace of growth slows down. Google, Apple, Samsung, and maybe Nokia are likely to remain dominant players. And so will RIM in the smaller business segment. In 2011 its share of the global smart phone market that it created had shrunk to less than 15%. From its peak, RIM's market cap has now fallen by more than 80%. The company could be taken over by a giant, lured by its business market franchise, but it could also survive independently, much as Apple did in the personal computer market a decade ago.

RIM's trajectory has followed a radically different path than Terry Chow's and reveals a very different facet of innovation. While Terry Chow pursued his lonely quest for a cancer cure, RIM was swept up in a race that demanded one innovation after another. For over 15 years, RIM launched a continuous gusher of new models that exploited the latest trends in technology and tapped an ever-enlarging customer base. Although driven by smart phone manufacturers, the race also involved telcos and application developers, all of whom relied on a complex web of exclusive and semi-exclusive alliances to further their own interests. But most of these alliances lasted only as long as they worked to the mutual advantage of the partners involved. Expedience demanded agreements on standards, interfaces, price plans, joint marketing, and division of the pie. But there was no place for long-term loyalty.

Newcomers like RIM led the race initially, but the big guys from peripheral industries soon joined the fray. Technology drove the race in its initial stages, but sustained leadership in the game of smart phone innovation depended on product management, networks, and alliances, and the leaders relied more on marketers and wheelers-and-dealers than they did on the scientists. At RIM, Mike Lazaridis would not have succeeded without a management partner like Jim Balsillie.

RIM is now in a new game. Its competitors are known. The product features are identified. Further growth will depend more on value than on new features. The game that RIM will play from now on will increasingly be typical of a more mature market.

New and Improved Tide

Tide has been 'new and improved' for more than 60 years. Launched in 1947 as the first detergent to hit the market, it has dominated the laundry market since 1960. Its manufacturer, Procter & Gamble, was founded in 1837 by William Procter and James Gamble as a family-operated soap and candle company. Tide came 110 years later. It then took only 15 years for Tide and its imitators to displace real soap in laundry markets all over the world.

Inventing the first detergent was a breakthrough. Soap has been around since ancient Babylonians used it to wash fabric. As the washing machine came of age in the 1920s and 1930s, soap's impact on colors and the rings of dirt it left in washing machines became real annoyances. In the early 1930s P&G set up a small team of researchers to develop an alternative that would work better with the colored fabrics that were becoming increasingly popular. Licensing a German technology, the team investigated chemical products known as surface-active agents or surfactants, which consist of large molecules that react with dirt within clothing and stay suspended in water until they're rinsed away. But surfactants have to penetrate into the fabric to reach the dirt. To allow them to do so, the team got them to interact with another type of molecule called builders. Often without much support from their superiors, in 1947 the researchers finally came up with the working formula. It had taken them more than 15 years in the lab.

Tide was an instant success and inspired many imitators. One year after its launch, it was selling more than any other brand of soap. For the next 15 years, detergent brands competed in a race of rapid innovation and fast growth. By the early 1960s, soap had fallen by the wayside in the fabric-cleaning business and Tide was the clear market leader.

Tide has remained the leader over the next fifty years, holding 25 to 30% of its market year after year. Despite being continually assailed by fierce competition, it has retained more loyal customers than any other brand of detergent. Tide has also remained among the most profitable products that P&G manufactures, a remarkable achievement made possible by a continuous stream of innovations that allowed it to meet changing consumer expectations and earn the well-deserved 'New and Improved' accolade.

P&G achieved this through an extensive product development program, continually improving the product while expanding its reach to a wide range of specialized applications: Tide with enzymes, Tide with bleach, Tide Liquid, Tide Concentrate, Tide HE (high efficiency), Tide basic, Tide for sensitive skin, Tide with lavender, Tide cold water, briskets, packets, sticks, and so on. The innovations extended to the format and the packaging, leaving no whim in consumer preferences unexplored.[2] Other innovations were less apparent to the consumer but of great importance to P&G, being aimed at cost reductions and process improvements. These innovations have enabled P&G to create and preserve the economic value in Tide for more than half a century.

Superior brand management has kept Tide at the forefront of its industry, with a strategy that rests on innovation and has kept the brand fresh and alive for 65 years now. That long brand franchise allowed P&G to demand premium prices for Tide products and avoid the pitfalls that turn many mature products into undifferentiated commodities.

Multiple Patterns

Terry Chow, RIM, and Tide are associated with different patterns of innovation. In diversified corporations, several patterns can coexist at the same time, making the management of innovation a complex endeavor. For instance, global oil companies, which make up half of the list of the top 15 largest global corporations, typically pursue several and very different innovation strategies in parallel. The authors have studied one of them, Total S.A., a Paris-based oil company ranking 11th on the Fortune Global 500 list. Total pursues innovation strategies in three very different areas, each demanding specific skill sets and each adhering to particular rules.[3]

First, Total seeks to improve its exploration and extraction processes. Oil companies' moves into the frontiers of production, tapping unconventional sources of oil such as deep water wells and oil sands, have called for new methods to be developed. Total works closely with oil production specialists such as Schlumberger and Halliburton and large engineering firms such Bechtel in order to develop more efficient and safer methods while lowering costs. Surprisingly, Total does not record these expenditures as R&D in its financial statements, treating them as normal production expenditures. Nevertheless, it is that quest for more efficient and safer extraction that drives the performance of its activities in deep drilling and oil sands production.

The second strand of Total's innovation strategies (and those of oil companies in general) aims at reducing the environmental impact of its products and activities, as increasingly stringent environmental regulations must be met. This strategic thrust motivates R&D programs involving everything from the removal of unwanted metal particles in gasoline to the development of bio-fuels. These programs are conducted in research centers and are fully reflected in the company's financial statements.

The third strand of Total's innovation strategies is the development of new polymer products and applications, mostly in partnership with entrepreneurial firms. A typical project would target the development of a family of polymers that meet stringent heat-resistance criteria, to be used for instance in polymer-based kitchen tools. This strand combines R&D with sophisticated product design, and product success depends on market research, venture capital, and test marketing that lie far beyond the traditional domain of an oil company.

Managing these three stands of innovative strategies in the same organization has its own challenges. Each approach must abide by the same capital investment rules and cope with the same corporate culture. To be a successful innovator on each of them within the same organization is a demanding undertaking.

Innovation is Manageable

The great variety of approaches to innovation may make it seem like a complex process. But when specific situations are examined, as we have done above, innovation appears well defined and quite manageable. Terry Chow, Mike Lazaridis, and Tide's product managers at P&G who manage Tide do not see innovation as peering into a black box. Each of them pursued a specific business strategy that has an innovation component, aiming at bringing to market a product or service with more value than anything currently available. Each of them combined patient development work, not always in the lab, with the necessary marketing and business maneuvers required to deliver a superior solution to their targeted customers.

At P&G, the Tide team has a fairly good idea of the 'New and Improved' variations they will bring to market in the next two to three years. Research in Motion has a clear view of the technological trends and customer expectations that will drive its new product plans for the next two or three years. Oncozyme has a detailed development plan covering activities leading, hopefully, to product registration by 2015. Moreover, Terry Chow's twin discoveries – the critical role of the endo-exonuclease enzyme in repairing DNA and the effect of pentamidine in preventing it from doing its job – have involved mostly systematic and patient analytical work. He followed the traces of endo-exonuclease as a DNA repair agent from the *E. coli* molecule to the human cell, and then through a process of trial and error (that better-endowed pharmaceutical companies have automated) discovered a drug that would stop it from doing its repair work. No walk in the dark was involved.

Innovation follows several paths. But in the final analysis, it is all about methodically developing and marketing a superior solution to a challenging problem. An innovator identifies the problem and then develops a solution that addresses it. An innovator's biggest uncertainty is not whether his or her solution will work, but the extent of its competitive advantage and whether competitors, building on the innovator's insights, will rapidly come up with an even better solution, the way the iPhone eventually caught up to and surpassed the Blackberry.

The Innovator Perspective

This book is the capstone of the professional career of its two authors. We have each spent more than forty years trying to improve the understanding of innovation. We met in 1970 as freshly minted professors hired by the University of Sherbrooke in Quebec, Roger coming from Columbia University and Marcel from Carnegie Mellon University. In 1975 we co-founded a management consulting firm, Secor, now one of Canada's largest, and Marcel left academic life to manage it full time, while Roger continued in academia, conducting consultation on the side. Although Secor's activities extended to all aspects of business strategy, a large portion of our own consulting projects involved innovation: research centers attempting to commercialize in-house inventions, governments developing science and technology policies, start-ups developing commercialization strategies, large companies assessing their research centers, and the like. In the mid-1980s we co-wrote *Growing the Next Silicon Valley*, in which we tried to decipher the formula behind the success of that legendary place. Finally, as an 'angel' investor, Marcel got involved over the years with over 20 start-ups, practically all of them in technological areas.

Throughout that period, our view of innovation gradually evolved as we looked at it from the perspective of the innovators with whom we were working. That perspective generally starts with an idea about an existing product that poorly meets a need in the marketplace. 'I can do better than that,' says the innovator. He or she starts with an existing solution that does not work well, and then borrows ideas from the vast basin of accessible experiences and know-how, tinkering with various concepts, he or she develop a new product, first as a prototype, which is tested, then as the the first series, which is usually full of defects and is rapidly replaced by a second generation.

We slowly realized that this approach did not square well with the conventional view of innovation, which sees the process as much more of a linear path from the lab to the market. We do not deny that many innovations appear to follow that path, and our vignettes of Oncozyme, RIM, and Procter & Gamble also suggest so. But while a linear model may capture some of the characteristics of innovation, it does not adequately explain how and why innovation emerges in the first place. R&D is seldom the starting point of the process, with 'inventors' assembling together the right ingredients that make a new product that is then marketed. That view, which emphasizes that most innovations can be traced back to a lab, has serious and sometimes expensive consequences when applied to both business strategies and public policies. For instance, it justifies setting up expensive but weakly performing links between business and universities where a lot of R&D is conducted. The linear model of innovation suggests that universities could liberate their significant potential for innovation if more funding could reach the likes of Terry Chow.

In the real world, most innovations take a different path. Innovators get their idea from the marketplace, as they observe something that is not done well or is not done at all. As they embark on an innovative project, they constantly adjust to feedback from the market, making their path toward innovation often fuzzy and unpredictable. The marketplace, not the lab, is central in their project. Innovators imagine solutions, test them, and perfect them. The process is highly heuristic: innovators may repeatedly change their minds, pause, reflect, start over, consider several approaches, and finally settle on one.

They tend to focus their inquiries on areas with which they're familiar. As a software developer, Mike Lazaridis was drawn to the challenge of enabling e-mail–addicted Waterloo University students to send and receive text messages anytime, anywhere. He imagined the potential for a device that would let them do this without being tethering to a computer. He made the connection with the pager technology that he was working on. Based on that insight, the product emerged, and the business model to profit from it came quickly afterward.

This is a much different approach to innovation than the linear, black-box model. But the view, although revisionist, is not original. There is a broad movement among experts on innovation to set aside the linear model, and many of our own ideas came from contacts with other experts in the field. When some 10 years ago we were presented with the possibility of conducting a global survey of innovative firms, we decided to seize this opportunity to test our evolving views of innovation. This book is the result of that research, presenting our ideas on how innovation occurs, why it occurs, and how it can be stimulated.

The Structure of This Book

This book is based on a simple idea: market conditions, not R&D, shape innovations and drive innovators' strategies. The patterns of innovation reflect the conditions of the market where they occur. That simple insight led to two fundamental questions.

First, what triggers an innovator's decision to look for a new solution? If we could identify the factors that turn the prospect of a new solution into a driver of action, we could develop programs and strategies to stimulate innovation.

Second, what conditions determine an innovator's success? New solutions do not necessarily make business sense at the outset. Competitors can copy an invention. Could we identify the factors that make it easier to bring new solutions successfully to market?

This may sound theoretical, but it is not. It is eminently practical, as we will demonstrate. The book is divided into three parts. Part 1 (chapters 1–6) sets the stage. Chapter 1 has introduced our basic ideas. Chapter 2 concerns the limits of the conventional linear model of innovation and the developments that are triggering its reevaluation. Chapter 3 deals with the research project that led to this book. In chapters 4 to 6, we describe the six patterns of commercial innovation, which we call innovation games, and the two market condition dimensions that define them.

In Part 2 (chapters 7–14), we examine each of the six games in detail, using actual cases of successful innovators and investigating the factors that define their success. The first game gets two chapters. Chapter 14 deals with transitions from one game to another.

Part 3 presents our conclusions, which concern the real-world application of the games model to innovation. Chapter 15 focuses on business strategies and chapter 16 on public policies. The final chapter sets this new framework within the broader context of the role innovation plays in supporting economic growth.

We hope that this book will provide business managers and entrepreneurs with a better understanding of the environment in which they develop and apply their innovation strategies. We also hope it provides them with a firmer grasp of the rules by which they and their competitors will play their innovation games. Finally, we hope that this work will enable policy makers to better define the way in which government intervention – and money – can make a difference in encouraging innovation.

2 Peering into the Black Box

If you go to Amazon.com and type the word *innovation*, you'll find more than 150,000 results. The existence of such a huge number of books on this topic reflects the great hunger for information about innovation. But the number of books on this topic is also a sign that innovation is not well understood. In many ways, innovation is in fact a dark art whose secrets are contained in a black box. What do we really know about innovation? More important, what don't we know?

Joseph Schumpeter's Paradox

Innovation as a basic economic concept took shape more than 100 years ago with the publication of *The Theory of Economic Evolution*, in which Joseph Schumpeter, a 28-year-old Austrian professor, presented a framework to explain how modern economies emerged during the Industrial Revolution. Schumpeter argued that the industrial revolution was shaped by successive waves of radical innovations,[1] starting with major advances in textile machinery and followed by the steam engine, which spurred waves of industrial investments, first in England and then in continental Europe and North America around the beginning of the 19th century.

Inventions in steel-making then led to the construction of railroads and steel ships, easing long-distance transportation of merchandise and spreading the Industrial Revolution to secondary cities. Building on discoveries in chemistry and electricity, entrepreneurs then developed the chemical, petrochemical, and power industries. At the beginning of the 20th century, the automobile industry became an economic driver, after Henry Ford, one car manufacturer among hundreds at the time, revolutionized the assembly line in 1910.

But Schumpeter saw more than technological long waves. He emphasized the central role of entrepreneurs in this process, and showed how
entrepreneurs combine emerging know-how and technologies to deliver superior benefits to the marketplace. Any innovation disturbs the
economic status quo and supports the cycle of economic growth. The
most radical innovations spur complete new cycles. Schumpeter coined
the phrase 'creative destruction' to describe the impact of these radical
innovations.

This entrepreneur-led model of economic growth can be called the
Schumpeter I view of innovation. Later in his life, Schumpeter moved
to Harvard. The Great Depression profoundly affected him, leading
him to abandon the optimism that informed his earlier work. His view
on innovation evolved, contradicting some of his earlier views, particularly on the role of entrepreneurs.

By the 1930s the modern industrial structure that we know today,
built around large corporations, had emerged. In a very influential
book published in 1932, *The Modern Corporation and Private Property*,
Adolf Berle and Gardiner Means argued that large corporations were
now dominating most industrial economies. For instance, the US economy was dominated by the nation's largest 200 corporations. But more
importantly, each of those corporations was more or less controlled by
its senior management.[2]

Schumpeter shared that view, but he also argued that innovation
now occurred primarily within these large corporations. In fact, they
had to pursue innovation to maintain their dominance in the marketplace and to ensure their profitability and survival. As a result, they
had come to dominate the innovation process. Only these large firms
had the financial resources to identify market opportunities through
extensive market research. Only they could invest in R&D on the scale
required to capitalize on technological discoveries made in universities and government laboratories. And only they had the capacities to
transform these innovations into products and processes suitable for
mass consumption. Innovation had become the privileged domain of
large corporations. Against these Leviathans, small entrepreneurs had
little chance of success.[3]

This was Schumpeter II, and it would dominate economic thinking
for the next 50 years. It reached its apex of popularity in the late 1960s,
when John Kenneth Galbraith published *The New Industrial State*, a pae-
an to the perceived foresight of governments and large corporations
working hand in hand to generate the bounties of an affluent consumer
society.

The Conventional Model of Innovation

Schumpeter's new view on innovation gradually gelled into the familiar conventional model describing the journey from the laboratory to the marketplace. It provided the intellectual foundations for post–World War II government policies in North America and Europe that emphasized significant public investment in research conducted in large government laboratories, and whose results could be transmitted to large corporations, which with further R&D would transform those results into commercial products. Government funding of basic research was the fulcrum on which future economic growth rested.

Around the same time, economists started to highlight the important contribution of technological progress to economic growth. Advances in mathematical and econometric modeling in the post-war years led to the development of a field of research known as growth economics. Robert Solow, who was to receive a Nobel Prize in economics for his work in this field, in 1956 published a landmark paper in which he suggested that 'technical progress' was as important to economic growth as increases in capital and labor.[4]

Six years later, another influential economist, Edward Denison, published an econometric analysis of the sources of economic growth, which attributed more than one-third of the growth of the American economy to innovation arising from advances in technology and knowledge. Governments used Denison's study to bolster the case for national investment in higher education and in research and development.[5]

In this linear model of innovation that prevailed among economists and policy makers, basic research leads to applied research, then to product development supported by market research and, finally, to commercialization of new products and new processes. The model also became embedded in official statistical data. Among government agencies and the Organisation for Economic Co-operation and Development (OECD), R&D expenditures and patents became the two most frequently used indicators of a country's capacity to innovate. The model ultimately led to national systems of innovation, which were built on the premise that government policies could create the right set of factors and conditions to spur innovation and stimulate economic growth through technological progress.

Likewise, businesses also based their strategies on the linear model of innovation. The experience of large firms serving well-structured markets became the source of best practices. To maintain their dominant market position, these firms committed resources to R&D, and they built the necessary competencies to investigate emerging technologies and develop the next generation of products.[6]

This linear view of innovation, from the laboratory to the marketplace, rests on several implicit assumptions.

1 *Markets pre-exist and wait to be discovered.* Latent demand materializes when marketing research identifies customers' needs and appropriate solutions to these needs appear in the market. Businesses rely on their R&D laboratories to develop these solutions, harvesting the bounties of the latest technologies.

2 *Businesses must exert strategic control of product development.* R&D should be done in-house, in a highly strategic, fully controlled process. Products should be fully developed before they are released. Consequently, by the time the products hit the market, the innovation process is largely over. To minimize learning costs and facilitate their adoption, the complexity of new innovative products is largely hidden from users.

3 *A new market is built over time through a managed diffusion process.* With proper marketing, the life-cycle model – pioneers followed by early adopters, then mass acceptance, and finally maturity and decline – is a manageable process.

4 *The best products win.* Buyers base their choices on relative utility, and customers clearly identify desirable performance attributes. The winning products are selected on the basis of their merits.

5 *Intellectual property is important to capture value.* Strong patents allow innovators to carve out dominant market positions and build strong, profitable franchises.

6 *Innovation depends mostly on new technologies,* which businesses must fully master to be successful innovators. They should not only invest in R&D but also keep in touch with scientific developments in universities and public research centers.

By the 1970s, these assumptions reflected conventional wisdom among business leaders, policy makers, and academics. Route 128 around Boston became the symbol of the mastery of the process of innovation described by the Schumpeter II model: the numerous government and corporate laboratories that proliferated in the Boston area generated discoveries on which the large number of high-technology firms that sprang up along Route 128 capitalized. For over a decade, Route 128 became known throughout the world as a model for the development of high-technology clusters. It was the home of several early successes in the computer industry, such as Digital Equipment, Data General, Wang, Apollo, VisiCalc, and Lotus. These success stories attested to the effectiveness of an economic growth strategy based on innovation.

But Route 128's triumph was not to last. Of the six companies just mentioned, not one remained in operation by 1990. Like these companies that once exemplified the model, Schumpeter II was to lose its credibility as a model for innovation.

The Triumph of Entrepreneurs

On the other side of the continent, an alternative model emerged in Silicon Valley. Its seeds were sown in the sixties, when a constant flow of entrepreneurs into the San Francisco Bay area began developing a vast array of commercial applications for rapidly developing information and communication technologies. Like Boston, San Francisco was a center of scientific discovery. But on the West Coast, opportunities were identified not by large corporations but by entrepreneurs and their venture-capitalist backers. Lean and nimble, these used their first-mover advantage to build a new generation of businesses, very much along the lines of the entrepreneur-based view of Schumpeter I.

Silicon Valley came of age about 15 years after Route 128. For a while, the two models of technological innovation competed for predominance. But Silicon Valley pulled ahead, favored by two factors. First, an entrepreneurial spirit was strongly imbedded in the business culture of Silicon Valley, thanks to entrepreneurs such as Bill Hewlett and David Packard, who had acquired mythological status. Silicon Valley's technological pantheon also includes eight young engineers who quit Shockley Semiconductors, founded by the inventor of the transistor, to start Fairchild Semiconductors, and after a few years, to create such spin-offs as Intel and AMD, who are still dominating the computer chip market. While engineer-led defence contractors dominated Route 128, Silicon Valley inspired technically oriented youngsters to start their own companies, capitalizing on the amazing growth potential of the computer industry.

The other factor that propelled Silicon Valley ahead of Route 128 was venture capital, which ironically had been first developed in Boston in the mid-1950s. Silicon Valley transformed the concept by putting successful entrepreneurs at the helm of venture capital firms, giving these

firms a business acumen that was second to none. As a result, entrepreneurs found a much more fertile breeding ground for their firms
in Silicon Valley. The presence of these entrepreneurs at the top of the
venture capital firms was a major advantage for the region, which it has
kept up to today.

The entrepreneurial drive behind the success of Silicon Valley has
been the object of numerous studies, including one of ours.[7] A rich
cultural ecosystem supports entrepreneurial experimentation and the
creation of firms in high-growth sectors, generating a virtuous circle
as success breeds confidence.[8] Entrepreneurs continuously explore
the slightest potential opportunity provided by the evolving information and communication technology. Capitalizing on their first-mover
advantage, entrepreneurial start-ups grew into dominant players such
as Intel, Oracle, Apple, and Google.

Silicon Valley is unique. It has sustained generation after generation
of new businesses poised on the frontiers of high technology. But in
most advanced economies, a similar process of rejuvenation occurs in
areas of low technology. In the early 1980s David Birch, a professor at
MIT, analyzed Dun & Bradstreet files to see where jobs come from in
a particular region. Birch found that most jobs in any region could be
traced back to a small number of high-growth businesses led by entrepreneurs. These businesses, which he called 'gazelles,' derive their
growth from a variety of innovative advantages, some of them having
nothing to do with technology.[9] They simply excel in whatever they
do. Whether the business involves a new chain of restaurants, a bicycle
manufacturer, a security firm, or a garage door manufacturer, the entrepreneurs who start them are unencumbered by the past and eager to
innovate. They do things differently, and illustrate clearly that growth
is not necessarily a high-technology phenomenon, but it is usually an
entrepreneur-led one.

Large firms grow too, of course, but at a much more subdued rate.
They are mostly in mature markets, large enough to support their size
but with lower growth potential. Acquisitions become their major mode
of growth. Their number of employees is more or less stable, as productivity gains allow them to grow without increasing employment.

Disruptive Innovation: Combining Schumpeter I and II

In 1997 Clayton Christensen, a Harvard professor, re-addressed the
Schumpeter paradox. In his book *The Innovator's Dilemma*,[10] he observed

that most businesses innovate to keep up with their competitors and abreast with regular advances in knowledge. But from time to time, in any particular industry, these day-to-day improvements in the sustaining technologies become irrelevant. This occurs when a major innovation associated with a disruptive technology sweeps through the industry. Christensen defines 'technology' as the 'the process(es) by which an organization transforms labor, capital, material and information into products and services of greater value.[11] These game-changing technologies can hit hard any incumbents that fail to recognize them early enough. Incumbents that stick to their conventional, tried-and-true practices risk falling by the wayside, as the disruptive technology renders obsolete their older technologies, upsets the industrial order, and allows upstart entrants to carve themselves significant market shares.

But incumbents can survive. A key contribution of Christensen was the development of adaptive strategies for large firms that have to cope with disruptive innovations. Christensen highlighted the fact that most disruptive technologies first appear as low-performance (although lower cost) solutions promoted by second-tier firms looking for a Hail Mary pass. Incumbents dismiss them too rapidly, feeling secure with their own well-developed and well-optimized sustaining technologies Their inertia creates opportunities for maverick entrepreneurs who are not burdened by installed equipment, market share, and a blind allegiance to proven ways of doing things. Although under-funded and under-organized, entrepreneurs running on disruptive technologies can grab a significant portion of a market, often in low-end segments neglected by incumbents, and then shake out the usual bugs, improve the product, and eventually displace more established players in the mainstream market. A classic creative destruction cycle occurs.

Sympathizing with the incumbents, Christensen explored ways for them to survive these entrepreneurial attacks by capitalizing on their inherent advantages of scale and resources. He mentioned two critical considerations. First, incumbents must accurately read the potential of any new technology, and even hedge their bets. Second, they must learn to cannibalize their existing production systems, often an essential move in surviving such attacks.

Inertia is an incumbent's Achilles' heel. Large firms under attack need far more than well-established R&D capabilities. In sectors exposed to disruptive technologies, they need the insights and the will to embrace change before they can create a successful innovation strategy, which sometimes can entail difficult moves. In a way, Christensen's prescription for incumbents facing disruptive technology is to do away with their Schumpeter II model and embrace a Schumpeter I entrepreneurial approach.

Disruptive technologies can also provide opportunities to create new markets, Christensen points out, giving the personal computer as one example. They also give rise to new market segments, such as Honda's small motorcycle that squeezed its way between the big Harley-Davidson–type motorcycles and the smaller scooters, creating a new two-wheeler segment. Another example of the creation of a new market segment is the emergence of the Health Maintenance Organizations, commonly known as HMOs, in the health care market in the United States. Such disruptive technological innovations, giving rise to new markets and to new markets segments, can be even more disruptive than technologies that merely pressure incumbents within existing markets, as these new markets and new markets segments can eventually crowd out the older, more mature markets.

Radical and Incremental Innovations

While Christensen's work highlights the importance of disruptive technologies, its wide diffusion in the management literature has created confusion over the nature and prevalence of radical innovation, as the notion became assimilated with any innovation that has a big impact. But this is a tautological definition. The concept of radical innovation, which goes back to Schumpeter (who used the term 'basic innovation'), characterizes an innovation that generates a structural discontinuity. Unfortunately, the term 'radical innovation' is now given a much broader meaning in the literature.

Christensen always preferred the term 'disruptive technology', which he carefully defined.[12] We will also avoid the term 'radical innovation', not because it does not exist, but because it is difficult to circumscribe. In fact, there are only two basic categories of innovation that can pretend to the 'radical' mantle. The first comprises innovations that create new markets, with the market being defined by a new customer base that has to learn about the product. The second category, which is the focus of most of Christensen's work, comprises new technologies that disrupt existing markets, either through structural change in costs or by bringing new features that render current products obsolete. But in both cases, it becomes difficult to define where the radical innovation ceases and improvement on it starts.

In fact, most innovations are incremental, representing improvements in existing products or in their technologies. Most of the long-term impact innovations have on economic growth and social change comes about via the accumulation of incremental innovations.[13] Hence understanding incremental innovation is fundamental to unwrapping the black box.

Reality Checks and Contradictions

Let's go back to the six assumptions behind the conventional model to see how they fare in light of current research.

1. *Markets pre-exist and wait to be discovered.* On the contrary, new markets are built after products that address them are launched.

Most new markets are constructed through interactions between buyers and sellers and evolve in ways that are difficult to foresee at their birth. Customers often start to intervene at the prototype and beta stage, guiding an innovator toward their real needs. Markets materialize as customers learn to use the product and discover additional uses, which are integrated into newer generations of the product.[14] Collaboration between competitors is often useful to foster complementary products and enhances market growth.

Development of the marketplace of new products can be described as a journey, during which those products evolve, grow, and adapt to the choices of a growing base of users. The needs addressed change along with the capabilities of the technology, leading to a continuous flow of product generations.[15]

2. *Businesses exert total strategic control over their new products.* This assumption is increasingly false, as many new products are part of systems controlled by third parties.

The better mousetrap is the traditional symbol of an innovation, but is outdated. A better illustration is a new application attached to a software platform, and which is partly controlled by that platform. Benefits demanded by consumers are increasingly delivered by systems, combining platforms, modules, and networks, as opposed to the stand-alone 'better mousetrap' products. With such dependency on a host platform, a product can become obsolete if its complementary environment changes too drastically.[16]

We must then ask: what is a system? Our definition is simple: a system is an array of multiple and fairly autonomous components or modules that must be attached to a platform to deliver their benefits. The

Internet and its content form such a system. In the same vein, without a computer or a smart phone platform, software applications are modules of little use. Conversely, a platform is of little use without modules. End products are increasingly integrated into a platform. A car, for example, is a complex system made of hundreds of different components. Wal-Mart is a distribution system, which, through proper category management, makes a well-thought offer of up to 200,000 products available in markets where it is present.

In this context, innovation policies and strategies have to acknowledge the additional complexity brought by the systemic nature of many new products. No longer alone in his or her basement, the innovator operates within a system and must abide by rules defined by the system operators. Modules have to meet interface criteria. Credit for the ultimate benefit of an innovation must be shared rather than attributed solely to the innovation itself.[17] The innovator's compensation depends on his or her ability to work within this system. System operators face a comparable challenge: they must inspire innovators to create a sufficient number of modules or applications to establish themselves in the marketplace.

This mutual dependency is well illustrated by the emerging market for smart phone applications. Apple enjoys an enormous competitive advantage with its iPhone and iPad because of its established competence in working with developers. Its competitors have yet to match Apple's competencies in that area, a huge competitive drawback.

Strategic interdependence has become a necessary condition for success in many sectors. It requires new skills that neither basement innovators nor large corporations possess in abundance. Was the free-wheeling Silicon Valley better at developing such alliances than the straight-laced Route 128? Absolutely! The skills involved in coalition formation and business diplomacy turned out to be a key factor in Silicon Valley's predominance over Route 128.[18]

3. *A new market is built over time through a managed diffusion process.* Contrary to this assumption, new markets often emerge from chaotic and uneven growth.

The early diffusion of new products is hardly a managed process. On the one hand, the first generations of products tend to be incomplete, often barely functional prototypes. The first Apple II personal computer, for example, did not have a screen. Innovators lack feedback from the market to identify the critical functions and benefits that the market wants. Moreover, in creating systemic products such as a platform, innovators often seek to interest potential suppliers of the missing complementary elements. Launched in primitive forms, new products reach their performance potential at a later stage (although some never do).

On the other hand, social interactions among pioneering users build early demand. This early interactive buzz leads to either growth or decay. Decisions to adopt a new product or service depend heavily on choices made by previous adopters. Earlier products may enjoy a network advantage as they are adopted in larger numbers. But it is very difficult to predict at the time of the launch how a market will develop.

4. *The best products always win.* This is simply not true.

Most executives still believe that the best products win. The duel between VHS and Betamax to become the prevailing format in video recording destroyed that myth. Meritocratic selection matters less and less for new products in the information age that operate as part of bigger systems. In adopting these products, consumers follow a non-linear selection process that takes into account numerous factors such as the reputation of the host, the availability of complementary products, and the emergence of meta-choice ('I'll take the package'). Such selection criteria for systemic products can often lead to an explosive growth in demand or, alternatively, to a stalled process.[19] This environment also allows second-class solutions to become entrenched while more worthy options are rejected, as high switching costs and prior investments in learning lead to inertia.

The strength of the support network can play a major role, as the VHS victory over Betamax illustrated. JVC, the lead manufacturer in the VHS coalition, early in its duel with Betamax enlisted a powerful coalition of movie distributors to stand behind its standards. It was clear that on the technical merits, the recording technology of Sony's Betamax was superior. But JVC won the battle on its superior access to a pool of films. Sony couldn't compensate for that initial drawback. Right at the outset when the market was still in its infancy, there were more VHS products, allowing the coalition to build a larger customer base. That initiated a virtuous circle, allowing the VHS format to capture a larger share of new releases. Within a few years, Sony's Betamax was outclassed and slowly fell by the wayside.

5. *Intellectual property is important to capture value.* R&D is increasingly externalized and innovation is open, leading to weaker intellectual property protection.

In the traditional model of innovation, companies develop their new product in-house. As one German car executive told us, 'Who wants to tell customers that we don't design our cars and understand their needs?' The process is secret, keeping competition in the dark. But increasingly, this practice runs afoul of a basic business trend, the increasing specialization of firms. To be first on the market place with a feature, businesses more frequently partner with specialists for product development, and R&D activities are conducted as part of alliances, contracted out to partners that have lower cost capabilities.[20]

This has led to the development of ecosystems, made of mostly smaller firms working in symbiotic relationships with large firms that have strong market position and deep pockets to develop and properly launch their next-generation products.[21] Ecosystems are increasingly seen as the foundation of the regional economies.[22]

Not only is innovation externalized, but it is also becoming more open, defying the long-held belief that controlling intellectual property is a strategic imperative. In fact, experience shows that owners of proprietary platforms often lose to open-source competitors. For example, the Linux operating system, the Firefox browser, and the Wikipedia encyclopaedia, three major Internet-based products, were developed through open collaboration between volunteer developers. Industry practices now accommodate free open-source software (FOSS), leading to the contention that there is an open-source alternative for every major software program.[23] Many entrepreneurs have capitalized on the benefits of an open-source product development. Investors also no longer hesitate to provide equity capital to open-source business models that rely on maintenance fees to generate income. Red Hat, one such company, now has a market capitalization of nine billion dollars.

Open innovation does not work in every sector. Where a high level of safety or reliability is demanded, the market still relies on closed systems, which ensure clear accountability and facilitate proper accumulation of data, monitoring of experience, and codification of knowledge. Airlines and their public regulators, for example, cannot accept the risks associated with open software or independent innovation.[24]

Moreover, open innovation applies more readily to applications than to platforms. The development of complex platforms can more easily be accomplished by well-coordinated management teams. Once the platform is sufficiently developed, it can then profit from external independent innovations.[25] Even Linux started as a proprietary system.

At a certain stage in platform development, however, open innovation often becomes a superior approach for platform orchestrators, allowing them to access a much bigger pool of ideas. Orchestrators may be better off with an open approach to innovation, stepping back into the role of coordinating the integration of improvements and new modules as these appear. What platform leaders lose in control and predictability can be gained on leverage and creativity.

6. *Innovation depends mostly on new technology.* Again, we're not so sure.

Twenty-five years ago, when 'high technology' had the mythical presence that the Internet has in today's economy, a Minneapolis-St Paul business coalition invited us to assist them in developing a strategy to spur high-technology investments in the Twin City area. Our first task was to get them to define what they meant by 'high technology.' After going through a mountain of statistics, we identified a limited number of industrial sectors that were characterized by a high level of R&D and the employment of a large number of engineers and scientists. These sectors included computers, software, pharmaceuticals, medical devices, robotics, communication material, aircraft manufacturers, instrumentation, and nuclear energy. We then calculated their aggregate contribution to GDP and employment. We were startled to find that these high-technology sectors represented less than 10% of GDP. When we expanded the definition to include bits and pieces from other industries such as medical equipment, machinery, and composite materials, the high-tech contribution to GDP rose to 15%, still surprisingly low.

If we were to repeat the exercise today, we would add the Internet and other new information-based industries. We would likely find roughly the same percentage, less than 15%, in the high-technology sectors of the economy. If, on the other hand, we had looked at an earlier time, say 1925 or 1900, we would have found different 'high-tech' industries, such as automobiles and electrical motors, but their contribution to GDP would still have added up to less than 15% of the economy.

What does that tell us?

'High technology' means 'new technologies.' Industries that exploit the technological frontier represent a small share of the total economy. The remainder of economic activities, relying on mature technologies, accounts for most of the value added by the economy. Governments that rely on innovation to support economic growth must realize that most innovation occurs in the mature sectors of the economy. We may associate innovation with the high-tech Blackberry, but the majority of innovation in an economy involves low-tech products like Tide.

Recognizing the Diversity of Modes of Innovation

These reality checks poke large holes in the basic assumptions that have shaped the traditional twentieth-century theory of innovation. Schumpeter's highly structured model of innovation built around large firms does not fare well in a world where the best products do not necessarily win, where markets are being defined by users as they experience a product, and where the development of a new product is shared, often with little direct coordination, among many developers, many of them start-up firms with limited means.

But as we challenged the linear model of innovation, we also had to answer a lot of questions. Should business rely more on in-house research or do away with most of it? Is open innovation good for all industries? When can a product be launched as an imperfect prototype without destroying the brand associated with it? Should intellectual property protection be strengthened or weakened? There is no right answer to these questions, whether we ask them as innovators or as governments developing their policies on innovation. It all depends on the specific pattern of innovation that is encountered in a particular industry.

We are not the first to challenge the linear innovation model. Two Stanford University professors, Nathan Rosenberg, an economist, and Stephen Kline, an engineer, published a highly publicized attack on the model in 1986, drawing attention to its multiple flaws.[26] They also proposed as an alternative the chain-link model of innovation, which highlights the important role that market feedback loops play in the development of innovations. Although science and R&D may be important factors, commercial success, design, and process development are usually much more important, and knowing their dynamics is critical to understanding innovation. The management science literature has pointed out for many years that innovations rest on a lot more than R&D and that marketing acumen and the organizational culture are much more important than R&D as determinants of successful innovations.[27]

Nor are we the first to draw attention to the many different patterns of innovation. Several researchers have emphasized the diversity of approaches to innovation and the importance to businesses and governments of recognizing that diversity. And several theories of innovation have explicitly identified elements of that diversity.

For instance, Keith Pavitt, a British economist, examined more than 500 innovations and identified four sector-based patterns of innovation: supplier-dominated, scale-intensive, specialized suppliers, and science-based. Each pattern, according to Pavitt, follows its own rules. Pursuing Pavitt's approach, other researchers have added a fifth pattern, information-intensive firms.

Nathan Rosenberg and a colleague from Berkeley, David C. Mowery, while examining the impact of technological progress on the U.S. economy in the twentieth century, have observed numerous paths to innovation as new technologies became embedded in the economy.[28] They found that the interaction of technical progress, division of labor, and effective utilization of resources continuously generate new patterns of innovation, each specific to a particular industry.

In an influential book about the nature of economic growth, *An Evolutionary Theory of Economic Change*, Richard Nelson and Sidney Winter described innovation as an evolutionary adaptive process fuelled by the continuous advances of technologies. Being adaptive responses, innovations are strongly influenced by topical conditions, and thus can take many forms.[29] Around the same time, Giovanni Dosi, an Italian economist, also drew attention to the existence of evolutionary paths with distinct dynamics, and importantly, a time-dependency: there is no going back in evolution.[30] These concepts were significant influences in the development of our framework on games of innovation.

Inspired by Nelson and Winter, economists explored further the sources of the diversity of innovation. For instance, Franco Malerba examined sectoral patterns and coined the term 'technological regimes' to categorize broad patterns.[31] Michael Best acknowledge the importance of science push innovation but emphasized the critical intermediary influences of suppliers of specialized machineries, large-scale mass production systems, such as the lean manufacturing system, and, more recently, systems integration.[32]

William Abernathy[33] of Harvard University and his colleague Jim Utterback from MIT, who both have written extensively about innovation, have distinguished between early radical innovations that create new markets and the more discrete efficiency-oriented changes that occur later in the life cycle of an industry, a view not unlike Clayton Christensen's.[34] For Abernathy and Utterback, radical innovations are the ones that create new markets, a view our research supports. Other researchers went on to draw finer distinctions.[35]

All of this research strongly indicates that there are numerous paths to innovation. Trying to integrate these disparate paths into a single unified theory, as many have attempted (including us), simply adds to the complexity and makes it even more difficult to understand innovation.

Some ten years ago, we decided to add our own two cents' worth to the discussion when we were given the opportunity to conduct a global survey of innovation practices. The project was designed to allow us to observe how businesses actually innovate, to catalogue their practices and explain the various patterns that researchers were pointing to. Until we conducted our study, no one had looked at a very large sample of firms, associated with a large number of innovations, encompassing all sectors of the economy.[36] Our central premise was that different competitive contexts call for different innovation strategies.

What We Do Not Know

Although our research provides numerous new insights on the process of innovation, there remains a lot that we do not know about innovation. Even with thousands of books on the topic, we still need to understand it better. Take Silicon Valley: we know what happened, but not well enough to replicate the phenomenon, despite attempts to do so in hundreds of regions and cities around the world. Governments are spending billions to support R&D to accelerate innovation. In fact, no other economic activity receives as much taxpayer support as research, all in the hope of stimulating economic growth. But does it work? We are not sure.

Well-ingrained conventional wisdom says that the future comes from R&D. But how much can we expect in return from a dollar invested in R&D to generate economic growth? No one can say with certainty. A direct link between fundamental research in the laboratory and development in the economy is hard to establish.

Moreover, much of the literature on innovation focuses on new technologies and new industries. But as we found in Minnesota, most of the economy is relatively low tech, and it still manages to innovate continually. Indeed, innovation in mature industries is a much bigger contributor to economic growth than innovation in new industries associated with new technologies.

We do not attempt to answer all questions about innovation in this book. Our ambition is more modest: we hope to add one more link in the chain of our understanding. We focus on the diversity of the modes of innovation and the implications of this diversity for business strategies and for public policies.

3 Searching for Patterns

The Industrial Research Institute, better known by its acronym IRI, is the oldest organization promoting innovation in the United States. Founded in 1938, it has around 300 corporate members, mostly large manufacturing companies and laboratories. Its mission is to promote technological innovation through better management and organization of research, development, and engineering activities, very much in the Schumpeter II mold. It organizes seminars, publishes the well-known journal *Research Technology Management*, and diffuses best practices and management tools.

One of IRI's programs is built around small working groups of chief technology officers and R&D managers who tackle specific issues in depth. A scholar who specializes in the topic is usually invited to join each group. In 2001 one such group set out to study the management of R&D in the context of the new economy. The group wanted to measure the impact of the Internet and new communication technologies on the management of innovation in large firms. Headed by Dr Ann Savoca from Sealed Air Corporation, the working group drew three other members from businesses, Mathew Cook of Armstrong World Industries, Salvatore Miraglia of Timken, and Larry Schwartz of Intellectual Assets. Roger Miller was the invited scholar.

Documenting Best Practices

The group sought to identify the best practices in the management of R&D in the new context of the information economy, and went looking for firms that explicitly took into account the realities of the new economy. Roger Miller was first asked to interview 75 CTOs and VPs of R&D in Europe, the United States, and Japan. That led to the identification

Table 3.1. Stimulating Innovation to Create Value: Ten Best Practices

Transforming academic research into novel products to gain intellectual property
Gaining approval faster than others for products subject to regulatory requirements
Developing safe and reliable systems through engineering capabilities
Coalition building to make platforms or products *de facto* standards
Aligning products with emerging architectures likely to become winning solutions
Reducing costs while improving quality on a sustained basis
Offering a continuous flow of new products and services
Developing partnerships with major clients
Customizing products from standard modules
Subsidizing products and services to grow markets

Source: Roger Miller and Serghei Floricel, 'Value Creation and Innovation Games,' *Research Technology Management* 47 (November/December 2004): 25–37.

of 27 superior practices, 10 of which are listed in table 3.1.[1] A survey questionnaire was sent to R&D managers in 125 industrial companies, asking them to rate the use of these practices in their business. These R&D managers were also asked to document the performance of their own firms in the area of innovation, supporting their observations with data on sales and new products.

When the results came in, the group was startled to find no correlation between best practices and performance on innovation. Did that mean the best practices were irrelevant, or was the questionnaire simply too crude to capture a complex reality? The group sought an explanation.

An important insight was indirectly provided by a best-selling business book that appeared at the time, *Blue Ocean Strategy*, written by W. Chan Kim and Renée Mauborgne, two professors at the INSEAD School of Management in Fontainebleau, south of Paris. The book proposed a new approach to game-changing innovations of the disruptive type that Christensen first wrote about in the mid-1990s.[2] The authors argued that a business creates real value only when it reinvents a product. To explain their theory, they used an ocean analogy. When it reinvents its product – and creates real value – a business moves from a "red ocean", where all its competitors operate, to a "blue ocean", where it operates alone with its new way of addressing customer needs. As an example, they use Cirque du Soleil, which has replaced animals with acrobatics, magic, and illusion as the basis of a circus performance.

Cirque du Soleil, they argue, exemplifies the successful application of a blue ocean strategy. In their book, Kim and Mauborgne provided examples of businesses that had successfully moved from red oceans to blue oceans, along with a set of best practices to navigate the passage.

It became clear to the IRI working group that these blue ocean strategies were not applicable to all businesses. Many more successful and innovative companies operate in red oceans than in blue. Procter & Gamble, for example, has successfully managed innovation at Tide for more than 60 years, creating a lot of value without leaving its red ocean. With that observation, the IRI group concluded that best practices in innovation are often situation specific. Value can be created by blue ocean and red ocean strategies alike. What works at Cirque du Soleil may not work at Proctor & Gamble.

Unknowingly, the 75 experts interviewed by Roger Miller provided such a perspective, identifying best practices that worked in their own specific environment. But when these best practices are integrated into a single list, the IRI working group discovered a mish-mash of strategies that did not add up to a single unified view of innovation. Indeed, some of the 10 best practices that topped the list, presented in table 3.1, contradict each other. Moreover, at best, several are motherhood statements.

No business will ever apply these best practices equally. The managers interviewed made it clear that their companies would choose specific configurations of complementary practices, depending on their own business environment. In rapidly changing markets, firms would choose value-creation activities that are quite different from those chosen by firms in more placid business environments.

The group concluded that different markets and products call for different innovation strategies and quite different best practices. Successful businesses can pursue very different approaches to innovation, depending on the markets and customers that they face.

Roger Miller developed the concept of games of innovation to describe the different pathways to compete on the basis of innovation. He brought the term back to Montreal's École Polytechnique, where he was teaching at the time. Unlike games played for fun or war-game simulations, these games involve a set of players whose innovating activities are governed by rules that define ways of creating value through innovation. In this context, the game is a metaphor that reflects the structured context that constrains and orients a business's approach to innovation. Played within the given rules, such a game offers ample strategic freedom as it unfolds over time.[3]

The idea that different business environments trigger different innovation patterns is now deeply embedded within the IRI. As the working group confirmed, when it comes to managing innovation, one size does not fit all. Much depends on the competitive circumstances in which businesses find themselves. The new economy reinforces this eclectic approach to innovation, as improving communications expands the capacity to innovate.

The MINE project

Back in Montreal, Roger Miller pursued his investigation. Capitalizing on the availability of government funding for research on the management of technology, Roger lined up the support of a group of Montreal-based companies to provide the seed financing for a major research project that would document the innovation process in a wide variety of business environments. The MINE project (Managing Innovation in the New Economy) was structured around a global survey of innovation strategies in companies known for being innovative. The survey would document how they managed innovation, the practices that worked most successfully, and, more important, whether multiple patterns of innovation existed.

Marcel Côté supported the project from the outset and assisted in lining up sponsors. He joined MINE as an outside challenger, whereas Roger was the principal investigator. The two also agreed to write this book, to diffuse the key findings beyond scholarly publications. The IRI and former members of the working group also agreed to support the project and participate in various meetings where the methodology and subsequently the findings were discussed.

Seeking Best Practices Worldwide

MINE was officially launched in the fall of 2003. Roger Miller had assembled a team of 10 research assistants, along with a few more senior collaborators associated with the Jarilosky Chair in the Management of Technology at École Polytechnique at University of Montreal, which he occupied. Following discussions with the advisory committee, two parallel streams of information were developed: (1) a quantitative stream built around a global survey of innovation strategies and practices, which involved the development of a large sample of qualified respondents, the development of a questionnaire, and its administration to more than 1,000 respondents; and (2) a qualitative stream built around 50 case studies of innovative companies.

To provide insights on the issues that surround innovation strategies, a list of 100 companies considered innovative was developed for the case studies on the role of innovation in their business strategies, and on the nature of the innovation strategies they pursued. Fifty of these case studies, involving at least four interviews conducted with senior executives, were completed.[4]

The MINE Survey

Developing the survey, conducting it, and analyzing the results took several years. The questionnaire targeted seven broad areas:

- The business context of the firm: markets, competition, etc.
- Their basic value creation strategies
- Investments in innovation: R&D, product development, IP, etc.
- Innovation strategies: products, costs, long-term goals, etc.
- Organizational design for innovation: leadership, support, etc.
- Management practices for innovation: monitoring, budgeting, decision making, etc.
- Performance: profitability, growth, returns on capital, etc.

A preliminary version of the questionnaire was tested in the spring of 2005, to assess respondents' understanding of questions and to see if the information we wanted was readily available. The final version of the written questionnaire had 335 questions and took about 90 minutes to complete, provided the information was on hand. At the same time, we built a list of 4,000 businesses or divisions and research institutes throughout the world, covering all sectors, regions, and sizes of business. We then identified a respondent in each organization, typically the chief technology officer or senior manager of R&D. In early 2005 we sent these individuals the questionnaire and, every three months or so, we did telephone follow-ups. By the end of 2007, 1,000 responses had been received and the fieldwork was closed.

After analyzing for coherence, ensuring that we'd received answers to all critical questions, and evaluating the overall quality of response, we ended up with 852 useful responses for further analysis. Fifty percent of the responding organizations were based in Canada and the United States, 24% in Asia, and 17% in Europe, with the rest based in

South America, Africa, and the Middle East. The average responding firm employed about 6,000 people, though the numbers ranged from a few to 50,000 and more. Respondents came from a variety of sectors. Most were involved in exporting, although a few were purely domestic-oriented organizations. On average, firms derived 53% of their sales from outside their home base.

We were not overly concerned about biases in the sample. We wanted a large sample of firms so we could document how they innovated, with the intention of identifying clusters of firms that played the same innovation games. Whether some clusters were over- or under-represented did not matter, as long as we had enough cases in each cluster.

We discovered in the later analytical phase that our questionnaire did contain three biases. First, it was still heavily oriented toward R&D and did not sufficiently cover several critical aspects of innovation strategies. The questionnaire emphasized the respondents' R&D decisions and strategies, but it under-represented the marketing strategies and investment related to the commercialization of the innovation. A second shortfall was the under-documentation of the way respondents manage rapid growth, a key concern of successful innovators. Finally, the questionnaire did not sufficiently probe the strategies behind the innovation decisions, particularly those that dealt with networks. These biases became evident when we developed the case studies and assessed the strategies of innovative firms. Fortunately, the case studies allowed us to compensate for the shortfalls of the questionnaire.

The Statistical Analysis

For the survey, a sophisticated statistical analysis program was then developed in collaboration with Dr. Bernard Clément, a professor of statistics at École Polytechnique in Montreal. The model, presented in figure 3.1, relied on three sequential types of analysis: factor analysis, cluster analysis, and canonical analysis.[5]

The first step was to aggregate the information provided by responses to the 335 questions into a manageable set. The principal components analysis yielded 27 composite variables. One interesting finding that came up at that stage was that there was no significant difference between regions. Businesses from different regions of the world face similar business environments, whether they operate in North America, Europe, or Asia. More specifically, no statistical difference emerged among businesses, whatever their location in the world, on such contextual elements as rivalry, market growth, knowledge production, and

Figure 3.1. Searching for Patterns: The Methodology

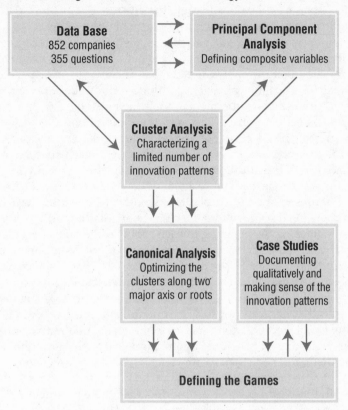

expertise of customers.[6] No matter where they operate, firms pursue with roughly the same intensity a range of similar competitive strategies such as technical superiority, cost reduction, and alignment with platforms. We concluded that a regional comparative approach would yield no significant insights about innovation strategies.

The second step was the cluster analysis. Using principal component as variables, we ran a series of statistical analyses to group together the organizations that innovated in a similar fashion. This required a long and tedious analysis to determine the proper composite variables that should be used to define the clusters. We eventually settled on a core set of composite variables that yielded seven relatively distinctive clusters of respondents. Organizations in each cluster were pursing innovation strategies sufficiently specific to be collectively and statistically differentiated from organizations in the other clusters.

The third step was canonical analysis. This type of analysis identifies another set of composite variables, which are called roots, that best explains the differences between the clusters. These roots are a weighted set of composite variables already identified in the principal component analysis. A canonical analysis is done serially, identifying first the root that discriminates the most among the clusters, explaining away a certain percentage of the variance; then identifying the second one and assuming the effects of the first one, thus explaining a lesser part of the total variance; and so on. The significance of each successive root, associated with the additional variance it explains, typically falls rapidly. This was the case in our analysis, where we kept only the first two roots. For presentation purposes, these roots can be seen as the axes in a two-dimensional space where the clusters are distributed.

Understanding the meaning of each root was the final step. This was done by analyzing the weight and polarity of each component of the roots, and asking what they signify collectively. For instance, several composite variables, such as ownership of intellectual property, level of rivalry, pursuit of disruptive innovation, and capacity to develop product variety, turned out not to discriminate between clusters, being of roughly equal significance in each of them. The variables that stood out in the first two roots generated by the canonical analysis, and that most clearly distinguished clusters from each other, were associated, respectively, with the maturity of the market the businesses were involved in and with the architecture of the product they were producing.

The first root defined a continuum from highly effervescent and rapidly evolving markets to mature, well-structured, and technologically stable environments. This dimension discriminated clearly between what we called 'emerging markets,' still in the process of being shaped and still attracting new customers, and better defined 'mature markets,' with their more stable customer bases. The second root was associated with the nature of each organization's products and more specifically their architectures. At one end were stand-alone products and at the other end were systems. Moreover, the latter were either closed systems, with a predetermined set of components provided by different partners, each with a specific role (a plane maker and its engine manufacturer), or open systems, defined by a platform and complementary modules provided by third parties, and each of which could evolve in its own way.

Figure 3.2. The Seven MINE Clusters

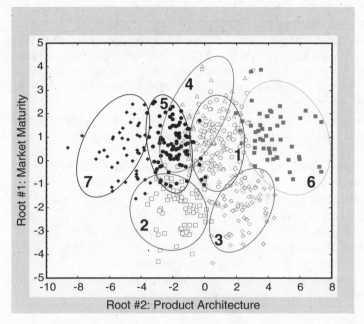

Figure 3.2 is a graphical presentation on a two-dimensional plane of the results of the canonical analysis. The seven clusters of firms are statistical constructs that minimize the variance within clusters and maximize it between them. The clusters are displayed on the two dimensions identified by the canonical analysis. The vertical dimension is related to the first root, market dynamics, whereas the horizontal dimension is related to the second root, product architecture.

The outlying cluster to the left is made mostly of non-profit support organizations, such as consultancies, research centers, and contract research organizations whose job is to assist businesses in innovating. Given their indirect direct role in ushering innovations into the marketplace, we set this cluster aside for later study.

The other six clusters comprised the bulk of the respondents. Three pairs can be identified along the horizontal axis: 1 and 4, 2 and 5, and 3 and 6. Clusters 1, 2, and 3 are respondents in emerging markets, whereas clusters 4, 5, and 6 are their counterparts in mature markets. The significant overlap between cluster 1 and cluster 4 reflects in part the continuum aspect of product maturity for stand-alone products. It could imply that the innovation strategies of firms that handle stand-alone products are less affected by the maturity of their markets. On the other hand, the overlap between clusters 4 and 5 could suggest that in mature markets, firms that deal with mature closed systems and those that deal with stand-alone products pursue similar innovation strategies. Both hypotheses are valid, and should be investigated further. (However, a third root could show that in a three-dimensional space the clusters are segregated.)

The statistical analysis of the database yielded two robust conclusions, which had a great impact on our subsequent analysis.

1 There are clear patterns of innovation, each with their own coherence. The clusters of firms, sharing similar business environment and pursuing similar innovation strategies, are easy to identify on the graphical presentation in figure 3.2
2 The clusters can be defined along two primary dimensions, the first and most significant one being the maturity of the market in which a company sells, and the second being the architecture of products sold, or more specifically, the level of dependency with other products required to deliver benefits to the customers.

These two conclusions were also confirmed by the case studies that constitute the second source of information in the MINE study.

Integrating the Case Studies

The case studies were based on numerous sources of information: public information provided by the companies to investors, articles about and analysis of the companies by third parties, and at least four interviews with senior officers in each company. These companies and the people interviewed represented a wide range of situations, allowing us to cover from various angles the six types of business environments that defined the clusters identified by the statistical analysis.

The case analysis also benefited from the accumulated experience of the two authors. We have both been consulting for the past 30 years, Marcel Coté professionally, Roger as an academic closely involved with a number of large firms. Marcel has also invested in a large number of technology-based start-ups and has extensive experience on the boards of public and private companies. Our experience has afforded us first-hand observation of strategic decision-making on innovation issues in a wide range of industries, from aerospace and telecoms to pulp and paper and mining. We were also in a position to observe the critical industrial processes, such as the working of the ecosystem, adaptation to radical changes, emergence of start-ups, and relations between business and universities. Finally, both of us have been extensively involved in public policy issues in Canada, giving us unique opportunities to observe the interface between the public realm and private business.

A New Framework

Developing the framework for the games of innovation involved a long journey. It started with a hypothesis by the IRI working group about the existence of very different patterns of innovation, shaped by the business context. The MINE research confirmed that hypothesis, identifying seven different patterns, with six of them defined by two dimensions, market maturity and product architecture. Our understanding was enriched by the case studies and the interviews that supported them, and by our own insights about business practices. We had some disappointments. The survey's questionnaire would be different if we could rewrite it on the basis of our findings, dwelling more on business processes, marketing decisions, and organizational culture. But on the whole, we are quite confident in the robustness of the empirical base that supports our conclusions.

We believe that the 'games of innovation' approach provides a unique and fruitful perspective on innovation. It is not a theory of innovation: such an encompassing theory probably does not exist. But it is a conceptual framework that facilitates understanding of the various factors that shape innovation in the economy, by explicitly segmenting products and markets into six classes, each one calling for specific innovation strategies. We are confident that further research that bears on all variables relevant to define and explain innovation strategies will validate the appropriateness of the framework.

The remainder of this book is devoted to the presentation of this framework.

4 The Games of Innovation

The shares of telephone companies, or telcos, used to be touted as widows' and orphans' stocks because of their stability, high dividends, and low risk. Some thirty years ago, the telcos were among the largest employers in most economies. AT&T, which dominated the US telephone market, was for a while the largest corporation in the world. Enjoying territorial monopolies, telcos' rates were regulated, but they ensured a fair return on capital. Dealing with regulators was a key competency and, not surprisingly, lawyers often rose to the post of CEO. Their marketing to consumers was mostly about the type and color of telephone sets. On the business side, their main competitors were mostly small and medium-sized PBX suppliers and operators that offered internal corporate communications equipment and services.

But life was too cozy and rumblings could be heard. Customers, especially on the business side, were complaining about the lack of competition. In the United States, an upstart competitor, MCI Communications, which provided long-distances services to large businesses, won an antitrust lawsuit against AT&T in 1981. In Britain, Margaret Thatcher was pursuing the privatization of Crown companies; in 1984, 50% of British Telecom was sold to the public. The same year saw the break-up of AT&T into seven regional companies.

Few people in the industry suspected at the time how much change would come over the next 25 years. Five game-changing disruptions brought a major restructuring of the industry:

Deregulation and the end of the operators' monopolies. This came rapidly and throughout the world. Competition was allowed in and price regulation was gradually eased. Newcomers rapidly invaded high-density markets, and in particular the business markets in major cities. Later, as their technology became bidirectional, cable firms moved into fixed-line telephony.

Mobile telephony. Appearing in the early 1980s, and unregulated at the outset, mobile telephony became an entry point for many newcomers. The market grew at a brisk rate. Mobile telephony is now overtaking fixed-line systems in most markets, and growth will continue as it expands beyond voice to Internet and payment systems, using the full capacity of smart phones.

The Internet. Originally conceived with military applications in mind, the Internet burst into civilian use around 1990, with e-mails and the Web as the major drivers. It is now an all-purpose network of networks, affecting not only the telecom industry but media and, increasingly, personal services. The Internet routing protocol has also replaced the old telco switch-based networks, allowing a 1984 start-up like Cisco, which manufactures routing material, to become a dominant equipment supplier to the industry.

Fiber optics. The traditional physical networks, the telcos with their microwave and cable backbone and copper wire for the last mile, and the coaxial networks of the cable companies are gradually being replaced by fiber optic lines, removing practically all capacity constraints associated with fixed lines. In parallel, wireless capacity has also improved, setting up the conditions for future competition between wireless and fiber communications, especially for the last mile.

Technical convergence of networks. Wired and wireless networks are slowly converging toward integrated high-bandwidth pipes. As expected, their owners are trampling on each other's territories. Telcos are getting into TV and cable companies into telephony, and both are fighting it out on the Internet.

These five shock waves have created opportunities for significant innovation, making the ability to innovate a key competitive factor in the industry. For incumbents used to a placid regulated environment, this became a major challenge. Surprisingly, most of them survived, although many merged. The seven regional Bell companies, for example, morphed into two surviving entities, Verizon and AT&T.

But what is more important is the place that newcomers have come to occupy in the industry. In fact, the network operators have mostly abandoned their leadership in the development of communication products to device and software companies such as Apple, Google,

Microsoft, and Research in Motion. The historic equipment manufacturers have faded into the background while newcomers such as Cisco,
Nokia, Samsung, and LG have replaced them.

In less than 30 years, newcomers have not only redefined the telecom
industry, but have captured most of the trillions of dollars in economic
value that has been created as communication products became ubiquitous. Why were the incumbents, with their huge cash flows, their solid
reputation with customers, and their deep reservoir of accumulated
know-how, outclassed by outsiders to their industry?

As consultants and investors, we were close to several companies
that navigated through this period in the telecommunications industry.
The telcos divided the markets accessible to them into three broad segments: network, access, and applications (or OTT, standing for 'over
the top' of the basic networks). The network business was their traditional carrier business. It was demanding significant investments to
increase capacity and quality of transmission, both in the wired market
– laying out fiber and agonizing over the last mile – and in the wireless market – setting up towers and backhaul connections to handle
rapidly expanding demand. In the access business, telcos connected in
the early 1980s with every household and business in industrial countries, usually as the single supplier of connectivity. They were to spend
the next 30 years fighting over these clients with other telcos and with
new entrants, as the service offering (fixed voice, mobility, Internet,
data, etc.) expanded and spending exploded. A continuous stream of
innovators entered their traditional network and connectivity markets,
typically with lower-price solutions in niche markets, from which the
newcomers expanded. In the fuzzier OTT space, which was developing
rapidly and where billions in market value was created by new Internet-based services, telcos hesitated, unfamiliar with the emerging revenue models and wondering if money would ever be made in this area.
With their territorial mindset, telcos also had difficulties assessing the
value of these Internet businesses, which were not territorially based.

All these developments challenged the telcos to embrace change rapidly. But there was strong resistance from within. Operation managers,
who were powerful because they generated the cash flows, were particularly reluctant to invest in new 'stuff.' New products had to meet
their traditionally high standards. They did not want to damage their
brand with a product that was not ready for the market. There were
constant concerns about cannibalizing their old products, which were
their cash cows. They had sunk costs to consider. They wanted to have

proprietary technologies and not be dependent on competitor technologies. So when it came to dividing the annual investment budget, the defenders of improving the status quo within the telcos had strong arguments. Comfortable with their old technologies, their first instinct was to improve them rather than switching to new technologies. And they won many of their battles.

Sensing that resistance, CEOs tried to reconfigure their companies through acquisitions. Following roadmaps developed by consultants and investment bankers, they continually examined a very large number of acquisitions, categorized along broad trajectories, some of which did not materialize as expected. Convergence was one of them: as the communication flows digitalized, the content industries, ranging from traditional telephone service to TV programming, would gradually fuse into an integrated offering. Convergence pushed them to control both content and connectivity. But it did not work that way, as synergies between the two did not materialize. AOL's merger with Time Warner was one of the biggest disasters of the 1990s. In Canada, Bell Canada Enterprise (BCE) bought the dominant TV network in Canada and the country's leading newspaper, along with Teleglobe, an international carrier. To pay for such acquisitions, BCE sold its mobile telephony business in Asia and in South America, which turned out to be a bad strategic choice, as mobility ended up expanding much faster than the expected convergence developed.

The telcos belatedly understood the fundamental changes that were occurring in their markets and recognized that there was a 'new game.' But they were hobbled by so many commitments and conventions inherited from their old games that they were left highly vulnerable to competitive attacks by more nimble new entrants. The traditional industrial order was being upset by technology, and they were lumbering giants attacked by hundreds of Lilliputians. Their competencies equipped them to play the traditional games that were becoming obsolete. Not only didn't the telcos know how to play the new games, but they did not have the organizational structures, the competencies, or the culture to be competitive in these new games.

Games of Innovation

What is a game of innovation? It is comparable to a game of sport. First, there is a context: a hockey rink, for example, two teams of uniformed players on skates, with sticks and a puck, goals at both ends, and so on.

Figure 4.1. The Elements of an Innovation Game

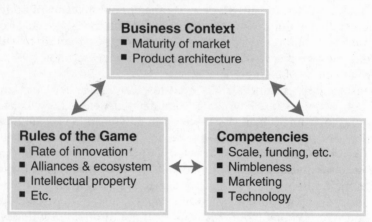

Then there are the rules, among them five players and one goalie on the ice, three periods of 20 minutes each, blue and red lines, the winner being the team that scores the most points. Finally, competencies and best practices define good playing: skating, speed, passing, body checking, back-checking, power plays, zone coverage, and the like.

Like hockey, an innovation game occurs in a particular context, a market with specific characteristics within which the players can pursue the goal of innovation. The MINE project identified the two key dimensions that define these market characteristics. Second, the game follows defined ground rules that determine how players compete in such a market, what they need for survival, how they create value, the importance of intellectual property, and so on. Third, to succeed in such a market while playing within these value-creation rules, the players require a set of specific competencies, among them nimbleness, technology, product management, economies of scale, alliances, partnerships.

Figure 4.1 presents these three basic attributes of an innovation game. Players self-organize within a particular market under competitive pressures. In pursuit of innovation, competing firms and their suppliers tend to follow relatively stable and coherent patterns that conform to a set of best practices executed according to rules of the game. The players thus apply a particular logic of innovation specific to the game, which transcends the preferences and actions of any single player, no matter how accomplished or well endowed.

Thus, the rules within which players win or lose logically flow from the business context, and not from the preferences of any particular competitor. Moreover, the rules and best practices vary significantly between the various types of game. In some games, for example, R&D investment may reach 30% of sales; in other games, it amounts to only 1% to 3%. In some games, players compete mostly by introducing new products, in others mostly by creating business alliances. Each game demands a particular set of competencies.

The game extends beyond the players to their ecosystems, involving interdependencies and shared interests in the success in the game. The firms in the ecosystem, under the leadership of the lead firm, collectively fashion their innovation game and are fashioned by it. Successful innovation usually involves collaboration between multiple players, who can be competitors, such as for the development of standards and industry regulations. Indeed, uncooperative competitors that fail to agree on standards can get trapped in very poor business environments.

Government and public agencies can play important support roles in these games. But the impact of a specific policy can vary greatly from one game to another. Whether it is public support for R&D, intellectual property protection, or competition laws, each type of game will be affected differently. As a result, public policies designed to support innovation often have very circumscribed impacts, as most government policies do not differentiate between games.

Businesses will identify competitive moves that are effective and avoid those that don't work in their game. As a result, in any game, competitors come to share a cognitive framework that reinforces the coherence of the game. This extends to the corporate culture, which reinforces the elements that contribute to good or great performance in a particular game. But changing industries demand fundamental changes in attitudes. A manager that moves from General Electric to Google has to adapt his or her managerial frame of reference. Work practices that apply in one context can have no value in another. For instance, some games may reward a company's individual efforts, while in other games going alone is unthinkable.

Table 4.1 presents the six games, as defined by the two relevant dimensions of their business context. As long as the contextual forces remain basically unchanged and the underlying processes of value creation remain valid, a game will continue. Knowledge will accumulate asymptotically, rapidly at first, then more slowly. A game will end when prevailing market characteristics change extensively enough to create new contexts for innovation.

Table 4.1. The Six Games of Innovation

	Autonomous products	Platform-based products	Closed systems
Innovations in emerging markets	1 Eureka!	2 Battles of Architecture	3 System Breakthroughs
Innovations within mature markets	4 New and Improved	5 Mass Customization	6 Pushing the Envelope

Let's now consider the six games.

Eureka!

This game is about the development of a new market for a stand-alone product. It starts with an entrepreneurial inventor at the confluence of technological developments who identifies an unmet need that can be addressed by an invention. The invention is first noticed by pioneering customers, who are usually familiar with the technology used, and thus at ease with the product, however crude it is initially. They start publicizing it through word of mouth. The game is starting, and can last for 20 years or more.

As soon as the invention gains traction, emulators jump in with improved versions. As they start to compete with each other, the race accelerates. New generations of the product come on stream, reshaping and refining it. As long as improving the product is still easily done, requiring imagination and smart moves more than anything else, the number of competitors multiplies. The customer base enlarges. But slowly, repeat business comes to represent a growing share of the market. As the product gets more complex and growth slows down, marketing, product reliability, and customer service become key differentiators. The industry suddenly consolidates.

Not all Eureka! games are identical. Some of them, such as in pharmaceuticals, emphasize the protection of intellectual property: patents play a key role. In markets where regulations hamper the rate of product development and hinder a player's ability to finance growth through sales revenues, deep-pocket innovators have an edge. Brands play an important role in most Eureka! games. Twenty-five years after 'reinventing' the circus, Cirque du Soleil still dominates it, with no significant competitor, capitalizing on the power of its brand to fight off imitators.

A fundamental characteristic of a Eureka! game is the relentless pressure to innovate as competition bears on the offering of new product features. Improvements between generations of product are substantial. In the MINE survey, Eureka! game participants spent on average 20% of their sales on R&D. Marketing is just as important: new customers are often unsophisticated and rely on clues to make their purchase. The pharmaceutical industry, for example, which is heavily involved in Eureka! games, spends $1.80 on sales and promotion for every dollar spent on research.[1]

Eureka! games generate rapid industrial changes. Winning companies typically go through several metamorphoses as they grow. Successful entrepreneurs in these games generally display an inherent talent for managing a rapidly growing organization, a skill that not all inventors master.

Eureka! games strike the imagination. Although these games represent only a small share of overall economic activity, most of today's industries have emerged from Eureka! games. But with the spread of information technologies, Eureka! games may become less important. Battles of Architecture may soon become the dominant game that heralds the arrival of new industries.

Battles of Architecture

This is the new game that incumbent telephone companies gradually discovered in the 1990s, as the Internet and mobile telephony challenged their traditional Mass Customization game. Battles of Architecture are fought over emerging open systems built around platforms to which an indefinite number of modules are attached. Benefits accrue to users from the combination of the platform and modules. Multi-sided markets emerged around these open-system platforms. Third-party module developers are attracted by the customer base associated with the platform. Customers are attracted by the wide choice of modules (or 'apps,' in Internet platform lingo). A key task of a platform 'orchestrator' is to manage the coherent development of such multi-sided markets built around its platform.

Battles of Architecture are characterized by strong network effects that enhance the benefits of enlarging customer and supplier bases. Network effects favor rapid concentration, as size becomes a key competitive advantage. As a result, Battle of Architecture markets get concentrated much more rapidly than Eureka! markets, which can remain fragmented for years. This rapid concentration often forces third-party suppliers to take a side in the game, giving rise to complex coalitions. The management of these coalitions and the diplomatic skills required are competencies for platform orchestrators at the center of these games.

The first Battles of Architecture were fought a hundred years ago by the mass retailers and their chain stores. Today, Battles of Architecture are prevalent in the information-based industries, where open platforms are common. Microsoft won its Battle of Architecture when it became the dominant supplier of operating systems for the personal computer. A Battle of Architecture is currently raging around smart phone platforms. Orchestrators such as Apple, Research in Motion, and Google scramble to line up application developers to make their platform more attractive to end users, to network operators, and to other developers. A similar battle is going on among e-book platforms. Battles of Architecture are also occurring in retailing, as new formats fight it out.

The potential of emerging platforms is often hard to detect in the early stage, which is why their funding often relies on astute venture capitalists. Given the huge benefits associated with network effects, both for suppliers and for users, only a few platforms survive in Battles of Architecture.[2]

System Breakthroughs

For several years in the early 1990s, Toyota worked closely with a subsidiary of the French aircraft manufacturer Dassault to revolutionize the way new car models were designed. Dassault had developed sophisticated software tools for new aircraft models and, working with Toyota, adapted them to the design of cars. The results were startling: a 44% reduction in the time and development costs of major car projects.[3] Dassault went on to commercialize the technology, now called Product Lifecycle Management or PLM, and on the strength of that product has become a global leader in the manufacturing design software market. Its success can be traced back to an engineering breakthrough, the development of the first 3-D industrial design software for planes. When it started to commercialize that technology, first with Toyota, then with others, it triggered a highly competitive innovation game among providers of industrial software.

System Breakthrough innovations result from close collaboration between a demanding customer and an expert firm that masters a particular technology and applies it to the customer's problem. Using a real challenge as a testing ground, the duo attempts to revolution-ize the way things are done in a particular area. Great products have come out of such games. Microsoft's operating system came out of nine months of intense cooperation with IBM. (A few years later, the game morphed into a Battle of Architecture.) SAP developed the first Enter-prise Resource Planning (ERP) system in a joint project with Imperial Chemical Industries of Germany in the 1970s and went on to popular-ize the system in all large businesses. Boeing intends to revolutionize the aircraft industry with the Dreamliner 787, which makes extensive use of composite materials and relies on close collaboration with a select group of industrial partners.

System Breakthrough games are highly R&D-intensive. In the MINE survey, firms that participate in these games as purveyors of solutions invested, on average, 32% of their sales in R&D. Both the client and the supplier of the technology take huge risks. Relations between the two can easily deteriorate as, inevitably, most projects hit unexpected roadblocks.

But the challenges go beyond properly managing the initial project. A player of this game has to build a proprietary system to commercial-ize it to other clients. This is a critical step, as both original partners can assert conflicting proprietary claims on the breakthrough.

Patents seldom play a major role in these games because proprietary solutions are deeply embedded in the products. Patenting them would force the divulgation of too much proprietary technology and 'tricks of the trade.' More important is the management of the intimate relation-ships with their customers, who are usually locked in and face high switching costs. Investing in the customer relationship is a priority for providers of the technological solutions to ensure good relations and a good reputation in the marketplace.

New and Improved

Procter & Gamble Co. continually ranks among the most admired companies in *Fortune* magazine surveys.[4] It has achieved this status by mastering the New and Improved game of innovation, the continuous development of an edge in the marketplace through product differen-tiation and cost reduction. Its success at this game allows it to minimize direct price competition and maintain its loyal customer base.

New and Improved games emphasize product differentiation, process improvements, and managerial innovation. Successful players reduce costs, improve quality and service, and maintain profitability in mature markets, preventing them from being commoditized. They search continuously for innovation that creates value. Customers are experienced and knowledgeable: the differentiation must be genuine.

The game is found in numerous markets, from industrial and consumer products and intermediate goods to services of all sorts. It includes, among other things, aluminum ingots, steel joists, food products, personal care products and services, household equipment, and legal services. Markets can be global (iron ore), national (breakfast cereals), or local (lawyers), and most are oligopolistic. Commoditized markets are not significant in the total. Considered globally, New and Improved is a game mostly for large businesses, but these rely extensively on an ecosystem of critical suppliers, primary small and mid-sized firms, that provide them with leading edge technological solutions.

In the MINE survey of participants in this game, which were mostly large firms, R&D expenditures represented only 3% to 4% of sales. Firms rely on their ecosystem to complement their in-house innovation capabilities. When a product line runs out of innovation potential and risks commoditization, the large firm often sells it.

Mass Customization

Between 1995 and 2000, the retail sector turned out to be the largest contributor to productivity growth in the U.S. economy.[5] That growth in productivity was brought mostly by several changes in retail practices during the period, larger stores, global procurement, efficient logistics, and collaborative inventory management. Economists sometimes referred to the phenomena as the 'Wal-Mart effect,' as Wal-Mart pioneered many of these changes and forced its competitors to adapt, in the process changing the face of the North American retail sector. Toyota engineered a somewhat similar jump in productivity in its automobile manufacturing operations, engaging not only its employees but also thousands of suppliers, relentlessly improving the quality of its cars while maintaining competitive prices. Through the effect of competition, Toyota's practices spread throughout the global automobile industry.[6]

When a Battle of Architecture matures, the parameters of the industry get settled. Mature open systems are still defined by platforms at their core and a large number of third parties providing proprietary modules (which can be applications, components, products, or services, depending on the platform). The platforms reach out to the customer base, offering a wide range of benefits that each customer can customize.

Mass Customization games are battles of brands catering to mass-market needs. The platforms fight it out among themselves, trying to differentiate their broad offering so that each customer can get what he or she wants. The generic strategy is increased segmentation of the final offering, while maintaining or lowering costs through the use of sophisticated systems common to all segments. A Mass Customization game rests on the continuous improvement of both the platform and the products that it delivers. Orchestrators such as Wal-Mart and Toyota integrate technological advances into their platform while managing thousands of suppliers to deliver continuously improving benefits to end users. The overall design of the offering, whether through category management at Wal-Mart or product management at Toyota, requires close interaction with a network of trusted suppliers. Competition results in a continually improved offering to the ultimate customer.

Mass Customization games will gain in importance as information technology penetrates the economy. Platforms, still in the mist of Battles of Architecture, will converge around dominant designs and will stabilize. But even when platforms stabilize, they are continually improved upon as logistics and information exchanges. With powerful brands, they will reach their customer base efficiently and reliably, delivering complex, always-improving and more customized offerings.

Pushing the Envelope

In Pushing the Envelope (PTE), players compete by redefining the state of the art in closed systems. The game may involve a new printing plant that operates with one-third fewer employees or a new bridge that spans a record length. Players incorporate the latest available technologies into major projects sponsored by industrial and government customers. Using the most advanced know-how available, engineers, architects, and designers push the envelope a little further with each new capital investment project, whether it involves a machine, a plant, a power facility, or an IT network.

Although they are evolutionary, achieving a little more with each successive project, PTE games are also generally risky, as they continually push up standards. The critical factors in this game are the selection of experts by the customer, the solidity of the partnership with these experts, and the project management competencies. PTE projects usually do not involve much R&D, since they rely on available technologies.

PTE innovations are critical to our well-being. They bring about improved infrastructures, from communications systems and bridges to financial institutions' back office operations and Google's computer farms. PTE games also improve reliability and quality in everything we consume. It is the game where governments are potentially major players, as big demanders of infrastructures. Unfortunately, the push for higher performance standards that drives PTE games is often set aside by governments, which are more concerned with cost considerations and with minimizing risks, and which rely on proven designs.

Supporting Innovation

Few firms innovate alone. Innovators generally receive support from their ecosystem of suppliers, and from a broader ecosystem made of research organizations, consultants, government agencies and, in the case of new firms, venture capitalists. This supporting infrastructure can have an important impact on a country's level of innovation. For instance, organizations such as Battelle, Forrester Research, and the Frauenhofer Institute network in Germany provide services, information, and tools that enable companies to make decisions about technological innovation. Consultants also provide knowledgeable individuals and advice about technologies and markets, identify partners, and facilitate access to publicly funded programs.

These organizations were included in the MINE survey. In the statistical analysis, they aggregated into their own cluster. Although they can play an important support role, they are not in the final analysis innovators. They can be directly involved in a player's decision to innovate and how to do it, but they seldom bear the risk and, more important, they do not manage the innovation.

A Dynamic Landscape

Table 4.2 summarizes the six games. They cover a very dynamic landscape. Not only do games evolve all the time, but in the case of emerging market games, they change quite rapidly. Companies in New and Improved games can at the same time also be involved in Mass

Table 4.2. The Six Games of Innovation Illustrated

	Autonomous products	Platform-based products	Closed systems
Innovations in emerging markets Innovation driving a rapidly evolving product and an enlarging customer base R&D and marketing-intensive industries 10- to 20-year competitive race, while the new market emerges	*Eureka!* A new stand-alone product, e.g., a new blockbuster drug, solar panel, Cirque du Soleil Often science or technology based Brands and patents are used to fend off emulators Marketing is critical	*Battles of Architecture* A new system takes hold, e.g., Microsoft O/S; Smart phone, Television in 1950s Success depends on vision, network effects, and coalition building VCs often key in early funding of visionaries	*System Breakthroughs* A major system component, e.g., SAP, CATIA, electric car battery Based on collaboration between an inventor and a demanding client Intense high-risk development
Innovations within mature markets Creating value through the improvement of products and processes Corporate culture is a critical element About 90% of the economy is in structured markets	*New and Improved* E.g., P&G, 3M, mining, much of manufacturing Continuous improvements (products, processes) Constant focus on innovation	*Mass Customization* E.g., Toyota, Ikea, Wal-Mart Battle of brands and of systems Managing global supply networks and maintaining evolving product integrity	*Pushing the Envelope* E.g., utilities, infrastructures, back offices Large clients improving their offering and systems, working with experts and suppliers

Customization games. Proctor & Gamble is one such case, involved in New and Improved games with its large portfolio of products, but also a critical supplier to mass merchants, whose retailing platforms compete in Mass Customization games and who are leaning on their suppliers to provide them with exclusive innovative products.

Industries face game changes, as telcos found out. Incumbents in mature markets can have a difficult time when their games fade away. Not only do they have to recognize and accept that their game is changing, but they have to acquire the competencies to compete in the new game, against new entrants that they do not always respect or treat as serious competition.

Change occurs more gradually when an emerging market slowly turns into a mature market, a very different type of transition. The aging of a market is generally accompanied at the player level by the 'graying' of corporate cultures. That can bring problems. Microsoft, the rabble-rouser of the early 1980s, is currently undergoing such a transition, and it is still questionable whether it will keep its ability to create significant value through innovation.

Some transitions are lateral, closed systems morphing into open systems. System Breakthrough games, involving an intimate customer–supplier relationship, can mutate into Battles of Architecture as new products evolve into platforms to which modules by third parties get attached. Microsoft managed such a transition quite well in the 1980s, when it established its operating system as the dominant platform for the PC and integrated thousands of applications. Large-business closed software systems are increasingly being pressured to open up, as customers move to 'best-of-breed' configurations for their systems, allowing the dominant platforms to coordinate peripheral systems, but still reducing their reach.

Managing a change of game is as important as managing the strategy of playing the game. In switching games, a company must acquire new skills and make fundamental changes in its culture. The first condition for success is recognizing that the game is changing, which is not always evident.

Quantifying the Games

The place that emerging markets occupy in the advanced OECD economies is generally overestimated. Although there are definitional issues about what counts as an emerging market and when it becomes mature, the share of GDP that is contributed by emerging markets is at best 10%. This may appear to be an underestimate, but upon analysis, it is easily understood. Emerging markets – better known at any given time as the 'new economy' – are the development component of the economy, at its fringe. Products in emerging markets haven't yet fully captured their customer base and are still gaining new customers, whereas mature markets basically churn their existing customer base. The addition of new customers allows emerging markets to grow at a much faster rate than the rest of the economy. As a result, they capture a greater share of the growth of the economy than their actual weight, around one-third of GDP growth, plus or minus 5%, according to our estimates.

We spent considerable time refining our estimates of the relative importance of each game in the economy, using data from the OECD

Table 4.3. Relative Contribution to Economic Growth

	Share of GDP	Share of GDP growth			
		Total	Autonomous products	Platform-based products	Closed systems
Emerging markets	10%	35%	*Eureka!* 15%	*Battles of Architecture* 15%	*System Breakthrough* 5%
Mature markets	90%	65%	*New and Improved* 30%	*Mass Customization* 20%	*Pushing the Envelope* 15%

and from US and Canadian national income accounts. Table 4.3 presents the results, in terms of the shares of GDP accounted for by emerging markets and by mature markets, and of the share of annual growth in GDP accounted for by each game and each family of games. These estimates apply to OECD countries and are intended to present a general assessment, as variations of 5% can be expected between countries. How we arrive at these estimates is detailed below.

The first step in the analysis was to estimate the relative importance to the economy, in terms of GDP, of emerging markets and mature markets. We first looked at the distribution of venture capital investments, on the hypothesis that venture capital would be concentrated in emerging markets. In the United States, according to the National Venture Capital Association, which publishes quarterly statistics about venture capital investment, 46% of the $23.3 billion its members invested in 2010 went to the 'information and communication technology' sector, a broadly defined sector that ranges from media at one end to semi-conductors at the other. In the same year, biotechnology captured 16% and closely related medical devices 10%, for a total of 26%. Industrial products and energy received 15%, and all other areas (consumer goods, financial services, retailing, etc.) 12%. These venture capital investment statistics tell us where the emerging markets are concentrated, namely in ICT and life sciences, which account for around 70% of venture capital investments from year to year. Similar results were obtained in Canada.

How important are these sectors in terms of GDP? Since 1987 the US Bureau of Economic Analysis (BEA) tracks the contribution to the GDP of the 'information-communications-technology-producing industries,' or ICTP. This category includes the following sectors: computer and electronic products, publishing industries, software, information and data processing services, and computer systems design and related services. It includes emerging markets, such as Internet-related software, and mature products, such as computers (or most categories of computers), semi-conductors, and other electronic components. What is startling is the size of the ICTP defined by the BEA: for the past 10 years, its share of the GDP of the United States has hovered around 4.2% ±0.1%.[8] Such an estimate concurs with other estimates of the ICT sector and of the Internet economy.[9]

Other sectors of the 'new economy' are much smaller. The pharmaceutical sector as a whole, a small share of which is biotech, accounts for less than 0.4% of the United States' GDP. Medical devices add another 0.2%. Thus, the three areas that attract 70% of venture capital investments account for less than 5% of US GDP. Moreover, of that 5%, only a portion, which we estimate at around 3%, is accounted for by emerging markets.

We combed the industrial statistics within the economic accounts data bases to identify three- and four-digit sectors with high annual growth rate and which could be qualified as 'emerging markets.' The total of their contribution to GDP (in terms of value added), including the ICTP and the pharmaceutical sectors, is definitely less than 10%, more likely in the range of 7% of GDP. By definition, the other markets are deemed mature, and they represent the rest. To be on the conservative side, and to take into account the situation of countries such as Finland, where the ICT sector had a bigger share of the GDP, we assume 10% as the share of GDP accounted for by emerging markets in advanced economies. It is an arbitrary cut-off, sufficiently high to capture all markets where the three 'emerging market' games occur. The other 90% of GDP is generated by mature market activities (which include governmental activities).

The next step was to estimate the contribution of emerging markets to the growth of GDP. The BEA measures the growth of the value added by ICTP sector to the US economy. In the period 2002–2007, which excludes both the 2000–2001 Internet bubble and the 2008–2009 financial recession, the annual rate of growth of the ICTP sector was 11.3%, nearly five times that of the rest of the US economy during the same period, which was 2.4%.[10] This rate is congruent with data from the OECD about the growth of emerging markets in other countries. So we assumed that the average rate of growth of emerging markets was five time faster than that of mature markets, that is, the rest of the economy. Applying that rate of growth to the emerging markets' 10% share of GDP indicates that these markets contribute roughly 35% of the annual growth of GDP. Numerous sensitivity analyses with different assumptions about emerging markets' share of GDP and their relative growth rate suggest that this is a relatively robust estimate within plus or minus 5%.[11] Conversely, mature markets, while representing 90% of GDP, account for about two-thirds of growth.

If one assumes that labor and capital contribution per unit of growth is the same in emerging markets and in mature markets, these calculations suggest that, measured by its contribution to economic growth, one-third of innovation occurs in emerging markets, which represent a relatively small slice of the economy, and two-thirds in mature markets, which account for 90% of GDP.

We also did an estimate of the relative contribution of economic growth of each game. We had much less data for that exercise. We did a rough allocation of each three-digit sector of the economy to each game, on the basis of what we could infer from the MINE survey and case studies. That led us to the distribution presented in table 4.2 for the contribution of each game to economic growth, assuming a 35–65% breakdown of growth between emerging market games and mature market games. In emerging markets, Eureka! games and Battles of Architecture have similar contributions. Breakthrough games are less frequent; we estimate their contribution to be about a third of the other two types of games. In mature markets, New and Improved games account for the larger share of economic growth. Over time, Mass Customization games should gain in importance as open information-based systems permeate the economy. Pushing the Envelope games are more important than Breakthrough games, as they include innovations found in business and public infrastructures.

These estimates are indicative at best. But they give a sense of the relative importance of each game in an advanced economy. They convey an important finding, namely the significant contribution to economic growth made by the mature sector of the economy. Most public policies to stimulate innovation have focused on developing emerging market enterprises, with a special emphasis on new businesses in the early phase of emerging market games. These estimates suggest that more attention should be paid to mature markets. It is, admittedly, counterintuitive to suggest that mature markets are a more important source of innovation in advanced economies than are emerging markets. But it may help us to understand why 'Old Europe,' with its strong position in mature industries, can keep up economically with the entrepreneurially driven North American economy. This paradox brings home how important it is, in any attempt to harness the powers of innovation, to develop a thorough understanding of the process of innovation itself.

5 Emerging and Mature Markets

In 1976 we were asked, by a commission of inquiry set up by the Canadian government to investigate corporate concentration in Canada, to conduct a case study of IBM Canada.[1] At the time, IBM dominated the computer market. Over 10 long meetings, the company's senior management presented their views on the computer market. They emphasized its competitive nature, despite their greater than 80% market share. In one meeting, we drew their attention to a news report about the development of personal computers by independent computer geeks. We both remember the swift reaction of the IBM executives: they saw no commercial potential in personal computers and dismissed their builders offhand as 'basement hobbyists.' Within IBM, in 1976, the personal computer market did not exist.

Eighteen months earlier, two Seattle teenagers had read an article in the January 1975 edition of *Popular Electronics* about a microcomputer kit. The Altair was a simple board, with no screen, no memory, no keyboard, and no software. It had to be plugged into a teletype machine. The two friends, who had been dabbling in computer programming, rapidly developed a BASIC program for the Altair and sold it to its manufacturer in return for royalties. Sixteen years after that first sale, the market capitalization of Microsoft, the firm founded by the two teenagers in the spring of 1975, overtook that of IBM.

The most common approach to the development of industries is to view their evolution in terms of the metaphor of a lifecycle, as shown in figure 5.1.[2] At birth, a new industry is unnoticed except by pioneering customers, who discover a new and innovative product that addresses their needs. The word spreads, emulators step in, the market enlarges, and early adopters come into the market. As the market enlarges, the product goes through rapid, continuous improvements.

Figure 5.1. Market Life Cycle

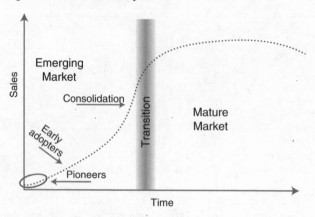

The more it improves, the less significant additional innovations become. Success increasingly depends on branding and distribution. The industry, highly fragmented at the outset, starts to consolidate. Laggards drop out, sell out, or merge. The industry matures as the market becomes saturated and sales flatten, some 15 to 25 years after being created. In mature markets, the remaining competitors tend to form oligopolies least on a territorial basis. Growth rates slow as demand stabilizes. As the market matures it gets more segmented: competitors discover new niches that they can serve efficiently with a targeted product. Innovation strategies still call for continuous cost improvements and product and service differentiation, as competitors shy away from direct price competition. Eventually, substitutes appear and the market starts a slow decline. Declining demand leads to spurts of product improvements and additional market segmentation. Producers drop out and the industry slowly thins out.

The MINE analysis indicates that the dynamics of innovation in an industry depend first and foremost on the maturity of the market. Table 5.1 presents the variables for which a significant statistical difference showed up between businesses in emerging markets and businesses in mature markets. We will use the case of the personal computer to illustrate these variables.

Table 5.1. Emergent Markets And Mature Markets:
Statistically Different Variables

Average annual sales growth (%)
Technical effervescence and pace of change
Need for collaboration with other businesses
Uncertainty about perimeter of the industry
Entry of new competitors
Focus of development efforts: disruptive changes
Focus of development efforts: new platforms
Focus of development efforts: cost reductions
% of revenues invested in R&D
% of employee time allocated to innovative activities
Contribution of innovative products to profits

Source: MINE survey

The Emergence of the Personal Computer

The personal computer industry was born in 1975, with the first shipment of the Altair. The market grew at a brisk pace for 25 years. In 2000, 60% of US households had at least one PC. It was also a watershed year, the last of a span of 25 years of continuous growth.

In 2001 worldwide PC sales declined for the first time. We arbitrarily set 2000 as the year when the market passed from an emerging state to that of maturity. Let's first analyze the emerging market journey of the PC.

The origins of the personal computer can be traced to the invention of the integrated circuit in the late 1960s. By crowding onto a single semiconductor chip an increasing number of transistor switches, researchers created an opportunity to significantly downsize computers. Electronic hobbyists had already started making all kinds of equipment with transistors, from pocket calculators to tone ringers that allowed free long-distance calls on public telephones.

Popular Electronics was a US magazine that attracted a loyal readership within the hobbyist community. Sensing that the personal computer was about to become a major presence, the editors of the magazine in the summer of 1974 invited a firm called MITS to develop a microcomputer for hobbyists that would be presented as the cover story for their next Christmas edition. MITS was a small 10-person firm based in Albuquerque whose main line of business was developing sophisticated calculators for the US Air Force. They were known at *Popular*

Electronics where they had previously written about calculators. The Altair microcomputer kit that MITS presented in the Christmas edition was a rudimentary product, a simple board. In the absence of a monitor and keyboard, users had to convey instructions by using toggle switches. But among the small hobbyist community that was developing electronic devices, the Altair was a big hit. Within a few months MITS started to ship it, and by the end of the summer it had sold more than 5,000 units.

Bill Gates and Paul Allen read the article and thought that they could develop a basic programming language for the Altair. They contacted MITS in early January 1975. A couple of months later, Paul Allen flew to Albuquerque with a program on a paper tape. A few weeks later, Allen and Gates founded Microsoft. Its first product was a BASIC program for the Altair, which it licensed to MITS on a non-exclusive basis. That key decision allowed Microsoft to sell BASIC software to other fledging manufacturers as they followed in the wake of the Altair success.

Two other teenagers, Steve Jobs and Steve Wozniak, also discovered the Altair in 1975, and within a year had developed their own board, named Apple, for the hobbyist market. In April 1977 they launched the Apple II. The Apple II was simply a box, with no screen, but small enough to sit on a table. An audio cassette recorder was attached to it to store programs and data. A video-controller screen was added to the basic kit. The Apple II is generally seen as the first full-fledged personal computer. Two months later, the Commodore PET 2001 was released. This PC had a small screen, and it quickly became much more popular than the Apple II. Radio Shack, a chain of electronics stores, followed in August that year with the TRS-80, which sold 10,000 units in its first month on the market. The age of the personal computer had arrived.

In 1980 more than 100 manufacturers were selling over one million personal computers worldwide. Atari, Commodore, and Apple were among the best-known brands. The central processing unit had progressed from four bits to eight bits. VisiCalc, the first spreadsheet product, and WordStar, the first word-processing software, were launched in 1979, enhancing the functionality of the PC. Other entrants followed, creating new models of PC and new software to run on them.

Sensing a movement in the marketplace, IBM, the global leader in computers, finally got moving in 1980. That fall it set up a small stealth-development team in Florida, with the mission to develop a PC in less than one year. To meet that deadline and reduce costs, the team decided to rely on outside suppliers for key components. Fatefully, the team asked Microsoft to provide the operating system for the Intel 8086 chips that they intended to use. As with all the components it used in its PC, IBM did not ask for exclusivity, providing an enormous break for Microsoft. IBM launched its PC in August 2001. It was an instant hit.

Within months, entrepreneurs in the United States and Asia had reverse-engineered the IBM PC and started to sell knock-off versions, euphemistically called IBM-compatible personal computers. In February 1982, only six months after the launch of the IBM PC, three seasoned Texas Instrument engineers launched Compaq (short for Compatibility and Quality), with the support of deep-pocketed venture capitalists. By the end of the year, Compaq was selling a fully IBM-compatible personal computer at a slightly lower price. Many more would follow. By the end of the decade, more than 85% of the computers sold in the United States were IBM-compatible. Compaq had the largest market share, beating the IBM PC by a wide margin. But no matter how the competitors shaped up, Microsoft provided all of them with MS-DOS software. The only significant player that didn't use Microsoft's operating system was Apple.

The 1980s brought great innovations in the personal computer industry. Intel provided most of the computer chips. It gradually increased their processing power through sustained improvement and miniaturization. It marked their progress by branding the chips, starting from the 8008 and moving to the 8080, the 8088, then the 8086, a slightly cheaper version created specifically for the IBM PC, then the 186, the 286, the 386, the 486, and in 1992 it introduced the Pentium.

Other developments were more readily apparent. In 1984, for example, Apple's Macintosh included a mouse and an icon-based desktop graphic interface. These two major innovations had been developed a few years earlier at Xerox's Palo Alto Research Center, but Xerox hadn't taken out patents on the technology. In only a few years, all computers incorporated the mouse and the desktop interface.

Around the same time, Microsoft launched Office, which grouped all common application programs, such as Word, PowerPoint, and Excel, into a single package, trouncing competitors who had remained in their respective niches. Even Apple, Microsoft's bitter rival, had to accept Office on its Mac computers. Complementary products became increasingly important. Microsoft invited independent software developers to create third-party applications for its operating system. The resulting applications ranged from Photoshop to tax-preparation software. Specialized graphic software, such as Acrobat from Adobe and Java from

Sun, also capitalized on the ubiquity of the Microsoft operating system. Computer games proliferated, from early versions of PONG, Arcade, and flight simulators to SIMS and scripted games that began appearing in the 1990s.

Meanwhile, computers became lighter but more powerful. The first portable computer, launched by Compaq in 1983, weighted 28 pounds (versus a few pounds today). With continuous improvement, portable computers assumed a new identity as laptops. In parallel, high-powered PCs appeared, while specialty companies manufactured peripheral equipment, from monitors and printers to memory storage devices. Quality improved across the board.

Dell was a late entrant into the field, in 1984. As a college student, Michael Dell assembled computers on demand (on 'spec' in the jargon), using stock components purchased from a variety of suppliers, a common business model from the early 1980s to the late 1990s. But Dell innovated by selling these computers by mail. By 2000 Dell had become one of the largest providers of personal computers in the world.

The Internet came of age between 1992 and 1995, transforming the use of the PC. Before the Internet, the PC was inward oriented, used by solitary individuals tapping away at a keyboard. With the Internet, the PC became a communication tool, no longer as important as the world to which it allowed access, its most critical function. The market's focus shifted from the PC itself to Web-related products. First came Netscape and Explorer, which allowed users to roam through the Web for information. Then came Yahoo and more specific Web-based services like e-Bay, Google, Amazon, iTunes and, more recently, the e-book. The personal computer itself has become just one of many devices that provided access to the Internet, along with specialized devices such as the Blackberry, the GPS, the iPad, and their imitators. All of these devices have computational capacity far greater than the personal computer of the mid-1980s.

Innovation Patterns in Emergent Markets

The PC industry's 25-year emerging market cycle is typical for a new product category. It illustrates well the fundamental characteristics of an emerging market:

1   At the outset is an invention, the result of a combination of ideas that defines a new product to address a specific unmet need in the

economy. The invention can linger around in the form of prototypes for a few years. The MITS Altair was the invention that gave birth to the PC. Thereafter, for about two years, emulators tinkered with the invention, greatly refined it, and developed its initial base of pioneering customers. Then the Apple II, the PET 2001, and the TRS-80 were launched and the market took off.

2 Swarms of entrepreneurs operate in the early years of an emerging market. Entry is easy, as the product is still unsophisticated. Differentiation through improved features is not difficult in the early stages. Five years after the Apple II launch, there were several hundred manufacturers of PCs in North America and Europe.[3] There is a rapidly growing base of customers who are eager to upgrade to new generations. As the product improves rapidly, no producer can stand still, and a strong virtuous circle of product improvement gets under way.

3 Large firms are not very present in the early years of an emerging market. There are exceptions, such as P&G's Tide and within the pharmaceutical industry, where product launches are dominated by large firms. But the delayed entry of IBM into the PC market is more common.[4] A corporate environment is not conducive to the 'needle-in-the-haystack' exploration that generates most inventions. Nor is it conducive to the continuous tinkering with a product required to maintain its differentiation. Entry by large firms, usually coming from 'neighbouring' markets, often happens later, through acquisitions, when the scope of the new market is clearly evident. We are seeing the same pattern with social media, the electric car, and solar panels.

4 Product management is crucial to sort out the winners and losers in emerging markets. Having the right products and the right upgrades is important at first. Soon, however, the positioning and marketing of the product become as important if not more, to cut through the clutter of competing products.[5] Indeed, the start-ups that make it through these initial years are usually led by marketers, who invest more on marketing and distribution than on R&D. The survivors also listen to customers, integrating their inputs into the firm's next generation of the product. Eventually, distribution becomes a discriminating factor. Many start-ups that hit the wall have good products, but cannot sell enough units to generate the cash they need to develop their next generation of products and keep up with their competitors. In a period of rapid product development,

that skill is critical. If forced to choose, a company should pay more attention to marketing and distribution than it does to R&D.

5 Complementary innovations play an important role in most emerging markets, expanding their reach. Such innovations were critical to the growth of the PC market.[6] With the introduction of a stream of new software applications, PC use extended from VisiCalc spreadsheet exercises in 1979 to a flight simulator game a few years later. Floppy disks and external hard disk drives expanded the PC's storage capacity in the early years. There were also printers, keyboards, mouses, and maintenance products. Most of these complementary innovations came from independent innovators.

6 The industry starts to consolidate even as the market is still facing double-digit growth. Several factors contribute to this consolidation. Standards gradually appear, both as guides of performance and for interoperability, giving more importance to brands as differentiator. Customers are more experienced and seek known brands as a promise of higher reliability. As the market grows, opportunities for economies of scale increase, favoring the bigger players. Price becomes a differentiating factor, putting pressures on margins. Distribution (or shelf space, in the jargon) gradually becomes more important as brands multiply and the market gets crowded. Entries become less frequent. (Dell Computers was the last significant North American entry, in 1984.) Smaller players start to drop out, short of funds to keep up with the race. Then large producers realize that their market share is slowly eroding and choose to sell out. In the PC market, consolidation occurred in the late 1980s at a time when the ubiquity of the Microsoft operating system was more or less forcing the Intel–IBM-compatible standard on the industry. Only a few mavericks, including Apple, chose to go it alone.[7]

7 Having a large market share at any given time does not ensure long-term survival in an emerging market. In the long run, only a few winners emerge. Of all the significant players in the PC industry in the early 1980s, only a few, such as Apple and Hewlett Packard, survived to 2000 as hardware manufacturers. Commodore, Atari, Radio Shack, Packard Bell, and Gateway, which were all at one time among the market leaders, have all faded away. On the software side, only Microsoft survived over the same period. A company that survives throughout the entire development cycle is more the exception than the rule.

8 Bold strategies can contribute significantly to shaping a developing

market and establishing leadership.[8] Microsoft's decisions to license its technology on a non-exclusive basis and to invite third parties to develop applications were critical in expanding the industry. Compaq shaped the PC market as well by entering the market in 1982 with an IBM-compatible PC. Apple survived as a non-IBM-compatible computer maker by incorporating the mouse and the icon-based desktop into its product. In the absence of these bold moves, the PC market would have been a very different place.

9 Where was the basic research behind all those PC innovations? The core R&D was related to semiconductor technology, as more and more capacity was integrated on the processing chips. Technological discoveries set the pace of change, but, with the exception of Intel, they did not in the long run confer significant competitive advantage on any particular player. New technologies spread rapidly, either through components or by licensing. Product engineering and product design were more important competencies, a typical pattern in most emerging markets where technological advances are usually rapidly shared.

Emerging markets are usually not well understood as they develop. Newness comes at a price, and uncertainty is one of the costs. Statistics are unreliable, since categories are not well defined and reporting is haphazard. Market information is sparse and unreliable. Companies have to rely on intuitive decisions and gutsy inferences about the direction of the market. This may be one reason why well-established companies do not fare as well as entrepreneurial ones in the early stage of a market's development. Established companies do better in mature markets.

Innovation Patterns in Mature Markets

Mature markets almost by definition are structured. Participants in these markets serve experienced customers with well-defined preferences. Competitors deliver similar product offerings incorporating the same technologies. Market shares are relatively stable. Yet a mature market is never static. Innovations still flow, oriented toward differentiating the offering by improving it, lowering costs, and improving business models. Typically, businesses focus their initiatives on these three areas simultaneously, although their relative importance will depend on the competitive landscape. Most innovations also occur at the margin. Very rarely will a business bet the farm on an innovation. Thus, innovations do not appear to be major strategic thrusts in mature industries. But they add up, and over time they come to matter significantly.

Product differentiation is the most visible field of innovation. In a mature market, product differentiation is pursued to avoid commodization and fend off price competition. It can bear on many attributes: product performance, reliability, added features, design, and so on. Given that all competitors pursue a similar strategy, standing still is not sustainable. The key decision is whether to be a market leader or a smart follower. Both strategies have their merits. Market leaders pursue systematic first mover advantages, enriching their brand appeal as they tend to be first with new benefits. But a smart follower can also succeed. Its strategy reduces risk by lowering investments in product development and experimentation, thus reducing the probability of costly failures. But lagging behind the innovators comes at a cost. Market leaders dictate the follower's product strategy, and that may not be optimal from the smart follower perspective. In the final analysis, it is a choice that reflects a firm's assessment of its capacity to innovate and of its appetite for risk. But whatever it does, it must continually improve its products.

The less visible ('under-the-hood') productivity-oriented innovations are just as important to improve profitability. Modern management practices keep constant pressure on costs. Most businesses are interested in productivity improvement, especially in mature industries where top-line growth is limited. The impact of these productivity-driven innovations is very significant in all advanced economies, given the dominance of mature sectors in the mix of activities.

The third source of innovation pursued in mature markets bears on the evolution of business models, such as sourcing and distribution. As the business environment evolves, new opportunities appear in the way a company can conduct its activities. The development of Internet shopping is causing retailers to change the way they sell; another example is the spread of loyalty-based systems. Competition tends to homogenize business practices and business models in any industry. But the same competition is creating pressure for continual improvements.

The PC as a Mature Market

After the dip in 2001, the global market kept on growing, especially in

China, India, and other fast-developing economies. As a result, more than 400 million PCs were sold in 2011, three times as many as in 2000 and an annual growth of 10%, which suggests that market penetration is not yet over. But the maturity of the market is revealed by several other indicators, such as relentless segmentation of the market and falling prices. Here are seven observations about the PC market since 2000 that yield useful insights about innovation in mature markets.

1 The pressure to innovate remains relentless, although the resulting pattern of innovation is different than in emerging markets The challenge in mature markets is not to reinvent the world, but simply to keep up with competition and, if possible, to nudge ahead. Adding an innovative new feature to a mature product makes only a small improvement in overall benefit and influences demand only at the margin. But such small differences still matter. With compatibility and common standards, customers can easily switch products. No competitor can afford to fall behind, even with strong brand and loyalty strategies.

2 Mature markets get increasingly segmented. The basic thrust of innovation is an ever-tighter match of features to the specific needs of customers. The PC market is divided at the macro level between business computers and home computers. Within each of these segments, competitors offer desktops and laptops. The laptop segment is further divided into regular and thin laptops, notebooks, tablets, and readers. At the periphery, the smart phone occupies a niche, protected by its voice functionality. Such fragmentation has been a fundamental characteristic of mature markets since General Motors segmented the automobile market to assume leadership from Ford in the 1920s. The more structured a market gets, the thicker the manufacturers' catalogues grow, as they compete by addressing ever more precisely the needs of their customers.

3 Prices fall continually, creating relentless pressure on costs. In the desktop PC industry, for example, a major brand sold in 2000 for $500. Ten years later, a much more powerful entry-level desktop sold for less than $400, despite inflation of 20% over the period. Innovation drives most of the cost reductions that allow competitors to support these falling prices. Manufacturers continually reduce costs in the value chain at the same time as they improve the features of their products. As a result, there are few structured industries where prices do not fall in the long run.

4 Mature markets are oligopolistic. Around 10 companies currently
  dominate the global PC industry: HP, Dell, and Apple in the United
  States; Sony, Toshiba, and NEC in Japan; Acer and Asus in Taiwan;
  Lenovo in China; and HCL in India. (HP is thinking about leaving
  the market.) A few subcontractors play a dominant role as well.
  Foxconn and Quanta, two Taiwanese contractors, account for more
  than half the notebooks sold in the world under major brand names.
  To varying degrees, mature market players control their innovation
  processes, which tend to involve big-business managerial decisions, not entrepreneurial ones. The players approach innovation
  with thorough planning and deep pockets. They build innovations
  around the evolution of portfolios, supported by brands and well-
  established distribution networks.

5 Stable ecosystems of suppliers and partners develop around these
  core players, sharing with them the slow evolution of the industry. The ecosystem is attuned to the relentless pressure to improve
  performance and lower costs. As the PC industry matured, the
  production of all commoditized components and their assembly
  were moved to low-cost regions and, in particular, southern China,
  where high-quality, low-cost suppliers abounded. But development,
  product management, and marketing activities remained close to
  headquarters. Typically, the PC industry ecosystems are dominated
  by small firms, both in advanced economies and in China and India,
  providing much of the downstream applications and the upstream
  components and peripherals. The relative stability of these ecosystems allows the development of collaborative practices. As a result,
  innovation strategies tend to be integrated throughout the industry,
  with each party knowing the others' expectations.

6 Predictability and manageability characterize mature markets. Big
  surprises are infrequent, and inertia prevails, both on the customer
  side and on the production side. Customers and producers share
  a vested interest in compatibility and gradual evolution. Buyers of
  PCs upgrade their machines to acquire more power as long as it
  doesn't involve extensive training or replacement of current software. In an industry with such a deep knowledge base, innovations
  migrate to the margins. When developing new products, manufacturers minimize cannibalization of their existing ones. As a result,
  there is little room in the marketplace for disruption: major innovations are usually introduced by fringe players who have little to
  lose.

7 Disruptive innovations generally appear in marginal segments
where customers are more sensitive to the disruptive features. The
attractiveness of disruptive features is sufficient to offset sub-par
performance in other areas, as Christensen pointed out. These innovations become disruptive only because dominant players ignore
them until it is too late. By then, new entrants have established
strong footholds in the industry. Incumbents generally survive,
adapting to the entry of a few upstarts in their ranks. Bill Gates
was initially dismissive of the Internet. But he woke up: Microsoft
eventually introduced Internet Explorer and, later, Office Outlook,
which have become dominant Internet-based software packages in
their categories. Advertising agencies initially dismissed Internet-
based advertising, leaving the field to start-ups. But by 2010 all
significant Web-based independent agencies had been absorbed by
global agencies.

8 For most markets, there comes an end, or at least a slow fade-out.
The horse carriage industry is still with us, but is a tiny fraction of
what it was. Some industries simply commodotize and get lost,
such as the salt industry, which a few century ago was the source of
incredible fortune, just as software is today. The automobile industry is centenarian, but is not likely to last another hundred years,
at least as now configured. The personal computer is getting old as
a product, at age 35, attacked on one side by cloud computing and
'software as a service' (SAS) and on the other side by tablets and
smart phones.

Mature markets not only dominate the economy, they are dominated by large businesses. As a result, a large share of the innovation in
modern economies arises from the corporate processes of large corporations, vindicating somewhat one of basic assumptions of the Schumpeter II model. The processes of these large corporations are designed
to maximize return on investment, minimize risk of failure, and properly channel the tensions that change generates within an organization. Innovating is a necessity for them. Every year, they must reduce
their costs and fend off intense competition. Innovations as investments compete against other ventures that aim to improve shareholder
returns. Thus the processes that frame innovations are important. But
they are very different from the processes that prevail in emerging markets, where there is much more uncertainty, and innovations tend to
represent bigger steps.

Inert Markets

There are mature markets in which little innovation occurs. Such inert markets are created by the convergence of three conditions: weak competition, little pressure for profits, and technological somnolence. Absence of competition is the most important factor. Quite a few economic activities in modern economies are organized as monopolies. The regulated ones such as utilities are well known, but government services constitute much bigger monopolies, organized around bureaucracies. Some are set by law, such as the police and the judicial system. But many other government bureaucracies crowd out competitors by offering their services for free or below cost. In most countries a large proportion of health care and educational services are delivered by de facto monopolies. Such monopolies hinder emulation, a major source of innovation. They tend to resist the testing of alternative solutions proposed by outsiders, something a competitive market does by its very nature. Moreover, monopolists face little risk of losing customers by sticking with the status quo, as long as they can channel those customers' complaints. Thus, little pressure for change comes from the customer interface.

The absence of shareholder pressures for higher returns can also favor the status quo. Such pressure in a mature market brings product differentiation and higher productivity, as both contribute to higher shareholder returns. Governments and non-profit organizations are affected by this absence. Treasury boards and budget offices will never be adequate substitutes, especially since the activities that they finance are usually prescribed by law and often prescribed in minute details by regulations that they cannot change.

Technological somnolence is a question of degree. The technological base of some industries is quite mature and is not changing rapidly. The extraction of salt, for instance, could be deemed a relatively stable process. So is the judicial process, although numerous lawyers will argue otherwise. There is of course no perfectly stable industry. Nevertheless, some industries are more placid than others, and that fact can be reflected in the industry's rate of innovation.

Large swaths of the economy are affected by these three factors, probably around 25% to 35% of GDP. These inert sectors do evolve, as they absorb technologies developed in other sectors. They also can innovate, and indeed, we continually hear about innovation in public services, in health care delivery, and in education. But the innovation imperative is much less intense. Innovation can always be driven by fiat, from the

Table 5.2. Innovation in Emergent and Mature Markets

Emerging markets	Mature markets
Fast changing	Slow evolution
Enlarging customer base	Defending market share
Fanatical users groups	Focus groups
Product management	Portfolio strategy
Designing the next generation	Implementing a product evolution strategy
Inventing the product	Improving the product
Seeking major performance gains	Seeking better features and prices
Improving reliability	Improving distinctiveness
Creativity	Efficiency
Life and death	Stability
Managing growth	Meeting growth objectives
Strategic insights, charisma	Good management
Worrying about exit	Good governance
Surviving stormy weather	Sailing on a red ocean, dreaming about a blue one

top, but it is rarely in the immediate interest of management to accept the turbulence that innovation forces on mature organizations. As a result, organizations in these 'inert' sectors tend to be laggard, soaking up new process and new ways of doing things from their environment, but careful not to be upset by too much turbulence. Anybody who has worked in government bureaucracies or in large regulated monopolies sees immediately the sharp differences between these organizations and others that face competitors on a daily basis and that must cope with shareholder pressures.

Two Worlds

Table 5.2 compares the nature of innovation in emerging markets versus mature markets.

In emerging markets, innovation drives growth. A typical journey lasts between 15 and 25 years during which the product gradually takes shape and the industry structures itself. The environment is turbulent. The priority is to enlarge the customer base as the market expands. The journey starts with a successful invention, which gives rise to a torrent of innovations to improve it.[9] Although they are fascinated by technological entrepreneurs, pioneering customers' true loyalty is to the avant garde. They will quickly drop an entrepreneurial company that cannot cope with the competition. As a result, most technological entrepreneurs get rapìdly pushed aside as competition intensifies. Performance in product management, marketing, and managing rapid growth sorts out the few winners from the large number of entrepreneurs that enter an emerging market.

Innovation appears to follow a more placid path in mature markets, which are dominated by a few large businesses that support large ecosystems of suppliers. Innovation occurs in an organized way, at a reasonable pace, as companies do not pursue a dream but simply try to do better than their competitors. Change is managed through processes of continuous improvement. Customers remain relatively loyal. A new feature offered by an unfamiliar competitor seldom persuades them to defect. The ecosystems generate many ideas for potential innovations, both in features and in productivity enhancements. Innovation may appear less spectacular, but it remains constant and ubiquitous.

6 Product Architecture

In 1979, under the leadership of its charismatic president Akio Morita, Sony launched the Walkman. It would become the emblematic consumer product of the 1980s and dominate the personal music player market for nearly twenty years. In its lifespan, more than 360 million units of the Walkman and its close cousin, the Discman, were sold.

The Walkman capitalized on Sony's experience with portable radio technology and sleek consumer product design to enter the nascent market for personal music players. Although not the first with a personal music player, Sony rapidly made the Walkman the market leader in Japan and, within a few years, a global marketing success. For more than 15 years, Sony continuously improved the product with a stream of innovations in performance, technology, convenience, and packaging, allowing it to stay at the top of the market. But eventually, with the combined impact of open standards and new technologies such as MP3, the Walkman lost its momentum, allowing the iPod to take over.

Twenty years after the Walkman, Research in Motion launched the Blackberry. It too became emblematic of a generation. Although there are many parallels between the two products, a close look reveals fundamental differences. The Walkman is a stand-alone product that delivers personalized music conveniently. It was designed and continuously improved by a group of engineers in a corporate lab, building on their accumulated expertise, and was sold by Sony, a global marketing powerhouse.

The Blackberry by contrast can be seen as a platform that offers a bundle of benefits. It belongs to a system that also includes Telcos and application developers. Research in Motion controls its evolution and its marketing, but in close cooperation with partners on whose collaboration it very much depends for its future. Indeed, a critical success factor for RIM is its ability to integrate third-party developers' innovations.

This chapter discusses differences in innovation patterns that are generated by the nature of the products or, more specifically, by the types of architecture, whether that product is a stand-alone one like the Walkman, an open system like the Blackberry, or a closed system like a steel plant. In doing so, we elaborate on a key finding of the MINE research: that the architecture of a product is a key determinant of the pattern of innovation that is pursued.

Products and Systems

The difference between the Walkman and the Blackberry is one of product architecture. The Walkman needed only recorded music to deliver its benefits to end users. The Blackberry, on the other hand, is a platform that relies on the contributions of telecom companies, of numerous independent application developers, and on its users' communicating with each other to deliver its benefits.

Stand-alone items such as the Walkman, Tide, books, pills, cameras, restaurant meals, and aluminum ingots represent a major share of the goods and services produced in the economy. But as the information economy advances, systemic products like the Blackberry are increasingly important. In the MINE survey, more than 60 percent of respondents were selling products or services integrated into systems rather than stand-alone products or services. The emergence and evolution of these involved different innovation processes than than do stand-alone products.[1] Yet until recently, the innovation literature focused on stand-alone products, such as a new detergent or electronic device.[2]

Systems have always been part of the industrial economy. Steel plants, which have been with us for more than 150 years, are systems built around a few core elements such as furnaces, casting machines, and rolling mills, to which are attached various modules such as coke ovens, power plants, repair shops, and slag disposal systems. The technologies behind most of these components are public. The progress of steel-making in the last 150 years cannot be understood without taking into account that systemic nature. Most of the innovations occurred at the component level: better rollers, more efficient furnaces, more advanced controls and, more recently, reduced emissions and better slag disposal methods. Moreover, the design of steel plants is typically done by third parties, namely by engineering firms. Innovation in steel-making for the past 150 years has emerged from a complex web of loose interactions between insiders and outsiders.

To distinguish between these different environments, we have borrowed the concept of architecture from engineering. Stand-alone products have a different architecture than systems. Furthermore, within the family of systems, one has to distinguish between closed and open systems. These distinctions are fundamental to understanding the innovation process, even more so as the development of the digital economy leads a proliferation of systems.[3]

Stand-Alone Products: The Better Mousetrap

A better mousetrap is an autonomous self-contained product that provides benefits without having to interact with other products or services. The analogy covers a wide array of products in today's economy, from aluminum ingots and plywood boards to wine, Aspirin, a bottle of Coca Cola, and the Walkman. Although these products can be used with complements, such as the mouse trap cheese bait, the complements are secondary and marketed separately. Here are the key characteristics of these stand-alone products that affect the innovation process associated with them.

Let's start with the invention of the product, the first of a long series of innovative moments. The inventor addressed a particular need that was perceived as unmet. The need precedes the invention. Not all products are in this situation, but a better mousetrap is. The pre-existence of the need influences the discovery process, focusing the inventor on the development of a solution that must meet certain criteria to address the need, whether it is a better mousetrap or a cure for cancer.

Second, an innovative stand-alone product is sold on its own merits, for the benefits that it single-handedly delivers. Its appeal is based on its performance on the attributes judged important by users, such as benefits, reliability, price, and image. Competing alternatives are judged on the same criteria, giving rise to merit-based competition. In other words, innovations associated with stand-alone products are assessed on their merits by customers.

Thirdly, the functionalities of a stand-alone product do not depend on its use by other people or on complementary products. It may come in and out of fashion as quickly as a Rubik's Cube, but its popularity does not depend on contributions of additional benefits from a complementary network. By contrast, the popularity of systemic products depends on choices made by a network of customers about continuing enhancements of functionalities.

Finally, the internal complexity of the product is largely irrelevant and is usually hidden. Innovative stand-alone products succeed on their superiority based on straightforward criteria that are important to prospective purchasers. A stand-alone product may be internally complex, but its complexity does not concern buyers, as long as it delivers what it promises.

Capturing the Value of a Stand-Alone Innovation

The relative simplicity in the way customers choose a stand-alone product has major competitive consequences. These products are easy to imitate. Competitors rapidly jump into the fray with a better mousetrap. Merit-based competition starts when the first imitator enters the market, and it continues throughout the life cycle of the product. This competition sustains a continuous drive for innovation. By being first with a feature, an innovator gains a lead time of mere months, not enough to eliminate direct competition.

In such a competitive game of innovation, a company can differentiate its product in three ways: first-mover advantage, exclusivity through intellectual property, and differentiation through branding.

First-mover advantage is ephemeral, unless continually supported by trend-setting innovations. But competitors can always leap ahead. A first-mover strategy places great demands on a company's product development and marketing. It also entails higher risk, betting on continuous success in the market. But since companies cannot risk lagging on product performance, almost inevitably they will pursue first-mover advantage, although they will not gain much from them as such first-mover advantages are fleeting.

A patent on intellectual property can provide relief from competition, but that protection varies greatly. In the pharmaceutical industry, marked by a combination of easy-to-copy products and complex regulatory process, patents play a major role in the innovation process. In general, if the product is unique, like the Rubik's Cube or a board game, a patent can keep imitators away. But a product's benefits cannot be patented and there is usually more than one way of delivering them. Thus, in most industries patents offer little protection to innovative stand-alone products as they are being developed and launched. Through clever design and engineering, competitors can circumvent patented processes and components to develop a similar product delivering roughly the same functionalities at little or no additional cost and with only brief delays. Patents also have drawbacks: they are in the public domain and force the divulgation of technological secrets. They can also invite costly legal disputes that may overwhelm a product's economics in a cloud of uncertainty. To minimize that risk, patent holders will often license their intellectual property, minimizing enforcement costs and building an alternative income stream.

Branding can offer better differentiation. Associating a proprietary brand with the specific benefits of the product differentiates it from other products, as customers want the 'real' thing. The classic case is Coca Cola, a brand whose value is estimated at $70 billion by Interbrand, a consultancy firm that publishes yearly estimates of brand value. In the same vein, copyrights provide strong and permanent ownership rights on a brand, and in fact on any expression of ideas, such as an exclusive design, a logo, a book, or a song. Louis Vuitton bags owe much of their value to the copyright that LVMH has on the brand, giving it the exclusive use of its logo.

When customers are still relatively unfamiliar with a product, which is often the case in an emerging market, a brand acts as a reference, providing sustainable differentiation to an innovative product. In an emerging market, establishing the brand of a new stand-alone product can be as important as developing the product itself, if not more.

Ecosystems

Ecosystems are important in stand-alone product games as a source of new ideas. The web of suppliers, distributors, key customers, partners, and service providers that constitutes an ecosystem know the product, and they have a shared interest in its success. This requires a firm to cultivate relationships within its ecosystem to stimulate exchanges beyond mere commercial transactions. Businesses that focus strictly on the cost of inputs and that delegate procurement to a specialized department deprive themselves of productive interactions within their ecosystem and restrict its potential contribution to innovation. Without rich interactions within an ecosystem, most innovative ideas must come from within the firm or from cues from their competitors: this is a position of weakness.

Distributors and key customers play a particularly important role in innovation, a fact that is not always well recognized. Many companies that produce stand-alone products keep an innovation secret until it is officially launched, frowning on any communications about it to its distributors prior to the launch. Their purpose is to keep the information away from competitors. A more enlightened approach to the trade-offs between secrecy and communication could be used to better exploit the full potential of an ecosystem.

Merit-Based Marathons

Success for a stand-alone innovation consists in delivering on its promise. But the goalposts of success are always moving, because competition entails relentless innovation, driving the advancement of competitive attributes, forcing a continual redefinition of the product.[4] Not surprisingly, market leadership usually changes several times over the life cycle of a product. Staying in the race over a long period is a great challenge, staying at the top even greater: few businesses survive throughout the whole cycle. The games that involve stand-alone products are never-ending marathons.

Open Modular Systems

The Blackberry is a typical platform supporting an open modular system. Research in Motion owns the brand, controls its design and develops its key software components, such as the operating system, e-mail and voice functions, and underlying signal-processing capability. It also integrates seamlessly several licensed proprietary software products, such as the Flash player from Adobe. The device is manufactured by contractors, mainly in China.

As orchestrator, RIM caters to three important communities: the customers that use the Blackberry, the network operators, and the third-party developers. Network operators provide the connectivity to wireless networks. They also distribute the product, often using it as a loss leader and participating in its marketing costs. For networks, Blackberry's clients are a rich source of revenue. Third-party developers develop applications for the Blackberry. Some of them are licensed to RIM, who pay royalties. Most are sold to users in the Blackberry Apps Store. Finally, some, such as Facebook and Twitter, are free, their owners getting their revenues from the advertising found on the application. (Apple, who operates a similar platform, is also seeking to get a cut of these revenues, just as they get a cut of any revenues third-party application providers receive.) The customers get a bundle of benefits, for which they pay network operators, which turn around and give a cut to RIM.

What the Blackberry platform does is to support multi-sided markets where each of these three constituencies draws some benefits from the presence of the other two. At the center, as the platform orchestrator, RIM ensures that each constituency is satisfied. That calls for managing the contributions and benefits received by its two 'complementor' constituencies, the network operators and application providers, and for ensuring that end customers get value for their money.[5]

Management of the complex coalitions of complementors as the Blackberry evolves in competition with other platforms is one of the main tasks of RIM and of other platform operators. All complementors have a stake in the success of the platform. RIM selects them with a balanced portfolio of benefits in mind. Managing the evolution of that portfolio of benefit is challenging. At any given time, RIM must identify attributes for improvement in light of what the competition does: a better phone signal, improved reliability of e-mail services, longer-lasting batteries, better Web interface, faster downloading, more applications, exclusive ones, an so on. In other words, RIM determines the bases on which the Blackberry competes. But RIM must also align its partners behind this evolutionary roadmap. Each of them has different claims on the attributes of the Blackberry. When incorporating an innovation, generated either internally or from a third party, RIM must consider the interests of the whole coalition to ensure that all parties will stay loyal to the platform. The presence of all these complementors with vested interests in the platform turns the management of innovation into an art. In this critical aspect, the innovation processes involved here differ radically from those of stand-alone products examined above.

Network Effects

The growth of multi-sided markets that open system platforms support is fuelled by network effects: the more, the merrier. Why are customers drawn to the Blackberry? As in the case of most open systems, there are many reasons. The platform offers a bundle of services, each of which provides a basket of benefits. In its early days, the Blackberry was a hit in the corporate world for its e-mail technology, enabling corporate executives to stay in touch wherever they were. The quality of the phone signal was important as well. But the Blackberry was also helped by its rising popularity, as the usefulness of a communication device increases with the number of people who can be reached on it. Its client base of high-income business people also interested greatly the network operators, which readily subsidized the price of the Blackberry. In addition, that client base drew application providers. The greater the number of applications offered, and the more the network operators subsidized the Blackberry, the more customers were drawn to adopt it.

'Network effects' refers to the mutual reinforcement of the attractiveness of a platform by the enlargement of its customer base. Open systems generate numerous network effects. As a system draws users, more third-party developers are attracted to it, in turn enhancing its attractiveness to users, in turn attracting developers, and so on. In an organization, the greater the number of employees using the Blackberry, the more devices the technical department keeps in stock and the better becomes the service users get. Having the same brand simplifies training sessions, upgrades, and assistance from colleagues.

Network effects relate to the benefits of being with the crowd. Open systems, whose appeal is tied to the number and quality of modules they offer, are generally associated with powerful network effects: more users, more and better modules, more attractiveness, more users. Powerful virtuous circles are triggered.

Network effects are also frequent when compatibility is a benefit. By accommodating a wide variety of applications within a single package, Microsoft Office, for example, became the leading business software for personal computers. Network effects enabled Office users to seamlessly exchange Word and Power Point files, ignoring perfectly good alternatives such as Word Perfect and FreeLance.

Network effects were first exploited in retailing, and they still are. Wal-Mart can attract more vendors and get better deals, which allow it to turn around and offer more deals to its own customers, which draws more of them, making Wal-Mart more attractive to vendors. Network effects also work for an airport hub. The more airlines fly to it, the more connections can be made, the more travellers flying through, more airlines flying in and out, more connection possibilities – but, alas, more congestion, the bane of network effects.

There are other limits to network effects. Complacency has hurt more than one successful platform, which has slowly drifted into blandness and lost its best customers. Managing size and the complexity that it entails offsets the benefits of network effects, as the platform starts to lose some of its edge. Network effects can lead to very high market share. Microsoft built a quasi-monopoly worldwide on operating systems on the strength of network effects, until a loose coalition of large users, regulators, and contrarians rebuffed Microsoft and popularized alternatives. Google and Facebook can also thank network effects for their high market shares.

There is a final downside to network effects: the best product does not necessarily win, as the VHS versus Betamax saga illustrated 30 years ago. From an innovation perspective, enlisting a strong coalition of third-party providers of modules can be more important than having the best performing platform.

High market share is not necessarily a bad thing, notwithstanding what antitrust authorities believe. There is real benefit in being with the crowd. If on the one hand a high market share can lead to undue market power and higher prices, which very much concern antitrust authorities, it can also lead to superior benefits to users, who can count on a superior offering made possible because of network effects.

Discovering New Needs

Who would have thought that the world needed a one-way communication platform limited to 140 characters, with no ability to respond? We are not even sure that the inventors of Twitter knew. Yet in 2011, five years after being imagined, Twitter claims several hundred million users.

Unlike stand-alone innovations like the better mousetrap or a cure for cancer, the innovations introduced in open systems do not always address apparent needs. The inventors of Twitter took a simple idea – combining mobile phone SMS messaging with e-mail push technology – and delivered it on the Web as an effective way of disseminating short messages. Before communities of users embraced it, the inventors had to imagine that some latent demand existed for such a product. Their intuition was correct. Within four years, Twitter had become the third most popular application on the Web.

New platforms typically emerge from the imaginations of creative promoters who can think system wide. At RIM, Mike Lazaridis crossed the pager's push technology with Internet's e-mail capacity to create an attractive product for people hooked on e-mail. But he had to convince mobile phone operators that a demand existed. He also had to design software that allowed mobile phone users to communicate with fixed-line e-mail users. In other words, he had to imagine a complete new system operating in parallel to the e-mail system already in use on fixed lines. With such system-wide thinking, new platforms are created. Then they get enriched by the development of a multi-sided market structure, with the addition of modules whose owners capitalize on the reach of the platform.

Open systems allow inventors to explore the potential of new product ideas that address needs which require the reach of the platform. The innovation activity moves from the platform and its initial benefits to new and improved modules that are attached to it. Then as network effects take hold, new vistas are opened. Farmville is a very simple game played on Facebook that in 2011 attracted over 100 million monthly users. It could not have been imagined without the reach of Facebook and the existence of an efficient payment mechanism for small transactions, which is the main source of revenue of Farmville. Again, the need for a simple fantasy game that involves building a model farming community was not really apparent in 2008, when its creators launched it. Yet a product that builds a 100 million customer base in less than 30 months must have addressed a real need.

Open systems are a boon to innovators, as they open new vistas, allowing innovators to explore concepts and ideas that were unthinkable until the platform arrived. When Netscape arrived as the first browser, suddenly the Web became a huge base for innovative products. Facebook and the iPhone did the same, but doing one better than the browser: keeping some control over the applications that were reached through their platform.

The potential contribution of third-party providers gives rise to one of the major strategic issues facing open platform orchestrators, namely the trade-off between the openness of the platform and the placement of constraints on third-party providers. Proper controls allow orchestrators to enhance the effectiveness, the performance, and the proper positioning of their platform.[6] But the same controls can reduce not only the attractiveness of a platform to third parties, but also the inventiveness of third parties. Tightly controlled platforms lose on creativity; they are less likely to be first on the market with new applications, which make them less popular with pioneering and trend-setting users, very influential communities in fast-growing markets. In the 1980s Apple ran a much tighter platform than Microsoft, and had the additional benefits of a superior product. Yet, Microsoft attracted more third-party developers and grabbed most of the market.

Success Factors

Capturing network effects and finding the right openness strategy are the two critical considerations for succeeding as an open platform.

The capture of network effects starts at the outset, with influential and dedicated early adopters. Their support is based not on the technical merits of the platform, but on its promises, in particular its promise of reach. The buzz they generate attracts complementors and later adopters. Proper marketing is thus critical at the launch, to reach an influential base of early customers and to get the product known among their communities of early adopters.

But early network effects are not sufficient to ensure long-term survival. A multi-sided market platform has to satisfy several constituencies, including the ambitious and sometimes greedy third-party developers, and this is challenging. It also explains why open systems witness frequent changes in market leadership. For every Microsoft that has managed to stay on top for decades, there are a dozen former early market leaders that could not stay ahead, from Atari and VisiCalc to WordPerfect and Treo. Early network effects have power, but it is not unlimited.

Maintaining the innovativeness of the system demands close cooperation between the platform orchestrator and the complementor community. A platform must maintain a compelling bundle of services as competition raises the standards. Under relentless pressures, the orchestrators must stay alert and guard against complacency. This is a tough task for platforms that are market leaders. Microsoft Explorer's market share is slowly eroding against Mozilla, Chrome, and Safari. Likewise, in the retail sector, chain store systems such as The Gap and Ben & Jerry's in the United States are locked into a once-winning formula that is rapidly aging. Wal-Mart is faced with tepid same-store growth in North America, a sign that competing platforms are encroaching on its customer base, offsetting any benefits from the huge economies of scale and network effects that the number one retailer has in the US market.

Aging platforms can ossify, making it difficult for orchestrators to modify their architecture and offering. Systems get more complex as they evolve, and complementors defend their vested interests. This sets the stage for possible Schumpeterian upheavals. These become even more likely since most platforms do not owe their dominance to some technological superiority, but to the fact that they were first to harvest network effects. That provides challengers with an opportunity to disrupt the existing order.

Creative Duets Developing Closed Systems

Tightly integrated systems, the third type of architecture, accommodate a very different pattern of innovation, best illustrated by IBM's 1981 decision to buy the operating system of its IBM PC from Microsoft. The dedicated IBM team set up to develop the PC had to meet two challenging constrainsts in the development of what was a relatively simple product for such a technical powerhouse as IBM: twelve months and low cost. These two constraints led the team to the fateful decision of relying extensively on off-the-shelf components. Instead of choosing an IBM chip as the brain of the computer, it selected the low-cost Intel 8086 chip. It then sought to license the operating software for the 8086 chip from Digital Research, a San Francisco firm. When the talks failed, IBM turned to Microsoft, on the belief that it also had an off-the-shelve solution.

Microsoft, barely a few months old at the time, did not have the software, but knew of another small Seattle firm that did. The software was called QDOS, or Quick & Dirty Operating Software. Microsoft quickly licensed it from its developers, without telling them what it intended to do with it. Within a few months, working closely with IBM, Microsoft adapted it and licensed it to IBM. In the following years, Microsoft kept improving it, turned it into MS-DOS, and licensed it to all computer manufacturers that chose to emulate the IBM PC by using 8086 chips and the MS-DOS operating system. From that foundation, Microsoft has grown bigger than IBM.

There are three observations to take out of this case.

1 The need that was to be addressed was well known at the outset – an operating software for the 8086 chips – and so was the client, IBM.
2 The innovation was well defined: the performance standard that the software had to meet was pre-defined by IBM and agreed upon by Microsoft.
3 Microsoft ensured that it could resell the innovation, by providing a non-exclusive license to IBM.

Other well-known software companies were born out of a similar experience. SAP traces its origins to a contract between ICI Germany, a subsidiary of the British chemical giant, and a group of fledging ex-IBM engineers to develop software that would integrate its various accounting and operational information systems. The engineers formed SAP and invented Enterprise Resource Planning (ERP) software, which now structures information systems in almost all large organizations, In a similar vein, Oracle developed its first relational database under a contract with the US Air Force and then went on to become a multi-billion-dollar company on the strength of its acquired expertise.

A tightly integrated system can be defined as a unique set of non-standardized components coherently integrated to deliver a proprietary solution to a customer. Not only does such a system require all its components to work, but these components must also operate together. By contrast, an open system is a platform on which an indeterminate number of modules are added, most of them working independently of each others.

Closed systems abound throughout the economy. Integrated industrial plants, from oil refineries to large printing plants, are closed systems. So are airplanes, bridges, ATM systems, and racing cars. In fact, a large proportion of capital goods are tightly integrated systems. Despite being neglected in the economic literature on innovation, which tends to highlight more visible open platforms, closed systems are major sources of innovation and technical progress. They also do it very differently.

In closed systems, an innovation typically starts with a customer who has a major problem and wants it addressed. The need explicitly precedes the innovation. The customer turns to an expert and challenges him or her to solve the problem, using the latest advances in technology and knowledge.[7] The two work together to develop and implement the solution. Subsequently, the solution can be packaged into a product and applied to other, similar situations.

The problem that is addressed is typically an industrial or an infrastructure challenge. Boeing, for example, wanted to build a new plane from composite materials. A bank seeks a totally integrated customer-focused information system that provides end-to-end services to its clients. A tycoon wants to build the tallest building in the world in a difficult environment. Toyota wanted to reduce the development time for new vehicles when it teamed up with Dassault Systèmes, which had tackled a similar challenge in aircraft manufacturing.[8] Regardless of the client, the problem is big and so is the ambition to address it. The client deliberately chooses a visionary expert. Together, they commit themselves to finding a solution to the problem.

Such an innovation process is very different from that of a stand-alone product or an open system. In a closed-system innovation, there is typically one customer with a specific and well-known problem. The solution that emerges has to address every specification, to the last coda. The process occurs within the framework of an industrial project, with a beginning and an end and a budget, all coordinated by a system integrator. From the outset, the customer chooses the experts and keeps them on the project until they solve the problem. Participants in the project apply the latest proven technologies. Within the project, a lot of advanced research development occurs. The solution that emerges usually stands on the leading edge of its technological universe. From such a process emerged products such as CATIA, MS-DOS, SAP, and the ubiquitous GPS. A highly focused and closely managed innovation process of this sort differs greatly from the processes involved in innovative stand-alone products such as the Walkman and in open platforms such as the Blackberry.

From Project to Market

The successful completion of a Breakthrough project is just the end of the first act of a game about to unfold. The system integrator and his or her team of experts typically search for an encore performance, in which they can apply the discoveries and the lessons learned from the original project. This is not always easy to do. Clients involved in such projects often feel that they have earned rights to the innovative technology. They also fear that their own competitors may have access to the solution, and will try to prevent this. Microsoft left a lot of corporate noses out of joint at IBM with its non-exclusive licence for its 8086 operating system. SAP and Oracle also remained in control of innovative technology developed for their first clients and went on to build their businesses around it.

The ownership, transferability, and subsequent applications of the technology developed through a closed system of innovation depend on several circumstances. When direct competitors are excluded, innovations may be freely transferred to other customers. An engineering firm that designs revolutionary technology to build a bridge or a skyscraper, for example, may carry the lessons learned to its next project without arguments from its initial customer. But the designers of a retailer's custom-built inventory management system could not sell it to a one of its competitors. In many cases, the contractual arrangement will prevent not only the sale of a system to a competitor, but also the sharing of the technology and expertise gained.

There are surely situations where clients kept full control of innovative technologies and no business emerged. But we seldom hear about them, as they are not marketed. Their commercial potential is often forgotten. Wal-Mart has kept tight control on the technology behind Retail Link, its in-store inventory control system that has allowed it to decentralize its inventory management and transfer to its suppliers responsibility for maintaining their inventory levels in all its stores. ('Indiana store number 19 needs more deep blue socks, size medium.') So far, competitors have failed to develop systems that can achieve the same low costs and functionalities that Retail Link delivers to Wal-Mart. Not surprisingly, Wal-Mart has gone to great lengths to keep full control of the technology. Contracts with third-party developers of the technology explicitly forbid them from sharing it. Moreover, Retail Link is not covered by patents. Wal-Mart chose to protect its intellectual property by guarding access to the code.[9]

Is such control a good thing? We can ask ourselves if the PC industry would have been less innovative if Microsoft's contract had prevented it from commercializing the 8086 operating system to third parties. Certainly, competitors would not have developed IBM-compatible PCs. But would the industry have been more innovative? Or less?

Different Architectures, Different Processes

Different product architectures lead to widely divergent innovation processes, each with its own dynamic. The classical view of innovation, in which the inventor carries his or her innovation from the lab to the market, protected by patents and a brand, may work well, but only for stand-alone products. In these markets, competition is based on continual displacement of established solutions by superior ones. Selection and the innovation process leading to it are based on merit.

Meritocratic selection does not prevail as much in platform-based open systems. Their evolution is shaped by strategic choices that take into account the interests of the multiple actors responding to network effects. As a result, the best technical solution does not always win. Winning solutions are not necessarily the best technologically, but rather those that were first to harness network effects and marshall a critical level of complementors' contributions.

In the third type of architecture, tightly integrated systems, a different dynamic, governed by its own rules, shapes innovations. It starts with an ambitious client with a big problem to solve. The client hires experts on the basis of their reputation, accumulated knowledge, and appetite for sharing risk. A critical issue is the freedom that these innovators enjoy to parlay their success into products for other clients, depending on their leverage and control of the innovative technology.

Table 6.1 describes these three very different innovation patterns. In each situation, the innovative spirit is driven either by the desire to

Table 6.1. Product Architecture and Innovation

Product Architecture	Stand-alone products	Open modular systems	Tightly integrated closed systems
The nature of the innovation	A new or improved product	A platform that delivers benefits	A solution to a complex problem
Key drivers	Relentless innovation, marketing	Network effects, complementary features	Project management, reselling the solution
Where does it start?	An inventor imagines a better mousetrap	An entrepreneur explores the potential of a platform	An ambitious client seeks a solution to a big problem
How is value created?	Product & brand differentiation ensuring good margins	Capturing network effect; building high market shares	Developing a breakthrough; selling it to others
Markets	An unmet or poorly met need	A market is created as buyers learn to use the product	Markets pre-exist but are enhanced by the innovation
How customers decide	Merit and brand, comparative shopping	The package of benefits, inter-operability	Very rational and risk managed
Methods of value capture	Temporary product superiority, brand, and intellectual property	Orchestrators and complementors split numerous revenue streams coming from a complex offering	A complex product, protected by contractual obligations and security policies

address an unmet need and turn a vision into reality or by capitalizing on available know-how to develop a superior product. But the nature of a product, and more specifically its architecture, inevitably orients the innovator toward a particular pattern of innovation. Successful innovation strategies and the resulting industrial dynamics stem from the product architecture. In other words, the kind of products that entrepreneurs and firms develop and sell shapes their innovation strategies and practices.[10]

PART TWO

The Six Games of Innovation

7 Eureka!

3M is one of the most admired high-technology firms. With annual sales close to $30 billion, it ranks 97th on the Fortune 500 list of the largest US corporations and 40th in terms of profits. It is widely admired for its innovations and has participated in more Eureka! games than most other major companies. Founded in 1902, its first product was abrasive sand for grinding wheels. That product and its lofty ambitions explain its name, the Minnesota Mining and Manufacturing Company, eventually shortened to 3M. The grinding-wheel-abrasive market did not pan out as planned, and the company gradually moved into the sandpaper market. It was a mature market at the time, but 3M thought it could establish a foothold in industrial segments.[1]

Success didn't come easily in the sandpaper market. A line of waterproof sand paper allowed 3M to survive. But in its diversification attempt in the sandpaper business it learned about glues. In 1925 it launched its first Eureka! product, masking tape, while establishing itself in the market for adhesives. In 1930 it announced another notable product, Scotch tape. This placed 3M solidly within the consumer marketplace.

By this time, 3M had institutionalized its innovation strategy. It had created a strong R&D center, significant marketing resources, and, more importantly, the belief among its leaders that the company's growth depended on new products. It mastered two technological areas, abrasives and adhesives, and kept on diversifying. During World War II, the company moved into magnetic tape, then into recording devices and a broad range of electronic equipment.

Today, 3M markets 55,000 products throughout the world, employs 75,000 people, and operates 35 research centers. In 2010 alone it obtained 589 patents. Over the 25 years from spring 1986 to spring 2011, its stock price grew at 7.95% a year compared to 5.8% for the S&P 500, not bad for a 109-year-old company. 3M remains a force in adhesives and abrasives, but it's involved as well in a broad range of technologies, from medical instrumentation to nanotechnologies. As a company, 3M has mastered the Eureka! game better than most other companies of its size and age. It owes its success essentially to its agility and to its marketing ability within the well-chosen technological areas that it masters.

Relentless Races

A Eureka! game involves competition between continually developing products in an emerging, ebullient, and fast-growing market. Standalone products target specific needs and include everything from portable music players and pharmaceuticals to AAA batteries and tennis rackets.

A Eureka! game starts with an inventor designing a commercially viable answer to an unmet need. The invention inspires emulators to build on the idea and improve the original design. The market can take off immediately, or it may take a few years for all elements to fall into place and for the product to take off commercially. As the market expands, new players enter the game. The game can last between 15 and 25 years. When the customer base has been fully developed, the industry consolidates, and the Eureka! game dissolves into a New and Improved game, which we will discuss in chapter 11.

The MINE survey included 139 businesses that were active, predominantly or solely, in Eureka! games. Furthermore, several of the case studies bear on businesses involved in Eureka! games. They provided good insights into the dynamics involved in the game:

Eureka! games are played mostly in sectors influenced by rapid advancement of knowledge. Stand-alone products are incubated in a nexus of technological advances, where inventors develop solutions for unmet needs. Although most inventions get lost in the archives of patent offices, there are always some that become commercially viable and create a market, attracting both customers and emulators.

As the product gets developed and refined, the customer base enlarges and the industry begins to structure itself. Entry is usually easy in the early phase of the game, but the failure rate is also quite high. Brands progressively get established and players accumulate knowledge. Both become barriers to new entry.

Products compete on their merits and are generally easy to copy. Superiority involves not only technical performance but also image, availability, reliability and, as growth tapers, price. Rivalry, crystallized around innovation, is significantly higher in Eureka! games than in any other game.[2]

Patents matter in some markets where products are easy to copy. Innovations involving new molecular structures for pharmaceuticals, for example, or a device like a Rubik's Cube can trigger races to the patent office.[3] However, for most stand-alone products, particularly in the early stage of Eureka! games, patents present more of a design challenge for competitors than act as a source of value for innovators. It is only much later that some of them become highly valuable.

Brands eventually become the most common product differentiators, displaying the promises of benefits while generating customer loyalty and higher margins. Marketing expenditures are as important, if not more, than R&D expenditures.

Change occurs rapidly in Eureka! games, as products are improved, new competitors enter, and new customers are drawn in.[4] Once products take off, annual growth rates of 20% and more are typical as products develop their customer bases.

Eureka! games involving regulated products that must meet strict criteria on safety or reliability, such as drugs, are characterized by more controlled competitive entry and unfold at a less frantic pace. We'll analyze this special case in the next chapter.

In Eureka! games, R&D expenditures are high, accounting on the average for 20% of sales in our survey. Most innovations, which are essentially improvements to existing products once the game has started, are largely developed in-house, requiring hands-on management.

Nevertheless, key players develop their ecosystem through symbiotic relationships with smaller technology-based firms, which help them to fuel the relentless process of innovation. Many of these small firms are eventually acquired by major players.

Two phases of Eureka! games are of particular interest, as figure 7.1 illustrates. Phase I follows the successful commercialization of a Eureka! product, when it attracts pioneering customers and emulators. Phase I lasts a few years and generates a fast-growing industry. Phase II is the consolidation that occurs when growth slows and winners and losers are sorted out.

Eureka! Moments: The Birth of a New Market

A Eureka! game starts when an entrepreneur connects a technical solution to an unmet market need. From this Eureka! moment comes the

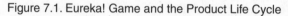
Figure 7.1. Eureka! Game and the Product Life Cycle

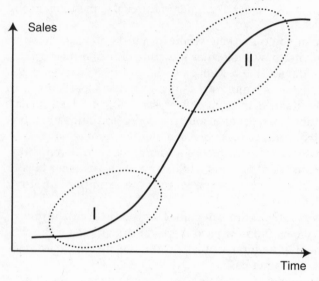

idea of a new product. The Post-It note is a classic example. 3M asked Art Fry, a product manager, to try to come up with a product based on a weak type of glue invented by a colleague in the 1960s, a product that had eluded 3M for several years. Losing his place in a hymn book one day at church, Fry realized his bookmark would work better if it stuck lightly to the page. Eureka! It then took Fry a few years and several market studies to convince 3M's top brass that people would buy poorly sticking note pads. When 3M launched the product in 1980, sales immediately soared. The simplicity of the product combined with a strong patent protection kept most emulators at bay. Post-It notes soon became one of 3M's best-selling products. Even now that the patents have expired, the Post-it note family of products remains one of 3M's major profit centers.

Products emerging from Eureka! moments appear continually. Some succeed; many don't. Even the few that succeed achieve varying degrees of success. In a 2005 list of products of the year, for example, Time Magazine highlighted an unusual planter box for growing tomatoes, invented by a serial inventor named Bill Felkenor. To protect tomatoes from insects and dirt, Felkenor's Topsy Turvy planter hangs upside down and has holes in the bottom that allow a plant's branches to hang down. In the last five years, Felkenor has sold more than 20 million units. But with several competing models on the market, no company will likely emerged as the dominant player in the marketplace for tomato planters.

Eureka! moments are associated with inventors. The small minority of them that succeed in translating their invention into a commercial innovation come from all walks of life. Some are scientists, exploring the edge of human knowledge in a particular technological area. Others are tinkerers. In between is a vast array of creative people who observe unmet market needs and who imagine solutions by drawing on their own technological knowledge.

Some inventors work alone, others in the laboratories of large firms, where they receive extensive support and enjoy access to a much broader pool of potential technical solutions. Since the days of Thomas Edison, who set up his laboratory in Menlo Park 130 years ago, some inventors have worked in creativity workshops where collaborative exchanges presumably enhance their creativity. Whether these work is still uncertain, although one of the best-known recent innovations, Twitter, came out of such workshop.

Whether unmet needs (the chicken) or a technology's potential (the egg) lies at the heart of an invention depends on the incubation process. Owners of technologies want to find a use for them. This was the case with 3M and its Post-its. But the process generally works the other way, as unmet needs trigger a search for practical solutions. The Segway, for example, the Walkman, and the breathing mask to relieve sleep apnea were all developed to address an unmet need. When developing a solution to such an unmet need is deemed achievable, ambitious inventors will seek to develop it. Drawing from available technology, they believe that they will succeed in developing a viable solution. But they don't necessarily succeed: bridging the gap remains a stochastic process.

Fertile Grounds for Incubating Innovations

In 1987 we wrote a book called *Growing the Next Silicon Valley*.[5] We were responding to the growing interest in recreating elsewhere the miracles of Silicon Valley, where a continuous stream of start-ups built up a global new-economy industrial base. We did not deliver a sure-fire recipe in our book, but we identified six desirable conditions for initiating Eureka! games locally through start-ups, outlined below. They are still valid today.

1 *Incubation*. Most Eureka! entrepreneurs get their Eureka! moments at work, where they are exposed to the two building blocks of invention, the need and the technology to address it. But their new product ideas do not always fit with what their employers do, and many inventors end up moonlighting on their invention on weekends or at night. They quit their jobs to work full time on their project only when they are sufficiently convinced that they have a potential winner. That incubation process creates significant kinship between the industrial base of a region and the start-ups created by entrepreneurs. For example, Intel, the world's leading semiconductor firm, was formed by a group of engineers who left Fairchild Corporation, where they had been working on semiconductors, to start their own company a few blocks away. AMD, Intel's cross-town rival in semiconductors, started in a similar way a few years later.

Most industrial clusters can be traced to this incubation process. Entrepreneurs who develop a new business generally have little time to move to a new community. The best place to start their new business is close to home and close to their networks of friends and business connections. Over time, that gives rise to a cluster of firms active in the same broad sector.

This explains the important role that large firms play in the incubation process.[6] While they don't usually actively encourage them, they enable ambitious, entrepreneurially inclined employees to assess technologies and market opportunities as part of their job. Some large firms have even become proactive incubators, setting up internal venture-capital investment units, encouraging employees to moonlight on projects of their own, and supporting new ventures by former employees as early buyers. Others also encourage start-ups through procurement, outsourcing, and collaborative activities.

Universities do not perform as well as incubators. Although they often allow staff members great access to technologies and leading-edge research, they are insulated from markets, thus falling short on an essential building block of great inventions. Most university researchers have little opportunity to assess first hand a poorly met or unmet market need. A sales-oriented business located close to a research-oriented university has a much better chance of becoming a good incubator, simply by hiring the university's best graduate students to work in product development, marketing, or sales. In Silicon Valley, HP, Fairchild, and Intel greatly benefited from their proximity to Stanford and Berkeley and the resulting pools of well-trained graduates.

2 *Models.* It is a tough decision to quit one's job to launch a business. Models of successful entrepreneurs who have already done it provide powerful stimulants for would-be entrepreneurs to get out of the closet: *If this guy can do it, why can't I?* The more innovative the product, the more skepticism an entrepreneur encounters, and the more important a role model becomes in getting him or her to take the plunge. The influence of models explains why new ventures often come in waves: success breeds success.

Models also stoke the enthusiasm of potential backers and bankers, who are helpful supporters in most start-up situations. Successful entrepreneurs often shape the attitudes of the business community they deal with. Thus promoting models is a key element of a local development strategy. Moreover, local chapters of groups such as the Young Presidents Organization (YPO) have an important impact by publicizing the achievements of their successful entrepreneurs.

3 *Pioneering customers.* We have all seen dollar bills pinned on the wall behind the cash registers of small businesses. Entrepreneurs always remember their first client, and for a good reason. By taking the risk of the first purchase, first clients vindicate all the previous efforts of entrepreneurs and play a major role in the early days of a Eureka! game. In the case of a new product, first clients often provide precious feedback to the inventor. Closed symbiotic relationships between innovators and their first customers can steer the product through several rapid and significant improvements.

This is one area where local development agencies can have a significant impact. By encouraging established local industries to act as pioneering customers for local start-ups, these agencies can significantly improve conditions for Eureka! innovations. Large firms that make it a corporate responsibility to support fledging entrepreneurial initiatives do a lot more for local economic development than is generally recognized. They are customers at a critical time in the birth of new businesses.

At a national level, DARPA is the model to follow. DARPA, whose

activity we will discuss further in chapter 16, is a US federal agency
tasked to stimulate innovations that could improve the United
States' defence capabilities. It has been quite successful as a pioneering customer in stimulating innovative advanced technologies solutions in a broad range of areas.

4 *A rich technological environment.* From technological progress comes
new ideas applied to unmet needs. The challenge is to get the technologies out of the ivory towers of researchers and into the hands of
tinkerers who are closer to the marketplace. This transfer of ideas,
from the scientists in their lab to the product developers close to the
market, is a difficult process that only a few research organizations
master well. Graduate students from research-oriented universities,
immersed in frontier technologies, tend to be good transmitters of
new ideas. By encouraging local businesses to employ them, community development agencies can encourage entrepreneurs to tap
the knowledge base of local universities.

5 *Business support.* Inventors are not necessarily good business people,
although they generally see themselves as entrepreneurs. They need
support to raise money and to make sound business decisions. Most
start-ups are initially financed by 'family and friends' and increasingly by 'angels,' the latter being well-heeled investors that invest
up to several hundred thousand dollars in start-ups that catch their
interest, providing both money and advice. Venture capitalists usually come after. The great majority of them specialize in later-stage
investments, often having little appetite or ability to deal with start-
ups.

   Silicon Valley is an exception. A large number of former entrepreneurs have joined local venture capital firms and they have an appetite for start-ups. Having been there themselves, they understand
that investing in Eureka! start-ups is not about returns on investment, controls, and spreadsheets. It's about recognizing the fundamental value of the innovation, steering the new business down the
right development path, and connecting it with pioneering customers and potential partners. These tasks require experience more than
financial skills.

6 *Social support.* Starting a new business on a Eureka! hunch is a
major decision. The psychological aspects cannot be underestimated. The more social support a community gives to the entrepreneur,
the more it can facilitate his or her decision to take the plunge. To
encourage start-ups to rejuvenate its industrial base, a community

must stimulate an entrepreneurial culture. Strong social support for entrepreneurship will attract other potential entrepreneurs into the region, initially perhaps as employees in local companies, where they will incubate their projects, and eventually as entrepreneurs themselves. Silicon Valley's culture contributed to attracting to the area people with dreams of striking out on their own.

This culture also nurtured a positive attitude toward moving on. Anna Lee Saxenian, a Berkeley professor, points out that Silicon Valley's cooperative and non-hierarchical culture provides it with significant competitive advantages. This fluidity makes the region very attractive to potential entrepreneurs, allowing it in the 1980s to beat out Boston's Route 128 to become the center for U.S. computer-based industries.[7]

Silicon Valley has never been replicated well, despite hundreds of attempts and billions of dollars invested by eager governments all over the world. Several technology clusters, such as in Cambridge in Britain and Waterloo in Canada, are often touted as replications of Silicon Valley, but in terms of size and diversity the comparison simply does not hold. Just like there was no duplication of Detroit in the 1920s, there has not been a real duplication of Silicon Valley in the past 30 years. The recipe to recreate it is clearly complex, and the proper mix of these six conditions is hard to duplicate. The first three conditions – incubation, models, and pioneering customers – bear directly on entrepreneurs and on the impact of their activities. They lie at the heart of a virtuous circle of development: success breeds success. But these three conditions also emphasize the importance to an entrepreneurial community of businesses already operating in the existing industrial base. In these companies, entrepreneurs of tomorrow are incubating their future businesses.

Early-Stage Market Dynamism

As soon as an original Eureka! invention hits the market and is successful with pioneering customers, the inventor can be sure of one thing: someone will soon get his or her hands on the product and say, 'I can do better than that.' A Eureka! success triggers emulators very rapidly among entrepreneurs knowledgeable about the need addressed by the product and who master the basic technologies. Most will also have more business experience than the original inventor.

How quickly they succeed in developing credible alternatives depends on the developmental requirements of the product, which can take a few months to several years. Patents may also throw obstacles in the path, but are generally not yet granted when emulators enter the scene. Those that are awarded mostly constrain some product features that are patentable. As we have said, outside the pharmaceutical area, early-stage emulators do not fear the threat of eventual lawsuits and usually find a way of circumventing patent protection. The high-profile patent disputes we read about in the media occur several years after the invention, and increasingly often involve 'patent trolls' who make a business of assembling patent portfolios and threatening users of related technologies with expensive legal disputes if they do not pay royalties. They have little impact on innovation, as they arrive when the party is over and it is time to divide the spoils.

The arrival of emulators starts a race during which the product is greatly improved as streams of new versions hit the market. The quick pace of product development persists until the product arrives at maturity. Innovations are not only technical; innovative marketing is as important, often putting original inventors at a disadvantage, since few of them are whizzes at marketing.

Pioneering customers interact closely with early-stage entrepreneurs. They like providing constructive criticisms as the product takes shape. But they are not always listened to, especially by Eureka! entrepreneurs, as good listening skills are not among the most common quality of inventors. Yet the ability to bond with activist customers may be the most important factor behind the success of a Eureka! product in its early years. Not only do such customers provide market feedback on the relevant features of the product, but they also contribute greatly to the market positioning.

Eureka! entrepreneurs also have to raise money, a skilled undertaking they do not always manage as well as their emulators. Money is always tight in the early years. The ability to raise funds as well as to spend resources where it makes the most sense, building a distribution network, reaching new customers, and the like, are critical success factors in the early years. Early entrepreneurs who are business oriented enjoy a great advantage.

Entrepreneurial Flurries

The early years of a Eureka! game are characterized by a large number of new entrants, usually already familiar with the technology or the market. Brands do not matter much in these early years, and the product is still easy to produce. But as the sophistication increases and the market expands, product complexity and cost start to rise and volume begins to matter. Building the largest customer base becomes the prize as the Eureka! game picks up speed.

Product superiority is very much a moving target. Product improvement is rapid in the early years of a new market. The brand also becomes important as the market expands, allowing the product to stand out in the crowded field and providing better access to distribution points or, on the Internet, reaching a significant share of potential customers.

The entrepreneurial firms that are best at marketing and product management gradually pull ahead of the field. The other start-ups that crowded the field in early-stage Eureka! games fail to build volume, throwing them into a vicious circle: not sufficiently attractive to distributors, they cannot invest in building a brand with some pull in the marketplace. They also do not generate enough cash to finance and promote their next generation of products. Eventually, they will be forced to sell out or cease operations.

Some new entrants set themselves apart with bold strategic moves. Compaq is the best example, with its decision to build an IBM-compatible PC and its ability to attract sufficient start-up funds. Its strategy, odd at the time, structured the PC market to its advantage for decades. Emulators that have enough confidence in a nascent market to strike out boldly and that are supported by sufficient financial resources, can often take a big lead with a daring strategy.

Where Are the Large Firms?

Large corporations seldom play early-stage Eureka! games. The game tends to be dominated by entrepreneurs; large corporations come in later. When Amazon launched the Kindle in 2007, for example, entrepreneurs had been selling e-book readers for almost 10 years, gradually improving the product, but sales did not take off. Sony became the first major company to enter the budding market in 2006, followed by Amazon a year later, both with significant marketing investments. The e-book followed the typical trajectory of a Eureka! game innovation. As entrepreneurs improved the product, the market grew slowly. As the product crossed a threshold of quality, sales took off and then large firms joined the fray.

There are exceptions to this pattern. 3M's Post-it notes and Tide were early-stage entries by large corporations. But there are not many of these, and for good reasons. Their decision making is seldom intuitive: they like ROI analysis to support a decision. But credible financial analyses are difficult to do for a budding or non-existent market. Moreover, the probabilities of success in an emerging market are low for most entrants, as a still ill-defined product takes shape. Finally, emerging markets demand fast decision making, nimbleness, and the ability to quickly change direction, all attributes of entrepreneurial firms. Such entrepreneurial business units are difficult to manage in the bosom of a large bureaucratic organization. So, failures abound. For instance, despite strong support from senior management, IBM did not excel in the PC market.

Wisely, well-established firms tend to stand on the sidelines during the turbulent early years of an innovative product or technology. They enter later, when the market becomes better defined. They then enter with a well-thought-out strategic acquisition. By this point, the game has reached the consolidation phase, and large corporations become prime players.

Consolidation

Emerging markets remain fragmented as long as no player builds economies of scale and as long as sales expand at crisp rates. But distribution channels eventually get saturated, growth slows, development costs increase, and reliability becomes important. Brands emerge as differentiators. Smaller players that are not in protected niches start to face working capital shortages. Consolidation becomes inevitable. The smart ones sell while their brand is worth something. But many refuse to believe that the game is over and persist, while financial pressures build up. Eventually, most have to give up.

Luckily for sellers, there are numerous buyers in a Eureka! market as it consolidates. The primary ones are the successful start-ups that have managed to build large customer bases. Acquisitions allow them to complete their portfolio, enlarge their customer base, and reap the benefits of synergies. Many of them have gone public and use their stock as currency to pay for acquisitions.

Large businesses in peripheral markets are also potential buyers. Once the market is well scoped and technology is stabilizing, entry decisions are easier to assess. These businesses look for healthy firms with growing pains that could give the buyer a good foothold in the market

Table 7.1. Eureka! Games: Key Strategic Factors

	Early stage	Consolidation phase
1	An invention responding to a real need, giving rise to a new market	Product management: continual and well-targeted renewal
2	Feedback from pioneering users	Distribution: partnering with the best
3	Developing a brand mystique	Strengthening the brand
4	Sufficiently funded to survive early stage	Cost control and process optimization
5	Product management: appealing to new buyers	Strategic focus on developing a portfolio of activities
6	Nimbleness: ability to quickly generate new versions of product	M&A*: choosing well and integrating their strengths
7	Organizing for growth: attracting and keeping talent	Building a strong team
8	Ability to attract investors: 5-year horizon	Appealing to analysts: short-term horizon

* Mergers and acquisitions

as it continues to develop. Their arrival, and their substantial resources, give new impetus to the development of the market. Their entry also provides a convenient exit for the early investors and, in particular, venture capital firms who can realize the value of their investments.

Surviving the Game

Not many firms survive Eureka! games. As Eureka! markets mature, they typically become oligopolistic, dominated by a few players. Hundred of aspirants do not make it to the finish line, usually including the original inventor. Large players can withdraw, licking their wounds. Smaller players will have either sold out or gone belly-up. Table 7.1 presents the key factors in the early stage of the Eureka! game and in the consolidation phase.

8 The Special Case of the Pharmaceutical Sector

Johnson & Johnson is the largest health care company in the world and ranks among the top 10 global companies on a market capitalization basis. Founded in 1886 by three brothers in the business of manufacturing sterile bandages, Johnson & Johnson claims invention rights to the Band-Aid, baby powder, dental floss, sanitary napkins, and first-aid kits. In 2010 it spent $6.8 billion on R&D, 11% of its sales, and the company employs about 15,000 people just in its R&D operations. Its organizational structure is unusual: it's divided into more than 200 operating companies in three segments – pharmaceutical products, medical devices, and consumer goods. This highly decentralized structure is designed specifically to spur innovation.

In 2009, a typical year, Johnson & Johnson's pharmaceutical segment launched five new products, along with several line extensions, which are new therapeutic indications (authorized therapeutic usages) and formulations for existing products. Johnson & Johnson is typical of the large research-oriented pharmaceutical companies that all pursue numerous Eureka! games simultaneously, targeting specific illnesses with innovative products. In most sectors, Eureka! games are dominated by small entrepreneurial companies. But in the pharmaceutical industry, Eureka! games are launched primarily by large global companies, the so-called 'big pharmas,' a consequence primarily of the heavy regulation of the pharmaceutical sector. Only large global companies such as Johnson & Johnson have the resources to play in the pharmaceutical industry's Eureka! games.

Unique Features of the Pharmaceutical Sector

To bring a new drug to market, pharmaceutical companies can spend between \$500 million and \$2 billion on laboratory work and clinical testing on animals and humans. The process takes as long as 15 years.[1] This particular situation makes Eureka! games associated with the discovery of a new drug quite different from all other Eureka! games.

Because they involve easily copied chemical formulae, the active ingredients in new drugs need strong patent protection against copycats. This gives their owners wide leeway in setting prices and allows the high margins they need to recover their development costs while patent protection lasts. But on the day the patent protection expires on a successful drug, generic manufacturers introduce low-price copies and take away the market.

Developing a new drug is very risky. According to an industry adage, only one in a thousand molecules that enter the development process makes it to the market. The stringent regulation of the drug development process imposes lengthy and expensive trials before a drug receives approval for sale: only a few drug candidates emerge from this to make it to the market.

Development can take as long as 15 years. When a company registers a drug for clinical trials, about half way in the development process, the drug's specific composition becomes public. To prevent competitors from copying it, patents are filed at that point. In most countries, they provide 20 years of exclusivity. But there is still between five to ten years of development before the marketing of the drug is authorized. As a result, a new drug has a commercial life of ten to fifteen years at best, before generics come in with low-price copies.

With such a relatively short period to recover its investment, a company relies on a commercial strategy that emphasizes intensive marketing. Over the life of a drug, a big pharma will spend much more on its marketing than on the R&D that leads to its production. Not only does launching a new drug require deep pockets, but a company also needs an extensive distribution system to efficiently exploit its market while patent protection lasts.

Unique Games

The combination of these factors defines the uniqueness of the Eureka! games built in the pharmaceutical industry. They also shape its structure around three types of players: the big pharmas that develop and market patented medicines, smaller R&D oriented biotechs that discover potential molecules that are subsequently (and mostly) developed by big pharmas and generic manufacturers that specialize in off-patent drugs.

These factors also explain the dominance of the big pharmas in early-stage Eureka! games. Johnson & Johnson spends one-third of its $7 billion annual R&D budget on the development of new drugs. At any time, it maintains 30 to 50 new drugs in various stages of clinical development and several times more than that in pre-clinical development.

Given the limited life of patents, time is a critical factor during the clinical development of a new drug, that is, the testing on humans, which typically takes five to seven years. The company must demonstrate to regulators that the drug is safe and, with statistical significance, that it is a more efficient treatement for a specific therapeutic indication than other drugs already on the market. Only once these have been proved will regulators approve the drug's commercialization. Once the drug is approved, it must also penetrate its market rapidly for the company to recover its development costs and pay for all its failures over the 10 to 15 years of patent protection. This explains why pharmaceutical companies spend more on marketing than research. That imperative favors large companies with extensive sales and distribution organizations that can quickly reach doctors who prescribe drugs.

It also explains the pharmas' pricing strategies for new drugs: they seek the highest price that the market will bear, and do sophisticated analyses to demonstrate the value of new drugs at these prices. Still they face strong resistance from third-party payers – governments and large insurance companies. In most countries, the price of new drugs is capped significantly below the price demanded by the pharmas. In the United States and Britain, where prices are not regulated, large-volume buyers such as the Veterans Administration, the National Health Care Service, and the major health-maintenance organizations (HMOs) get significant discounts. Big pharmas, with their deep pockets and diverse drugs portfolios, are in a much better position to hold their own in these negotiations.

Product Development

In addition to marketing, product development is the other critical function in the pharmaceutical industry. Most new drugs can be traced back to fundamental research at publicly financed research institutions and universities, where, worldwide, more than $100 billion is spent annually, more than the pharmaceutical industry spends on its own proprietary research. The results of that fundamental research are disseminated in the public domain, through scientific publications and conferences.

Pharmaceutical companies select promising findings, generally therapeutic 'pathways,' and investigate them further, focusing on identifying mechanisms that could be exploited for therapeutic purposes. This leads to the screening of new molecules, which the companies patent and put into development as new drug candidates.

Most of the leads are eliminated at the pre-clinical stage. The ones that show promise are patented, and the most promising ones are registered with regulators and entered into clinical testing. Given that the new therapeutic pathways are usually public, several drug companies will pursue them with slightly different molecules, called analogs. Being first on the market with an indication is a major competitive advantage. Pfizer launched Viagra in 1998, for example, opening a huge market. Its two key competitors, Cialis (Eli Lilly) and Levitra (Bayer), arrived in 2003. But more than seven years later, Viagra held 50% of the market and Pfizer had managed to double its price since its launch. (Viagra's patent expires in 2015, which will expose the whole class to intense price competition. This will likely destroy not only Viagra's franchise, but also those of Cialis and Levitra.) These races to the market are very public, as all clinical trials are public. Reaching the market ahead of others depends on three factors: being first with an approved candidate for clinical investigation, the duration of the clinical trials, and the quality of the evidence on the safety and efficiency of the candidate.

Once a new drug hits the market, a pharma will attempt to extend its reach with additional clinical research trials and, on their basis, will submit to regulatory authorities new proposals for line extensions. Most common line extensions involve new formulations such as once-a-day, extended duration, and timed-release tablets; combinations; and new indications, that is, using the drug to treat conditions other than the one for which it was originally approved. Pharmas also use these line extensions to prolong patent protection, adding a few years of commercial value.

Once patent protection lapses, the drug becomes uncompetitive relative to the low-cost generic version, typically priced at 25% of patented drugs, and most pharmas abandon the market. Recently, drugs with strong franchises as patented medicines have been kept on the market after their patents expired to compete, even at a higher price, with generic versions. Tagamet, once the world's best-selling drug for the treatment of heartburn and peptic ulcers, is still sold as a prescription drug, competing against the cheaper generic Cimetidine. Zantac, used for a similar indication, has been off-patent for several years and is now sold in a milder form, as a non-prescription medication under its original brand name Zantac. As we were writing this book, Pfizer announced a similar strategy for Lipitor, the best-selling drug ever, patent protection of which lapses in 2012.

But the big money does not lie in extending an old drug's commercial value. The industry creates value mainly by developing and marketing new drugs. This leads us back to the discovery process.

Public Research and Biotechnology

In the pharmaceutical world, most Eureka! moments occur not in pharmaceutical companies but in universities and public research centers, where new mechanisms of action associated with specific adverse physiological or psychological functions are discovered. These discoveries are the fountainheads from which new drugs emerge. Pharmas latch on to these mechanisms and seek molecules that will interfere with them in a therapeutic way to alleviate the adverse function. The pharmas stay in close touch with leading researchers, striving to get a leg up on the competition by being first to find and patent a lead compound. Novartis even moved its research headquarters from Switzerland to Boston to be closer to biotechnology research activities at MIT and Harvard.

The journey between the discovery of a mechanism of action and the development of a drug is a long one. Moreover, there are not enough pharmas around to develop all the potential drug candidates. Thus, as public research expanded in the 1970s and 1980s, and new mechanisms of action were discovered, the biotech industry developed to handle a growing share of the early development of drugs.

Genentech, founded by Dr Herbert Boyer of Berkeley and Robert Swanson, a venture capitalist, is widely regarded as the first biotech firm. Set up in 1976 to develop new drugs based on the research of Dr Boyer, Genentech announced its first product, a synthetic version of insulin, two years after its foundation. That success sealed its reputation and paved the way for thousands of enterprising researchers striving to add value to their discoveries by pursuing their development in for-profit biotech ventures.

Several thousand biotech companies of different sizes and financial conditions now exist, and some have significant portfolios of drugs in development. Every year, hundreds of new companies are formed. Initial investments generally come from friends and increasingly from early-stage financing organizations set up by governments and universities. Start-up expenditures can be significant. Identifying a lead compound can easily cost a million dollars. Pre-clinical testing can cost several millions more. At that point, the biotech will have done a proof of concept, verifying that the new drug works in a Petri dish and in animal testing and confirming the mechanism. Then the company patents the drug and prepares for highly regulated clinical research on humans. From then on, friends, family, and early-stage financing organizations can no longer afford the required investment. At that point, most biotech companies that have survived thus far turn to professional investors.

The Limits of Venture Capital

Venture capital firms typically invest in a biotech on the basis of positive indications about safety and efficiency. But even at that stage, the probability that the new drug will make it to the market is still less than 10%, making biotech one of the riskier types of investment that VCs face. Most new drugs consist of molecules that have never before entered a human body. Within the human body, they must reach a specific target area and effectively derail a mechanism without causing significant dysfunctional effects elsewhere. Not surprisingly, most molecules fail the test. Compounding the difficulties, early-stage biotechs typically have a portfolio of only one or two leads. The failure of one product can destroy a company's value and prevent a biotech start-up from raising any further funds. Even if the trials succeed, the company still faces clinical research expenditures of several hundred million dollars to get a drug on the market.

Nevertheless, Genentech's early success made biotech the darling of VC investors for the next few decades. However, the enthusiasm has cooled recently as biotechnology has failed to live up to its promise. There are no publicly available statistics on the performance of private venture capital investments in biotech. But Gary P. Pisano, a professor at the Harvard Business School, has analyzed the performance of publicly traded biotech companies in the United States from 1979 to 2003,[2] and found that their financial performance has been abysmal. Investors would have done better with Treasury Bills than with a portfolio of biotechs that went public during the period. Furthermore, if we exclude Amgen, the largest and most successful biotech company, from the portfolio, the whole sector operated at a loss every year over the whole period.

Pharmas Need Biotechs

Despite these poor results, the biotech industry has survived. At the same time as venture capital was pulling out, the pharmas started to invest heavily in biotechs, dramatically improving their fortune. Since the mid-1990s, the productivity of the pharmas' internal R&D has been shrinking. Despite growing R&D budgets, the approval of drugs based on new chemical entities has declined. Between 2006 and 2011 approvals fell from more than 40 a year to fewer than 25, a 35% decrease, despite an increase of 75% in global R&D budgets from 1999 to 2009 and the contribution of new chemical entities that originated in biotechs.[3]

This slide had started in the 1980s, although the long leads and lags in the industry prevented pharmas from recognizing it for more than a decade. By the early 2000s, the pharmas became convinced that internal research alone would not support a portfolio of innovative, patent-protected drugs. So they gradually partnered with biotechs in developing and acquiring high-potential leads. Since 2006 pharmas represent a more important source of financing for biotechs than venture capital firms, saving the industry.[4] Whether the pharmas will do better than the VCs remains to be demonstrated, but private equity already feels the positive impact of the arrival of their new partners. A recent study of private equity investment in biotech suggests a turnaround in performance since 2000, when pharmas started to provide financing to biotechs in a big way.[5]

But the pharmas had no choice. It was a two-way deal: in saving the biotechs, they also ensure their own commercial future, allowing them to replenish their pipeline. Partnerships are usually done through licensing options against up-front payments and regular payments upon reaching specified development milestones. If subsequent results look promising, the pharma will pick up its option, which entails a royalty to the biotech firm. This provides the biotech with funds to further develop its pipeline. The risk is thus shared, as are the rewards.

Twisted Eureka! Games

Played under such conditions, Eureka! games in the biotechnology sector are highly constrained. The high level of public funding of fundamental research creates easy entry conditions early in the development cycle, explaining the high number of biotech firms in operation. They can survive in the early phases of the game, when the funds required are modest by industry standards. But deep pockets are required to bring a new drug to the marketplace, and that excludes most biotechs. They generally pass the ball to a pharma as the expensive clinical studies get underway. As a consequence, most new chemical entities that make it into the list of approved drugs emerge today from about 25 global pharmaceutical firms. Only they have the resources to manage a balanced portfolio of drugs in development and to provide marketing and distribution support to generate sufficient cash flow in a drug's limited life span before it gets copied by generic manufacturers.

This makes the Eureka! games played in the pharmaceutical industry unique, involving large firms, thousands of smaller biotechs, and significant public funding for basic research. The games are also structured by the heavy regulatory approval regime for new drugs, which precludes the trial-and-error processes associated with new products in other industries. Regulations not only limit interactions with customers in the development phase of a new drug, but also impede the rapid product improvement that occurs after its launch. In the pharmaceutical industry, a product is fully developed by the time it hits the marketplace. Without question, safety considerations demand tight regulation of new drugs. But one could ask whether it wouldn't be better to concentrate regulatory efforts on safety, leaving the trial-and-error process of the market place to assess the efficiency of new drugs. This could allow more rapid commercialization of new drugs, more competition, and most likely lower prices.

Current regulatory conditions may explain the growing difficulty the industry faces in coming up with new products. Stock-market pharmaceutical-industry indices point to a secular decline compared to the broad market as a whole. Discovery, even when assisted by biotechs, is simply not productive enough to support the huge development and marketing infrastructure that a new drug requires. As long as advances in medication involve the absorption by the body of new chemical entities, safety approvals will remain stringent, as they should. But perhaps we could stimulate greater efficiency by relaxing regulatory controls on the drug's non-safety performance, allowing the industry to play Eureka! games more vigorously.

9 Battles of Architecture

The story of Facebook is well known, thanks to the combination of a best-selling book, *The Accidental Billionnaires*, and a blockbuster movie, *The Social Network*, which even garnered a few Oscars. What is most amazing is that the company was founded only in 2004. Seven years later, as we write this book, Facebook is vying with Google for the title of the most popular site on the Internet, with more than 600 million visitors a month. It is a unique story, saying much about the power of the Internet and how it has connected the whole world at warp speed.

Facebook was not the first Internet social network. The genre can be traced to a site called SixDegrees.com, which appeared in 1997 and allowed people to post their profile and connect with their friends.[1] Six-Degrees folded in 2000, but by then numerous similar sites had sprung up on the Web. Social networks became the flavor of the year in 2003 and the darlings of Silicon Valley investors, with the emergence of well-known sites such as Friendster, MySpace, and LinkedIn. Facebook came in 2004, first targeted to Harvard students and then to students from other elite universities, allowing it to acquire a special cachet from the outset. It used this cachet to expand to all universities and high school students by 2006.

By then, established media companies were taking an interest in social networks, seeing them as new high-potential media. In 2005, for $580 million, Rupert Murdoch, the Australian press baron who built News Corp, the world's biggest media company, snatched MySpace, at the time the most popular social network, with 27 million unique monthly visitors. For a few years after, Murdoch took a personal interest in the strategic direction of MySpace with the purpose of developing synergies with his other media properties and to benefit from News

Corp's clout with advertisers.[2] For Facebook, which still focused only on college students at the time, MySpace was the competitor to beat.

Social network sites evolved rapidly in the following years, as new features were added, enriching communications between members. More importantly, evolving computer and Internet technology allowed faster connections, better graphics, and more complex sites. Competition was fierce, but Facebook turned out to be the site that grew faster, slowly gaining on MySpace, the market leader. The genius of Mark Zuckerberg, Facebook's founder, was reflected in his ability to steer the evolution of its features, keeping its cachet as *the* social network to join. By 2007 Facebook finally expanded access to the world, without compromising its high-quality image. New features were added and others were improved, paying close attention to user feedback and building a strong sense of community among members. Facebook also strongly encouraged its users to develop applications and publicized the revenues generated by the most successful ones.[3] Finally, borrowing from Google, Facebook maintained a clean front page, which clearly distinguished it from the brassy and loud appearance of MySpace.

By 2008 Facebook and MySpace were running neck and neck worldwide, but Facebook had the momentum. In early 2009 it surpassed MySpace in the US market. By 2011 Facebook world-wide membership exceeded 600 million, 10% of the world's population. Meanwhile, MySpace had tumbled. The monthly unique visitor statistics of May 2011 in the United States tell it all, as shown in figure 9.1. In June 2011 News Corp sold MySpace for $35 million. Around the same time, Facebook was valued at $70 to $80 billion on private exchanges.[4] The team assembled by Mark Zuckerberg had beaten the largest media empire in the world.

What Facebook won is a battle of architecture – but the battle is not over. Facebook's triumph is likely only one phase in the game. MySpace is probably history by now, but Facebook will encounter new competitors with better platforms. It has happened before. Yahoo, for example, triumphed over Lycos, AltaVista and other search engines in the early 2000s, then lost out to upstart Google. A similar competitor will eventually move onto Facebook's turf.

Open-System Economics

An open system is defined by a platform to which can be attached an indefinite number of modules that deliver specific benefits. In partic-

Figure 9.1. Facebook versus MySpace: Monthly US Unique Visitors

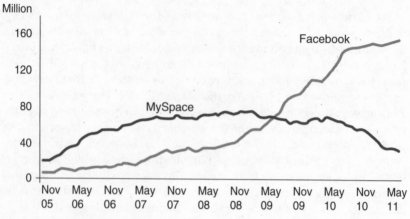

Source: comScore Media Metrix

ular, web-based open systems can develop complex architectures, as their platforms generally support multi-sided markets, that is, a set of managed exchanges between users of the platform, third-party application providers, and advertisers, bringing benefits to all. The battles are fought over attracting participants to multi- sided markets through a continual refining of the complex offering of benefits available to participants.

Open systems and Battles of Architecture predate the Internet, as David Evans and his colleagues at MIT document in their 2006 book *Invisible Engines*.[5] From their infancy, supermarkets were new platforms that brought branded goods to neighbourhoods, instigating Battles of Architecture. Visa and Mastercard credit cards are 60-year-old multi-sided platforms, facilitating transactions by connecting merchants, banks, and consumers.

Battles of Architecture occur with increasing frequency in today's economy. The industrialization of information brought by digital communications facilitates cooperation between economic agents, allowing them to bundle their respective contributions into a joint product or service, which we conveniently call a system. Before, complex systems generally required physical proximity of agents to ensure cooperation. Toyota City, for example, established in the 1960s to host the auto manufacturer's just-in-time suppliers, was a pre-computer arrangement to facilitate cooperation. Information goods do away with the requirement of physical proximity.

Innovative open systems ignite Battles of Architecture, as competitive alternatives rapidly appear. Open systems are easy to copy in their start-up phase, before they engage their participants irreversibly in a complex web of relationships. The Internet as a widely accessible communication platform has stimulated a plethora of new open systems. The Battles of Architecture involving smart phones and social media are getting a lot of publicity. But many of the OTT opportunities that the telcos have passed over in the past 15 years were in fact budding open systems that, when successful, entered into Battles of Architecture.

The development of Internet communications has also brought about many Battles of Architecture beyond the Web. Urban transportation offers a few examples. Urban bicycle-sharing systems, popularized by Paris's 2007 introduction of the Vélib', are based on a business model that combines on-the-spot subscriptions and advertising revenues. Similar systems have emerged in many large cities in Europe and North America. They would not have been possible without an Internet-based communication support, which handles credit card transactions, inventory control, usage metering, and return confirmation. Car-sharing are also developing rapidly, adding GPS to the standard Web technologies. One of the oldest, Communauto, founded in 1994 and based in Montreal, has 21,000 members and more than 1,000 cars. Zipcar, founded in Boston in 2000, has more than 8,000 cars, a market capitalization of $175 million, and annual revenues of nearly $200 million. The popularity of these sharing systems is stimulated by new Internet-related technologies such as smart cards, mobile communication, and GPS.

Car-sharing is now embracing the electric vehicle. New entrants are also entering the market. In Paris, a French tycoon, Vincent Bolloré, has invested $2 billion to develop the Bluecar, a battery-based urban car-sharing service that will start in 2012. Daimler, Avis, and Vinci, the giant parking lot operator, are also testing the market. An Israeli start-up, Better Places, has raised $350 million to commercialize a model of electric car with switchable batteries. Better Places believes that electric car sharing will eventually account for as much as 50% of the urban travel market. All this activity suggests that a new mode of urban transport based on car sharing is about to take off. We are currently observing the under-the-radar experimentation with various architectures that precedes the establishment of a new system. The same jockeying for the right formula occurred before social media took off in 2003.

What We Learned from Our Research

The MINE survey included 159 organizations that were participating in Battles of Architecture. Case studies also provided us with valuable insights into the nature of these battles. We gathered additional insights from the abundance of literature available on the topic, although most writers refer to these battles by other names. From these sources, the MINE project identified the following eight characteristics of Battle of Architecture games:

1 Battles of Architecture involve the organization of communities of complementary interests around platforms that can deliver benefits to multiple markets. They occur in a highly effervescent business environment, where technologies and markets evolve rapidly, generating numerous new product ideas. Battles originate in entrepreneurs' experimentation with concepts for new systems, a phase that can last for a few years. Although most concepts do not last beyond that experimentation stage, some of them take root. As Battles of Architecture proceed, competing designs emerge into the marketplace from the experimental phase. A dominant design can take decades to emerge and mature, feeding on continuous innovation; the underlying Battles of Architecture can last a long time.
2 In the early years of a Battle of Architecture game, innovation is based less on scientific prowess – as in the case of Eureka! games – than on leveraging the opportunities created by the evolving market conditions generated by competing platforms. Pioneering customers and suppliers hanging around emerging platforms discover new applications. A key asset of an emerging platform is an interconnected web of creative supporters, which becomes a brand that appeals to third-party developers and to new users drawn to 'where the action is.'
3 Sooner or later, network effects emerge as key growth drivers. They stem from an expanding customer base and from the synergies of benefits provided by continuous enrichment of offerings by third-party suppliers of modules. Successful platforms can grow rapidly as Battles of Architecture become highly dynamic. In the MINE survey, companies involved in Battles of Architecture recorded average sales growth of 20% a year.

4 The orchestrator behind a successful platform carries a vision that steers its evolution while stimulating both customer demand and third-party application developers. Although new platforms tend to be launched by entrepreneurial firms, larger established companies often wedge their way into Battle of Architecture as orchestrators through a combination of acquisitions and investments. For instance, in the early years of credit card systems, Visa and MasterCard started as coalitions of banks who consolidated smaller operators.

5 Successful platforms operate within a coherent business model. On the Web, many models are built around a three-sided market configuration involving users, advertisers, and application sellers. Users, who are often called members, get most of their benefits free, on advertising-supported applications. But in the variant called a Freemium model, they can also get a higher level of benefits by paying for selected services or becoming subscribers. Advertisers are attracted to Web platforms by the high level of qualified traffic, a key function of a platform being to characterize its users. As a result, advertising can be targeted toward users interested in the subject matters, dramatically increasing its effectiveness. In the Freemium variant, application developers give away a basic model and sell a premium one; the orchestrator's revenues come from three sources: advertising, premium membership subscriptions, and commissions on sales by application providers.

6 Revenue-sharing can becomes complicated on the Web, as platforms often become stacked. YouTube, for example, is available on Facebook, and Amazon is available on the iPhone platform. Many magazines and newspapers balk at having platforms such as Facebook or Apple's iStore take a 30% commission on the sales of subscriptions. It will take years to develop complex arrangements for splitting commission revenues between stacked platforms.

7 A Battle of Architecture demands coherent platform development. A platform must continually evolve and integrate a continuous stream of new modules competing for user attention. An orchestrator's ability to manage coherently the development of its system, which includes both the platform and the modules, is a key determinant of its success. In the opinion of most observers, MySpace fell out of favor because of incoherent development.

8 Of the six games of innovation, participants in Battles of Architecture rely most heavily on open innovation and external parties. The coalition of partners committed to a platform can become fairly

complex to manage. Orchestrators tend to concentrate on marketing and on ensuring coherence and to count on third-parties' application providers for innovation. In the smart phone market, the orchestrators – who control handset-based platforms – partner with network operators, device assemblers, and system software providers such as Google and Microsoft. As their market grows, systems evolve, applications are added, and the relative importance of complementors shifts. This requires constant fine-tuning of the coalition. For an aspiring Bill Gates, Steve Jobs, or Mark Zuckerberg, managing that complex evolution may present the most formidable challenge, requiring a great deal of skill.

Key Strategic Issues

Battles of Architecture are generally won on a combination of bold strategies and good management of the coalition. Four strategic factors emerge as critical in sorting out the winners from the also-rans: capturing network effects, locking in customers, managing the openness of the platform, and tapping open innovation. These are reviewed below.

Harnessing Network Effects

Steve Jobs was a master at harnessing network effects. The iPod was launched in 2001,[6] among a crowded field of portable digital music players. But its many unique features, such as the classic click-wheel control panel, attracted a solid group of early adopters. The cool design aura of the Apple brand also enlisted Apple's core clientele. But more importantly, acting on his view of the computer as a digital hub, Steve Jobs connected the iPod to iTunes, a music database manager recently added to the Mac computer. Not only did he add functionalities to the iPod, but he also extended its reach to all Mac users. Two years later, Apple opened the iTunes Store, allowing users to buy songs online from most music distributors, and allowing anyone to obtain songs legally. Within months, the iPod became the leading portable digital player.

The complex but well-managed interactions between the iPod, iTunes, the iTunes Store, and the Apple brand had created network effects that propelled the iPod to market leadership. What Apple had never been able to do with Mac computers, Steve Jobs did in two years with the iPod, tapping several elements to create a strong pull in the marketplace. Strongly associated with the Apple brand, the iPod was launched by Steve Jobs himself at the industry's major trade show, appealing directly to the core followers of the Apple brand. The sleek design of the iPod broadened that appeal to another segment of customers. The iTunes application made it easy for Mac users to transfer their music library to their iPhone. Finally, the iTunes Store, the first legal site to allow the downloading of songs on a pay-per-song basis, addressed the insecurity of a large group of music listeners concerned about the legality of peer-to-peer downloading.

Five years later, in a different market environment, Apple applied a similar strategy to the iPhone. But this time, the competition was much better established, as Apple went head-to-head against Nokia, Samsung, Motorola, Sony-Ericsson, and Research in Motion. As with the iPod, sleek design and the loyalty of Apple aficionados were instrumental in attracting the iPhone's initial customer base. Apple also positioned the iPhone as a personal statement, representing modernity and signalling an avant-garde sensibility, reaching image-conscious users. As well, Apple chose an exclusive mobile phone operator in each market. This gave the operating companies privileged access to Apple's exclusive customer base, but it also gave Apple access to a larger potential customer base.

Even with this well-managed strategy, Apple had a difficult time breaking into the smart phone market. By July 2008, one year after its launch, Apple had sold only about 6 million units, a small number in the telephone market. But then the App Store was launched and sales took off. At first, the App Store carried only 500 applications, a quarter of them free. But from the outset, Apple strove to attract more third-party developers. Not only did these developers broaden the benefits offered by the iPhone, but many customers also believed that they needed an iPhone to get access to these applications. With the surging demand, stories abounded of moonlighting developers making fortunes from apps developed in their basements. A virtuous circle of feedback ensued, as more developers flocked to the iPhone. By 2010 Apple boasted of offering more than 300,000 applications on its iPhone. In early 2011 iPhone and iPad users had initiated 10 billion iStore downloads. In the first quarter of 2011, the iPhone accounted for 50% of Apple's sales.[7]

Network effects such as those that propelled the sales of the iPod and the iPhone result from strong self-reinforcing dynamic relationships and feedback loops on the demand and supply sides alike. The popularity of a platform attracts new users on the basis of two drivers. First, risk reduction is very important in an emerging market still crowded with inexperienced first-time buyers. The Apple brand provides an effective security blanket for new buyers, who then get hooked on the numerous applications on the platform. Second is the synergy between users. By sharing the same network, they enjoy the same benefits, talk about them, discover new ones, and share applications. The enlargement of the customer base attracts suppliers, whose contributions expand the product's appeal even further. Thus, demand and supply reinforce each other.

Network effects can easily trump other competitive features of a platform, such as technical capabilities. Users and third-party developers select a platform first and above all for its reach and not because of its technical superiority. A platform's value depends mostly on the number of users it attracts and the availability of complementary goods and applications attached to it. These network effects subside only when the market gets saturated, by which time only a few platforms dominate the market.

A customer base must cross a certain threshold before network effects can take hold. In the initial stage of a platform, its orchestrator must attract a minimum number of users and third-party developers to deliver a sufficient bundle of benefits. This requires a different strategy that has nothing to do with network effects. To get quickly to that threshold, Apple delivers the perceived benefit of association with a cool, high-quality, and usually exclusive product, appealing to Apple's loyal core of supporters, the usual early adopters of Apple's new products. Lesser known brands give away their products or rely on heavy promotion to create a base of customers sufficient to cross the threshold. Amazon, Google, Facebook, and Twitter all went through their initial years without advertisers or subscribers, using mostly viral marketing to build a critical mass of customers. These early years without revenues require strong investor support to carry the platform through the profitless stage of building an initial customer base.

Locking in Customers: Winner-Takes-All

Once network effects kick in, winner-takes-all situations often develop. The phenomenon is called hyper-selection, as fragmented markets coalesce around a few brands while demand grows explosively. Hyper-selection is the normal outcome of network effects. As new customers discover a new market, many choose to go with the flow, relying on the decisions of others in selecting their brand, instead of trying to assess the relative merits of competitive offerings. Siding with the expected winner is a risk-free decision. As a result, in hot new markets, promotion is often built around the buzz coming from early users and reviewers. Technical superiority matters less. The Matsushita VHS victory over the technically superior Sony Betamax video recorder has become the emblematic example of the phenomenon:[8] customers chose the VHS because it had a wider choice of Hollywood movies. It does not really matter whether the most popular platform is technologically superior or not.[9]

Hyper-selection is stimulated by lock-in effects.[10] Users who have invested time and effort in learning about a particular platform do not see much gain in changing or even in exploring alternatives. Switching to new options, even superior ones, is hindered by inertia. For instance, Internet Explorer has successfully resisted the encroachment of Mozilla for more than a decade in the browser market, even though Mozilla generally receives better ratings in expert comparisons. Lock-in effects can also be designed into the product, increasing the inconvenience of switching. This is achieved, for instance, by a platform's development of complex interactions with users, associated with storage of pictures and documents and contact lists. Unique features that require learning can also be barriers. The lock-in effect paradoxically imposes industry standards that can fall short of ideal, since dominant platforms leave little room for incompatible products and services, even if they are superior.[11]

Hyper-selection is not guaranteed: a platform can get trapped under the threshold,[12] critical complements can be missing,[13] and network effects can get stymied by chicken-and-egg paralysis. Making small payments using mobile phones took off in Japan several years ago. Why didn't electronic wallets catch on in Europe and North America? How come it takes so much longer to align the key actors: network operators, device manufacturers, merchants, transportation agencies, and so on? Why all these delays, for a solution that's bound to be adopted? The hesitation of key actors justifies the hesitation of others, a classic chicken-and-egg situation. Under such conditions, even highly valuable business models or superior technical options will not take off.

Managing Openness

An open system can accommodate modules of all shapes and sizes, as long as they add to its performance without impairing its integrity. The iPhone accommodates applications that range from weather reporting to financial planning. It is also an emergency flashlight. The integrity of a system depends solely on the platform.

In Battles of Architecture, managing the openness of a platform to third-parties' modules is a central strategic issue. Open systems generally encourage innovation by third parties, but in return, those parties must respect the rules set by the orchestrator of the platform. In software, openness has been a fixture of the industry. Already in the 1980s and 1990s, Microsoft was distributing beta versions of its new platforms months in advance of their release, to stimulate the development of third-party applications.

Orchestrators must outline the conditions of access to their platforms. Some allow access to third parties only under strict conditions. Others provide third parties with almost open access, in the belief that fewer constraints will allow independent innovators to be more creative. The orchestrator must also decide how much of the content grafted onto the platform will be centrally managed and how much it should leave to the discretion of third parties. When innovation is an imperative, this is an important choice.

Apple has clearly hit the proper balance with the iPhone and its App Store. The iPhone platform remains relatively closed and stable, fully under Apple's control as orchestrator. But Apple counts on third parties to add features and let innovation thrive at the periphery, while protecting Apple's income stream. For instance, third-party applications cannot redirect traffic to a proprietary site, where users could conduct transactions without paying a commission.

All open platforms impose rules, but some are less stringent than others. Apple has always been stringent. Google allows device manufacturers to customize its Android mobile phone operating system, within well-defined rules. The open-source Linux platform can also be customized by users as long as the changes remain in the public domain. On the other hand, content developers on most Wiki sites have no access to the platform, and they must respect editorial rules when contributing material. Wiki sites also prohibit advertising and self-promotion.

More openness is a basic trend for complex products and services, through protocols and contractual arrangements. The industrialization of communication makes it easier to manage interfaces. In addition, new systems designed as open platforms are easier to integrate into a legacy structure. Openness greatly expands a platform's scope, facilitating the customization of any service provided by a system.

Yet thousands of systems on the Internet still do not allow third-party attachment or customization, especially in business software.

Open-Source Innovation

Openness applied to the innovation process itself has a different meaning. In the context of open-source innovation, software and inventions enter the public domain at their inception and evolve through collaboration by numerous developers. This open-source movement began in the 1980s as a reaction to the domination of companies like Microsoft, to encourage the creation and distribution of free software. Beyond the software industry, Wikipedia emerged from an open-source movement to democratize the compiling and publication of information.[14]

The debate continues about the relative merits of open versus closed (or proprietary) innovation. The metaphor of the cathedral and the bazaar has been used to characterize the two approaches.[15] The bazaar of open innovation attracts a large number of contributors but suffers from looser and weaker management and control, major weaknesses when it comes to innovation. The cathedral may represent bigger ambitions, and is built on stronger foundations, but it is one view, limited in its offerings.

Companies that rely on the commercialization of open-source software have to capture sufficient value to justify their development costs, making many companies hesitant about getting involved in open-source innovation. Yet it can be done. Red Hat, the leading distributor of the Linux operating system, has built a market capitalization of about $10 billion. Fully committed to the open-source philosophy, Red Hat earns its revenues from installing and maintaining open-source systems. In addition, it invests in the development of open-source software. IBM also promotes the Linux operating system. In some areas of software development, free open-source software (FOSS) holds a significant share of the market. Mozilla, one of the best-known FOSSes, has captured 30% of the browser market. Google's browser, Chrome, was developed as open-source software and is slowly encroaching on the market leader, Microsoft's Internet Explorer, which is proprietary. In other words, open-source software can be a viable commercial alternative, and there are numerous systems that demonstrate it.

Patents

On 30 June 2011 a consortium led by Apple, RIM, and Microsoft announced that it had just won the auction for the intellectual property portfolio of Nortel, the bankrupt Canadian phone manufacturer, paying $4.5 billion for its 6,000 patents that covered mostly mobile phone applications. Forty-five days later Google, which had been on the losing side of that auction, announced the $12.5 billion acquisition of Motorola Mobility and its 17,000-patent portfolio. Ten days later, Apple obtained an injunction in Germany preventing the sale of Samsung's smart phone, which is based on Google's Android platform, on the ground that it infringed on Apple's intellectual property. Samsung did the same to Apple in Australia, on the same ground. HTC, a manufacturer of mobile phones aligned with Google, also sued Apple for patent infringement in the United States.

These are all illustrations of the important role that patents have taken in Battles of Architecture unfolding in the computer and telecom markets. Major platforms are now using patents to trip each other. Of course, the patent as weapon is not new in the field: the industry had been dealing with patent trolls for more than a decade. For instance, in 2006 and in 2008, RIM paid closed to $900 million to two patent trolls that threatened to seek a court injunction to shut down the whole Blackberry system. Another troll, Lopsys, is now going after application developers for the major smart phone platforms, on the ground that the platform payment systems they use infringe Lopsys patents. But in 2011 patent fights changed theatres, bursting out among major platform owners and their surrogates.

In general, patent fights are frequent in emerging industries, where numerous new technical contributions crop up within the span of a few years. Thomas Edison was a famous patent litigator, with highly publicized court fights involving most of its major inventions, from the telegraph and the alternative current to the telephone and the light bulb. The emergence of a new industry with complex products creates numerous opportunities for 'inventors' to lay claim to technological contributions. Patent fights are a rite of passage for most new industries, as their technological structure gels. What is different about the Battles of Architecture involving today's information-based open systems is, first, the complexity of the final products, linking ever-evolving platforms with tens of thousands of applications, and, second, in the United States, the recognition of patent claims for new 'business methods,' that is, claims about a new way of doing something using software. The best-known business method patent is the one received in 1999 by Amazon for buying something on the Web with a single click of the mouse.[16] The buyer, being recognized by the seller from previous transactions, and having already given his or her shipping and credit card information, needs only click to do a new transaction. Although the one-click patent can be circumscribed by simply asking the buyer to confirm the purchase with a second click of the mouse, tens of millions of dollars in lawyer fees have been spent to assess the validity and scope of that patent. And this is the issue: the entanglement of the slow, inefficient judicial process, and the uncertainty and delays about its outcome, with a rapidly developing product, where competitors are continually churning out new variants and applications. As a result, patents have become highly prized chips in high-stake business negotiations between companies with claims on bits of technologies, on the one hand, and operators of complex multi-sided market platforms that aggregate a large number of technological applications, on the other.

That is not the intent of the patent system. Its primary purpose is to encourage innovation by ensuring that inventors profit from the success of their invention. But as we have discussed, there are often better ways of capturing value than patents, with their cumbersome granting process that unfolds several years after the technology has started its commercial life.

This does not mean patents are not valuable. IBM generates about $1 billion annually from its intellectual property, most of it from licensing income on patents. In 2010 patents represented 5% of its pre-tax profits. But these royalties amounted only to 15% of its R&D expenditures. Yet this was sufficient to justify its filing close to 6,000 patents that year. IBM is probably the technology company that derives the most income from patents. Patent trolls are in a somewhat different business, exploiting the fact that platform orchestrators engaged in a Battle of Architectures are reluctant to get involved in lengthy and costly judicial skirmishes that may force them to withhold some applications or benefits. Instead they agree to a licensing agreement or settlement with the patent trolls. It is a different story when the claimant is a competitor. Apple is using its patent portfolio to slow down Android's penetration. Its intervention in Germany was a clear signal. But then, Google's purchase of Motorola Mobility gives it sufficient munitions to stare down at Apple with its own patent infringement claims. It also explains why RIM, Microsoft, Ericson, and EMC, a leader in cloud computing, were able to join Apple in its consortium: what these companies were seeking was the bargaining clout associated with the Nortel patents.

The rapid progress of communication technologies and of open systems creates ample opportunities for patenting, compounded in the United States by the recognition of patents on new business methods.

But as a spur to innovation, the importance of patents is far from certain.[17] Competition is what drives innovation in Battles of Architecture, and patenting is too slow a process to have a significant influence. As Holman W. Jenkins, an influential *Wall Street Journal* columnist, puts it, 'Invention is more collaborative, more a matter of stealing, copying, or to put it nicely, "standing on the shoulders of giants," than the patent system likes to think.'[18]

When investing in a new platform, venture capitalists consider first and foremost its ability to attract a user base and a developer community sufficient to create network effects. The possibility that the software may infringe on existing patents will be assessed, and if that is the case, VCs will require either licensing of the patented technology or circumventing of the patents. On the other hand, they will pay little heed to patent applications for an exclusive intellectual territory whose commercial value remains to be established. They are looking for a commercial success, the best guarantee for superior returns on their investments. Patent protection is obtained well after the market has already decided whether a platform will fly or not. Google, for example, obtained its basic patent in 2003, when it had already become the leading search engine. In open systems, intellectual property is best protected by a trademark or by keeping it secret. If a competitor fraudulently obtains access to corporate secrets, a company can sue for theft of information. Patents reveal too much information, allowing competitors to circumvent them. For instance, Google has not patented its algorithms; it simply guards their secrecy.

Patent fights occur regularly in open-system markets. Fights erupt several years after the system has emerged, when the bulk of the innovations associated with the system have matured. Because they occur so late in the game, these disputes have only a minor impact on innovation. They have more to do with sharing the spoils of a well-established successful innovation, but that occurs long after the innovation hits the market. Open innovation that does not bother with patents and relies instead on General Public License (GPL) and Free Documentation License (FDL) may turn out to be as productive as proprietary innovation in the development of open systems. The growing popularity of Mozilla, Linux, and other open-source systems confirms this.

Winning Strategies

What does it take to win a Battle of Architecture? How can a company

Table 9.1. Battle of Architecture Game Dynamics: Winning Strategies

	Emerging systems	Stabilized systems
	New systems that emerge from thousands of entrepreneurial experiments	Consolidation as the network effects are sorting out the players
Orchestrators Running Platforms	• Invest in a platform that can support a high-potential system • Develop a beta version that will attract a core group of pioneering customers • Open the platform and attract enthusiastic and innovative third-party developers, through simple interfaces • Define a clear vision of the trajectory pursued • Make bold investments to build up a significant base of loyal users • Be among the first to harvest network effects, with the proper marketing and pricing model	• Acquire solid management • Adapt the system to changing technology and competitive landscape • Lock in evolving targeted audiences (needs and preferences) • Ensure coherence among third-party offerings • Develop attractive third-party application agreements that ensure a fair split of revenues • Keep the platform simple; late-coming users are less sophisticated • Manage growth: organization, finance, culture, etc.
Complementors Providing Modules	• Align with the platforms most likely to win and try to negotiate a privileged status • Develop applications that will appeal to early adopters • … and that work seamlessly with the selected platforms • Develop a strong brand • Build traffic with a basic free offer and extras at a price (Freemium)	• Manage growth of the customer base • Invest in partnerships with orchestrators • Develop bargaining power with a strong brand and destination traffic • Improve and expand applications, staying ahead of competition • Keep applications simple

turn the particular market dynamics of a Battle of Architecture to its advantage? Table 9.1 presents some of the strategies that can be used by platform orchestrators and complementors in Battles of Architecture, both in the emerging phase and when the system has stabilized.

In the emerging phase, an orchestrator has to build a platform with legs. It doesn't have to be the best platform technologically, and not even be first in its class. But it has to appeal readily to a core group of users and draw enough third-party developers, as the objective is to cross the threshold for creating a network effect and 'get going.' Amazon, Facebook, and Apple's iPod, iPhone, and iPad pursued such winning strategies. None was the inventor of its system; but when they entered the nascent market, they already knew what they wanted to achieve and had a clear idea of the trajectory. That helped their initial positioning, which was well defined, and which strongly appealed to a core group of users sufficiently large to serve as a springboard for chasing network effects. All of them invested significantly at the outset, positioning themselves as leading brands of tomorrow, an image very attractive to insecure new users.

Good management is important for young companies as they maneuver through a powerful spiral of growth. Google and e-Bay founders went outside their companies to get top managerial talent early in the game. In some companies, such as Microsoft and Amazon, the founders themselves turned out to be good managers; but they could be the exceptions. (Companies whose founders were not good managers and did not hire good managers are likely to be forgotten.) Management's biggest challenge is steering the system toward the right destination as the company grows rapidly. Without such control, a company can easily take a wrong turn or go down a dead-end. Despite its early lead, for example, MySpace never really succeeded beyond the market of music-loving teenagers, while Facebook captured the much bigger mainstream American social network market. Despite the pressure to compromise on graphics and functionality, Mark Zuckerberg kept Facebook on its trajectory, gradually adding features but keeping the original look and feel and maintaining the positioning of the system as it evolved. A clear vision of the product's future made the critical difference.

The complementor space is driven by a similar dynamics. When the founders of Zinga decided to enter the market for networked games, they did not try to reinvent the wheel. They took their inspiration from an existing game, Farm Town; made a few critical improvements, mostly simplifying it; carefully chose their initial target audience; and launched Farmville. They partnered with Facebook, the leading social media for the age group they were initially targeting. They also used a Freemium model, with a generous free basic service and a well-priced premium package. They carefully managed the evolution of the model, rapidly crossing the threshold for network effects, and then systematically broadened their targeted audience. In early 2011, less than three years after its launch, Farmville dominated the interactive game market, with nearly 100 million users, generating more than $500 million in sales.

A Game That Reshapes the Economy

As the world moves into an information-based economy, an increasing number of industries will be built around the management of information. Most of them will have gone through Battles of Architecture. Although Microsoft initially regarded its initial contract with IBM in 2001 as a development assignment, it was smart enough to keep control of the software, and went on to capture the huge network effects that resulted from the emergence of IBM-compatible PCs, laying the foundation for its dominance of the computer industry.

Like Microsoft, many companies do not always realize that they are engaged in a winner-take-all Battle of Architecture. Telcos, for example, whose origins are in network operations, are currently fighting for significance in a totally changed industry, competing against companies that have originated in the Internet space, such as Google, Microsoft, and Facebook, and with device manufacturers such as RIM, Apple, and Nokia. We still do not know the architecture that will eventually channel personal electronic communications in the future, and who will control the platforms. But if the winning architecture does not depend on their physical network, then how should the telcos reposition their billion-dollar assets? Should they buy a content provider? Should they reinvolve themselves in producing devices or merge with a software company? Or should they simply fight tooth and nail to retain ownership of their customers, accepting that, in the overall communication value chain, they will generate less value by connecting A to B but still provide an important and valuable service?

Battle of Architecture games are high-stakes market-creation tournaments where platforms fight it out for dominance in a new market.[19] New platforms emerge from the convergence of new technologies, generally creating opportunities for multi-sided markets. Although many of these battles are Web-based, they also occur in old-line industries. Urban transportation is a case in point: major platforms that could be thorns to auto makers might currently be brewing.

Many entrepreneurs dream of being the next Bill Gates or Mark Zuckerberg, believing that they are in the right place with the right idea. But they are usually not alone in that position. Emulators abound in early games of architecture. The winners are those who manage to steer their platform in the right directions and lead in capturing network effects. Their platform does not have to be the best, but it should be well liked by core groups of users and module developers. They should invest significantly in building coalitions with developers. Their platform should also be biased toward simplicity and be easy to adopt. Finally, they should continually improve their offering, and be good at managing growth, avoiding big mistakes along the way. The few that end up winning, win big.

10 System Breakthroughs

As the airline industry was taking off in the 1950s, one its major problems was the handling of reservations. Airlines were using a manual system, with telephone operators recording the number of seats filled on cardboard charts, one for each flight. The actual number of seats available was not known in real time, except on the day of a flight. Because computers played little or no role in the process, booking a flight and issuing the ticket took an average of 90 minutes.

According to industry folklore, the president of American Airlines sat by chance next to a senior IBM salesman on a flight from Los Angeles to New York.[1] During the seven-hour flight, the two men discussed the way American Airlines could adapt software developed for the US Air Force to streamline its cumbersome reservation system.

Within weeks, IBM sent a proposal to American Airlines. In 1957 the two companies set up a joint project team to develop a computerized reservation system. A prototype was completed in 1960. In 1964, more than 10 years after the fortuitous conversation, American Airlines started using the SABRE system to handle all of its reservations.

SABRE rapidly became an important competitive asset for American Airlines. IBM also realized it had gained valuable expertise in designing and building the system. SABRE had not yet become fully operational when competing airlines asked IBM for similar systems; it obliged. (Large European airlines also developed their own systems, using local system integrators.) Around the same time, IBM launched its 360 line of computers, which were perfectly suited for these large system, having the capacity to handle high-volume transactions and maintain real-time inventory records, two key features of SABRE and similar systems. IBM capture the market as it emerged.

On its side, American Airlines fully exploited its first-mover advantage. In the mid-1970s the airline extended access to SABRE to travel agents. American also opened the system to all flights on all airlines, which convinced travel agents to make SABRE their system of choice. Despite the arrival of several competing systems and growls from US antitrust authorities, SABRE's dominance continued into the 1990s.

Only when the Internet arrived and passengers began booking their own reservations did systems like SABRE slowly fade into competitive obscurity. Nevertheless, today's online reservation systems, such as Expedia and Orbitz, can trace their origins back to American Airlines' first SABRE system.

The SABRE system was a major breakthrough, allowing the airline industry to handle the surge of reservations that erupted in the jet age of the 1960s. For the two companies that developed the system, it provided a foundation for steady future growth. By better managing its customers' reservations, American Airlines gained significant market share in all regions where it competed. IBM built a core franchise around high-volume transaction systems, which included hardware and software.

The development of SABRE demonstrates clearly the dynamics of a breakthrough game. It started with a radical restructuring of a critical airline industry process that had become a bottleneck. The breakthrough was brought about by two innovative companies working together: American Airlines, a visionary and deep-pocket client, and IBM, a system integrator whose team of experts could think outside the box. Such situations can involve huge technological risks. Some of them, like the Concorde airplane, end in failure. Others, like SABRE, end in triumph. Not only do such breakthrough systems generate years of continuous progress, but they rapidly attract competitors who contribute to its sophistication, to the benefit of a whole industry.

System Breakthrough games unfold on the verge of broad technological waves that sweep through industries and revolutionize the way they operate. In the past, these games typically involved new mechanical machinery, such as the electric motor and robots, and new chemical processes. Today, information technologies and software applications are stimulating similar breakthroughs that transform industries.

System Breakthrough games do not account for much of economic growth, around 5% as table 4.3 suggests (p. 57 above). But as they spread throughout the economy, they can bring substantial productivity growth, as the Enterprise Resource Planning (ERP) business software does. (ERP is discussed below.) The games themselves can last as long as 20 years.

Major Problems Crying Out for Solutions

A breakthrough results from removing a bottleneck that holds up the expansion of a system, such as the manual reservation systems of airlines in the 1950s.[2] Today, in an age of ever-rising fuel costs, the weight of long-range airplanes presents such a bottleneck. Boeing is currently attacking it with the newly designed 787 Dreamliner.

How do innovators attack these bottlenecks, which are often taken as inescapable by most businesses affected by them? Residents of large cities accept rush-hour traffic congestion as 'the way things are': too many people, too many cars. Yet there are some people who believe that information technology can significantly reduce congestion through a more efficient approach to the management of traffic. That breakthrough is yet to come. Their recipe will be to use the latest technologies to redesign the established way of doing things. To attack major bottlenecks, it usually takes a pair of innovators, a customer that has much to gain by eliminating the bottleneck and will finance the attempt, and an expert that will develop the solution.

One form of System Breakthrough game that is gaining in popularity is the 'challenge' approach. In 1996 an entrepreneur named Peter Diamandis established a $10 million prize to be awarded to the first non-government organization that built and launched 'a spacecraft capable of carrying three people to 100 kilometers above the Earth's surface, twice within two weeks.'[3] The prize, which was won in 2004, is considered to have been highly instrumental in the development of a non-governmental space launcher business, which has developed rapidly since then. The challenge approach dates back to the 19th century. In particular, such challenges, sometimes offering substantial prizes, were common in the early years of aviation, at the turn of the 20th century.[4] Another example is the Bill and Melinda Gates Foundation, which has so far allocated nearly a billion dollars to the Grand Challenges in Global Health grant program and related challenges that target specific global health issues.[5] NASA is pursuing a similar track with the Centennial Challenge program that addresses specific space-related issues that are unresolved but attainable. An interesting aspect of the challenge approach lies in its stimulation of a large number of competitors, many of whom become emulators once the breakthrough has been achieved, facilitating the development of an industry.

System breakthroughs are more common than is generally assumed. Computerized flight simulators have addressed the explosive demand for well-trained pilots. High-voltage power lines have tackled the need to transport electricity over long distances. Automated design of computer chips has crammed exponentially increasing processing power onto a single chip. The computerized designing of cars has sped up the introduction of new models, improved their reliability, and lowered their cost. And Boeing is using composites to reduce the weight of the Boeing 787 Dreamliner and increase its fuel efficiency.

The breakthrough itself is only the first step in a fascinating game of innovation. The competitive race that follows as the breakthrough technology is refined and integrated in competitive products is significantly different from those of Eureka! games and Battles of Architecture.

One striking difference is the size of the organizations involved at the outset. Eureka! and Battle of Architecture games generally begin with inventors and entrepreneurs, who smart small, addressing needs that most people don't even perceive, and sometimes must persuade people to take them seriously. Breakthrough games start differently, with well-known big problems that appear so insurmountable that most people have given up on resolving them. The organizations that can address such problems have to be big as well.

The airline industry provides many examples. In the 1970s, airplane manufacturers faced a huge demand for new aircraft, as jet travel attracted a rapidly growing number of passengers throughout the world. A major bottleneck in the design and production of such aircraft at a reasonable price was their complexity. The Boeing 747, which began flying in 1970, incorporates three million different parts and three million fasteners. For many decades to come, it was the most complex piece of equipment that ever came off an assembly line. Such complexity posed a big problem, and it called for a major breakthrough. The breakthrough came from Dassault Aviation, the French military aircraft manufacturer.

That company is still today a family business controlled by the Dassault family. Best known for its Mirage jet fighter, Dassault has to compete against much larger aircraft manufacturers, most of them American. Its biggest challenge, as a small player in the aircraft manufacturing industry, has been the high cost of designing a new plane. In the mid-1970s it succeeded in addressing that cost by considering how to design a plane faster and do it right the first time.

The company's president and sole shareholder, Marcel Dassault, believed that the design process could be automated using the emerging computer technology. At the same time as the personal computer hit the market, Dassault set up an in-house project to computerize the design and testing of new planes and their components. By 1978 the firm had begun applying its computerized design system to its current projects, with astounding results. Within a year, Dassault dramatically increased its productivity in design, giving it the competitive edge it needed to compete with bigger players. It had made a major breakthrough, and initially, it kept it to itself.

But the system was too valuable to keep under wraps indefinitely. In 1981 it created a subsidiary, Dassault Système, to commercialize the technology, and in partnership with IBM began to sell it to other aircraft manufacturers. Within a few years, every major aircraft manufacturer used a computerized design system based on Dassault's technology. In the early 1990s Dassault moved into automobile design, partnering with Toyota. Since then, CATIA, as the system is named, has become the dominant software tool for designing industrial equipment and machinery. It has also attracted several competitors.

Computerized design of complex equipment had to happen sooner or later. Dassault simply took the risk before others did. The company had a deep-pocket client, Marcel Dassault, who happened to own the business, and a group of experts that he trusted. But if Dassault hadn't moved, somebody else would eventually have tackled the problem.

Moving first is never an easy decision. It means treading on untested ground. Budgets and timelines are highly uncertain and generally over-optimistic. When Boeing decided to build the Dreamliner in 2004, it thought it could ship the first plane in 2008. As a next-generation airplane, the Dreamliner relies on extensive use of composite materials to lower its weight and improve its fuel efficiency, something that had never been done on that scale in the industry. Indeed, Airbus, its chief competitor, had decided against it. But Boeing pressed on. The weight of an aircraft presented an unmistakable bottleneck, and overcoming it would provide an enormous competitive advantage. To spread the risk and share the cost of the project, estimated initially at $10 billion, Boeing made a second major decision: it shared the design, manufacturing, and financing with partners from several countries. That decision created a management challenge of daunting proportions.

In pursuing a Breakthrough game, the customer knows from the outset that budgets and timelines are uncertain and are likely optimistic. Boeing was no exception. On the promise of delivery of the first Dreamliner in 2008, Boeing attracted several hundred aircraft orders, each accompanied by a hefty deposit. Were Boeing and its customers so naive as to think the Dreamliner would arrive on schedule? Or were they simply playing a game in which Boeing could raise cash and the customers got a spot at the head of the line and a chance to reduce the cost with penalty payments for late delivery? The answer is: probably a combination of both.

Boeing announced the first delays in 2006, and several more followed. The first Dreamliner was delivered in September 2011. The development had finally taken eight years, 45% more time than had initially been foreseen. Such a delay is actually par for the course for a breakthrough project of that magnitude. The development costs also surged by more than 50% to over $15 billion by the time the first plane flew commercially in September 2011. And that did not include the penalty fees for late delivery that Boeing will have to pay, and which could amount to several billion dollars.[6] Again, this is par for the course.

Considering these breathtaking figures, we don't wonder why Breakthrough games tend to be initiated by deep-pocket customers. Nor will we be surprised if all future commercial planes are constructed from composite materials.

Duets under Stress

Breakthrough games begin with the vision of a customer who wants to remove a systemic roadblock by redesigning the way things are done. At first glance, the problem defies conventional solutions. But the customer wants to address the problem differently, and has the resources to do it. Breakthrough customers tend to be atypical organizations with strong leadership. They can afford to take a large risk, and are not deterred by conventional wisdom or by the possibility of delays and cost overruns associated with an out-of-the-box solution, as long as it addresses their nemesis, the bottleneck. American Airlines, Dassault Aviation, and the Boeing Group are typical of Breakthrough game players. There are occasional exceptions to this model, as when the bottleneck is so big that it can be tackled only on an industry-wide basis. This is what happened with flight simulators, which we will discuss later in this chapter.

To tackle a bottleneck, the customer teams up with a system integrator, who assembles a team of experts. The customer and the integrator then steer the project. The customer provides the money and usually the field for experimentation, while the system integrator develops and delivers the solution. The system integrator may come from the same organization as the customers, as occurred at Dassault and Boeing. More often, the integrator comes from outside the organization, as was the case with IBM when it developed an airline reservation system for American Airlines, or with Microsoft when it designed the operating system for the first IBM PC. The system integrator has overall responsibility for coordinating the experts. The team is multidisciplinary, drawing individuals from a wide range of fields. Challenging the way things are done requires a radical departure from convention, and it helps to be able to assess the problem from a numerous viewpoints. The system integrator has overall responsibility for coordinating the experts.

Breakthrough games usually place great demands for engineering resources. In the MINE survey, system integrators involved in Breakthrough games devoted 30% of their sales to research, development, and engineering. They devoted another 14% to building capabilities in engineering, marketing, and production.

System integrators tend to come from large organizations that can marshal a wide range of resources and provide adequate assurance of success, no matter how ambitious the project. These engineering breakthroughs usually lie beyond the capabilities of small entrepreneurial firms. But there are important exceptions. SAP, Microsoft, and Oracle all got their start by working on a breakthrough project. These three companies were led by visionary technologists that were able to convince a deep-pocket partner to finance the breakthrough they had in mind.

Breakthrough projects inevitably give rise to tensions between the partners. The stakes are high and the paths unexplored. Budget overruns and unplanned delays are common, creating financial strains. Fatigue often sets in within the customer's organization. Moreover, the customer's expectations may shift over time, resulting in ever-rising performance thresholds as the system develops.[7] Experts can fall out of favor, and system integrators often buckle under incessant customer demands. What begins as a very tight partnership between customer and integrator can rapidly unravel. For the smaller partner, failure can be costly.

The Game Starts

Once the initial breakthrough occurs, the competitive game of innovation starts in earnest. The game is usually triggered by competitors of the initial customer, who seek a similarly high-performing system. At this point, the system integrator responsible for ushering the breakthrough into practice usually faces a dilemma: does it stay faithful to the original client or does it deal with the enemy? If the original customer is indifferent or is contractually powerless in preventing the system integrator from working with competitors, the decision is easy. But generally, contractual arrangements give temporary exclusivity over the breakthrough to the original customer, at least within its industry. Inevitably, other system integrators will propose competitive solutions inspired by the original breakthrough. As this occurs, the original customer that addressed the problem and financed the breakthrough gradually fades in importance, and system integrators take center stage.

As this happens, the competing visions of system integrators and their marquee customers structure the Breakthrough game. Although all emerging competitive solutions usually incorporate the original breakthrough, they generally also diverge.[8] As the game progresses, competitive advantages lie less with scientific advances and more on the patient and imaginative redesigning of processes and products. As these competitive solutions integrate the latest available technologies, the integrators tread on unexplored territory. One of their challenges is to harmonize their leading-edge solutions that work in novel configurations with the legacy systems of their customers.

Accumulation of Knowledge

Success in Breakthrough games depends on several factors. Project management and leadership are important, especially early in the game, when the ramifications of the breakthrough are still being explored. In these early years, integrators and customers must develop relatively intimate relationships, sharing information gathered from pilot testing and incorporating solutions into the next iteration of the breakthrough innovation. The accumulation of knowledge becomes a critical success factor for system integrators. The more contracts a system integrator obtains, the more knowledge it accumulates. At the same time, it also enhances its reputation and builds its technical expertise, leading to more assignments. For instance, Lurgi, the large German petrochemical equipment builder, considers its library of projects as its most important asset, reflecting the high value it places on accumulating knowledge. The library dates back more than a century, and it houses solutions to most chemical problems. Such accumulated knowledge becomes a key competitive advantage in Breakthrough games.

Breakthrough games can shape a new industry, as the emergence of the Electronic Design Automation (EDA) industry in the 1980s illustrates. The industry began around 1980 when manufacturers of computer chips began to pursue ever more powerful products. To meet the demands of Intel, AMD, National Semiconductor, Motorola, and IBM, a flurry of start-ups teamed up with them to develop increasingly powerful EDA software. The ensuing competition triggered a classic Breakthrough game that continues to this day. In our MINE project, we studied the case of one of these initial start-up firms, Cadence Design Systems, formed in 1984 in San Jose, California. Now the second-largest firm in the industry, Cadence spends about a third of its $1 billion in revenues on R&D. Its main asset is its accumulated knowledge, which enables it to keep up with the ever-increasing demand for higher performance from its customers, who are themselves caught up in their own races to deliver better-performing chips every two or three years to the makers of cell phones, PDAs, digital TVs, routers, computers, and other electronic devices.

Knowledge accumulated in Breakthrough games often allows a few competitors to dominate an industry, creating an oligopolistic structure and leaving room for smaller players only in highly specialized peripheral niches. In EDA, the hundreds of start-ups that existed in the 1980s had within 15 years distilled down to three major players. Customers depend on their accumulated knowledge about their chosen system, creating significant switching costs. Furthermore, the knowledge base of the three large EDA firms has become so complex that patents hardly matter anymore. Proprietary solutions that cannot or should not be patented (revealing their secrets) dominate the industry.

The case of SAP also illustrates how a successful system integrator involved in Breakthrough games accumulates knowledge. Since its invention of the Enterprise Resource Planning (ERP) system at the German subsidiary of ICI, SAP has not only expanded the ERP market to large businesses in all sectors of the economy, from basic manufacturing to banking and retailers, but has also diversified in numerous other business software markets. For over 30 years now, it has been codifying and redefining business processes and organizing them into integrated information systems that formalize best practices. That experience has allowed it to accumulated extensive and detailed knowledge about a wide range of manufacturing and operational activities. SAP has also developed the skills to integrate independent business functions into coherent systems. Its website mentions expertise in 24 industries and 11 lines of business (human resources, governance, etc.). For each line of business, it identifies between five and ten processes that it supports with accumulated expertise and best practices.

Opening Up Closed Architectures

Contradicting the trend toward open systems, most breakthrough solutions are closed and proprietary. Integrators place a high value on system integrity and control. They aspire to build global solutions, portable throughout an industry, and they are not too keen on having many third parties participating. Initially, customers appreciate the high productivity gains associated with a breakthrough solution and do not seek improvements by third parties. But as systems mature, some customers lean toward 'best-of-breed' approaches, a variation on open systems, that better accommodate their legacy systems. This resistance to a single-system solution opens the market to specialists that offer vertical modules, forcing system integrators to accept hybrid solutions. Thus, as a Breakthrough game matures, best-of-breed approaches gain market shares, and system integrators lose their tight grip on their solutions. New kids on the technological block come up with enhancements, enticing customers with higher-productivity add-ons. System integrators, meanwhile, have to reinvest continually in new generations of products to keep their market share and fend off direct competitors and niche players.

Industry Challenges: The Case of Pilot Training

Some bottlenecks are so big and complex that they can be addressed only by broad coalitions of stakeholders. Civilian pilot training provides a good example. Training pilots on actual planes is both expensive and dangerous. For commercial planes in particular it's entirely impractical. A missed landing could cost millions of dollars in damage, and that's assuming the apprentice pilot and the trainer are the only two brave souls aboard and that they survive the botched landing.

As early as 1910, pilots began training on ground equipment. Ed Link, an organ builder and amateur pilot, constructed the first cockpit simulator in 1928, a crude contraption that made no claims as a substitute for in-flight training. The electro-mechanical Link Trainer merely augmented a pilot's in-flight training, but it was a breakthrough of sorts, leading to the peripheral use of mechanical simulators. Only when the simulators started to incorporate computers and audio-visual projections in the 1960s did ground training become an acceptable way to reduce in-flight training requirements.

The jet age arrived around the same time, and pilot training became a major bottleneck for the airline industry. Not only did the surge in demand outpace the supply of trained air force veterans, but pilots had to fly increasingly complex planes, each of which demanded specific skills and training. Even experienced pilots needed regular retraining, particularly in mastering the difficult and dangerous procedures for landing and take-off. For airlines and for regulators who oversaw the certification of pilots, pilot training became a major issue.[9]

Under the leadership of the largest airlines of the time, such as Pan Am, BOAC (now British Airways), and KLM, the industry developed hybrid training programs that mixed low-cost ground training and in-flight training. Regulators accepted this approach to training, but when the time came to qualify a pilot for actual flight duty, regulators allowed only in-flight testing, as flight simulators were not sufficiently advanced. This regulatory requirement created a costly bottleneck for the industry. Better simulators were needed.

The ideal flight simulator must faithfully reproduce an actual flying environment and duplicate the specific aeronautical flight behavior of each type of plane.[10] If a simulated environment does not recreate actual aeronautical flight conditions, pilots develop negative responses. In flight, a pilot who has developed negative responses may take the wrong actions during situations such as turbulence, landing, or take-off that demand instinctive reactions. In other words, the pilot may pull up instead of pushing down, with disastrous consequences.

As the power of computers progressed in the 1970s, many in the industry suggested that the only solution to this bottleneck was Zero Flight Time (ZFT) training. They proposed using simulators to replace in-flight sessions for all pilot training as well as all evaluations conducted by regulators. This would drastically reduce the cost of training while allowing for increased duration of training sessions. It would also allow for periodic evaluations during the career of a pilot. In addition, ZFT would allow the development of global standards for pilot certification. But to work successfully, ZFT simulators had to replicate perfectly the stressful conditions encountered in flight, such as take-offs and landings in hailstorms or with a mechanical failure.

Developing faithful simulators was challenging. Because of the safety issues involved, the usual trial-and-error approach associated with most innovations could not be used. Comparable to the development of an innovative drug, which allows for no failure, an acceptable first-generation flight simulator had to work perfectly from the outset. To avoid negative learning, the simulated environment had to reproduce faithfully and in every detail the actual aeronautical conditions of flight. The conventional pattern of breakthrough innovation, which is perfected through successive competitive generations, was not acceptable. The first ZFT simulator had to work perfectly right out of the box.

Organizing the Breakthrough

No single airline had the resources to finance the development of simulated flight training. Moreover, the simulator had to incorporate endless amounts of data to duplicate accurately the flight conditions encountered on routes around the globe. To allow for international certification, it also needed the approval of regulators in every major industrialized nation. Airlines could collect the required information, but they would have to share it with simulator manufacturers. Simulator manufacturers, however, were fierce competitors, and each one wanted the industry to adopt standards that reflected the characteristics of its own technologies.

Despite these challenges, ZFT presented an enormous opportunity for airlines and simulator manufacturers. Airlines could reduce their costs while meeting the demand for new pilots. Manufacturers could create a lucrative new market for their technology. No one wanted to give up on ZFT.

In the mid-1970s, a Canadian manufacturer of military simulators, CAE Industries, engaged in quiet discussions with aircraft manufacturers, competing simulator manufacturers, and some large airlines to find a way to circumvent the bottleneck. Gradually, a coalition emerged among simulator manufacturers, which included all major players. They started to rally the airline industry behind a collaborative approach to the development of ZFT.

The coalition persuaded the Royal Aeronautical Society of Great Britain, a learned society for the industry, to convene a meeting of all stakeholders in London to explore the feasibility of ZFT. The meeting, held in 1980, included regulators from Britain, the United States, and Canada along with manufacturers and airlines. Participants at the meeting, known as the London Group, agreed to initiate an open dialogue among experts in the field leading to intensive cooperation about standards and requirements. The Group also served as an umbrella for the highly competitive simulator manufacturers to join together in exploring all possible options for designing and manufacturing a simulator that would have sufficient integrity to convince airlines and regulators to abandon in-flight training and focus on ZFT training.

Each member of the London Group held a piece of the puzzle: the air carriers knew about the design and cost of training programs; aircraft builders had accumulated extensive flight and cockpit data for each of their models; and simulator manufacturers had accumulated years of experience and knowledge about designing their own machines. Now each participant had to reveal its proprietary information to other members of the group, with whom it had competed fiercely in the marketplace. Simulator manufacturers, for example, had to share their design technologies and the knowledge behind them. Finally, public regulators had to promote common rules for assessing simulators and simulator-based training programs, and they had to evaluate the performance of simulators compared to hybrid programs.[11] Overcoming the politics and practices ingrained in each group of participants posed a major obstacle.

The London meeting led to further meetings. Working groups investigated specific aspects of the program, options were investigated, and gradually the participants reached a consensus, supported by participating regulators, about the standards that simulators should meet before they would accept ZFT training. No simulator in existence at that time could meet these standards, but manufacturers said they could create such simulators within a few years. Spurred onward by standards that anticipated their innovation, they began work in earnest on the next generation of technology. The Breakthrough game of innovation had begun.

In this Breakthrough game, regulatory standards for ZFT simulators agreed upon by regulators, airlines, and manufacturers created a market for technology that didn't yet exist. Not only did simulator manufacturers set out to achieve the standards, they did it much sooner than they'd anticipated. CAE began marketing a ZFT-compatible simulator in 1984. ZFT training then spread like wildfire. By meeting the minimum fidelity level required by airlines and regulators, simulator manufacturers delivered a breakthrough innovation that worked right out of the box.

The flight simulator market today represents sales of $500 million a year in products and services. The industry has consolidated around a few major players, including CAE in Canada, Thales in Europe, and L-3, formerly called Link Simulator, in Binghamton, NY, where Ed Link built the first mechanical simulator more than 80 years ago.

Unlike most breakthrough innovations, the flight simulator did not address a demand by a single customer to overcome a bottleneck. Instead, a consortium of airlines, regulators, and system integrators identified the challenge and then rose to the occasion to overcome it. In this case, the Breakthrough game that led to the ZFT flight simulator involved collaboration as well as competition.

Conclusion

The flight simulator breakthrough is an exception. Most breakthroughs involve a visionary customer who decides to tackle a major problem, and a well-financed team of experts that departs from convention to explore a new way of doing things. When and if the breakthrough occurs, a wave of innovations follows as competitors of both the original customer and the original system integrator exploit the technology. The initial breakthrough is just the first step in a work in progress.

The breakthrough is typically a new system, whose development and successive improvements call for the inputs of a wide range of expertise. Nevertheless, the role of two initial key players cannot be underestimated: the client, who faces a problem and finances its solution, and the expert, who leads the system-integration team and, in a typical Breakthrough game, eventually sells the solution to other customers.

By definition, systems involved in breakthrough are complex. Otherwise, the problem involved would not seem insurmountable and the solution would already have become an industry convention. The system integrator who participates in developing the breakthrough gains a competitive advantage over competitors, typically being the first at mastering the technology behind the innovation. But contractual constraints can restrict the integrator from selling its know-how to the original customer's competitors.

Over time, System Breakthrough games become less intense as the innovative solution slowly becomes a legacy system, ripe for an overhaul. The significant productivity advantages that customers discover in the early years become standard, as the technology behind the breakthrough joins the mainstream. Successive generations of the system offer fewer advantages.

In the process, however, Breakthrough games lead to the creation of great companies. American Airlines, for example, owes much of its success in the 1980s and 1990s to the competitive advantage of its SABRE system. SAP and Oracle have installed large enterprise-planning systems in global corporations, creating billions of dollars in shareholder value as they compete. CAE has also become a billion-dollar corporation, firmly in the lead in the pilot-training industry.

Breakthrough games occur mostly on the production side of the economy, bearing on industrial processes. They begin as huge bets that would seldom meet the approval of corporate bean counters. Their initiation and ultimate success depend on a visionary customer who believes that the time has come to do things differently. In the ensuing stages of the game, a system integrator untangles itself from the grip of the original customer and commercializes the breakthrough to other customers, some of whom are competitors of the original customer. Other systems integrators join the fray, often stealing employees from the original system integrators to build up their expertise. It all makes for a fascinating game, watching the limits of loyalty in the corporate world as a breakthrough process get diffused and improved upon.

11 New and Improved

On 18 February 2004 *The Onion*, a satirical newspaper and website, published a purported internal memo from the president of the Gillette Company responding to the launch of a four-blade razor by Schick-Wilkinson, their main competitor. The president challenged his team to develop a five-blade razor that would replace the company's three-blade Mach III razor as Gillette's primary shaving product. If 'Gillette is to be in the vanguard of the men's shaving industry,' the president argued, it had to have a five-blade razor. 'We could go four blades ... like the competition ... Why innovate when we can follow?' he asked rhetorically. Then he answered his own question: 'Because we are a business, that's why! ... From now on, we're the ones who have the edge in the multi-blade game ... Gillette is the best a man can get.'[1]

The memo was a spoof, typical for the front page of *The Onion*. But lo and behold, 18 months later Gillette announced that it had developed the five-blade Fusion razor. The company started delivering the Fusion in early 2006, in a standard format and in a premium battery-operated power model that featured a microchip to regulate the action of the blades. The Fusion was aimed directly at the competition, Schick's Quattro.

The world-wide razor blade market at the time was worth $10 billion.[2] It was a mature market, dominated in most parts of the world by Gillette and Schick. Since then, Gillette has introduced several versions of the Fusion razor, including Fusion Power Phantom, Fusion Power Phenom, Fusion Gamers, Fusion MVP, Fusion Pro-Glide, and Fusion Power Cool White. In parallel, it also launched a family of razors for women under the brand Venus. Schick has done more or less the same, with several families of multi-blade razors targeted at both men and women.

Why so many? Because it is a *business*, wrote *The Onion*, and it was right. How do you stay on top of the competition and get your year-end bonus in such a mundane industry as the razor? By continually improving the offering through small incremental innovations. This is the New and Improved game, a phrase that is also associated with Procter & Gamble, which acquired Gillette in 2005 for $57 billion.

The battle of the blades involves more than smoke and mirrors. Razor companies spend hundreds of millions of dollars a year to improve on the design of razors. They make them lighter and less irritating to the skin. The improved razors shave closer and leave behind a feel-good sensation. Gillette's corporate motto is 'Advanced technology for proven shaving performance,' and the company marches to its own marketing drum. New models keep on coming, offering new designs in new configurations. *Consumer Reports*, the magazine of the Consumers Union, has even tested a six-blade razor available from an American pharmacy chain.[3] Can a ten-blade model be far behind?

The New and Improved game is the most common innovation game in the economy. Companies playing the game account for about 45% of the GDP, according to our estimates. They compete on the basis of regular improvements that differentiate their products and processes, improve product benefits, and lower product costs. They are found in most mature sectors: natural resources and commodities; basic materials such as petrochemicals, glass, and steel; industrial products such as equipment and machinery; building materials; consumer goods such as soap, razors, clothing, shoes, toys, and food products; and services such as car rentals, electric power, insurance, and restaurants. These markets are mature, customers are familiar with the products, and the technologies change slowly. Keeping customers satisfied and away from competitors while improving profits drives the dynamics of competitive innovation in the New and Improved game.

New and Improved games are first and foremost the province of large businesses, although small businesses are also very present, both in ecosystem of large firms and in local markets, from mom-and-pop restaurants and convenience stores to local law firms and small printing shops. In these local markets, convenience, service, and intimacy are the prime drivers of competition, but local businesses can also innovate with 'First in the market ...' types of innovations borrowed from elsewhere.

What MINE Has Taught Us

New and Improved games drew 167 MINE respondents, mainly large businesses with an average of 8,900 employees. The game is observed in three primary areas: local markets; upstream producers of basic material such as lumber, steel, chemical products, and utilities; and downstream companies, closer to the final users, involved in manufactured goods, equipment, and consumer goods and services.

From an innovator perspective, upstream businesses compete in technologically stable markets with lower rates of change, knowledge production, and rivalry. New knowledge is generated mostly internally, and mostly from the accumulation of experience. These businesses engage in low levels of R&D. In the MINE survey, they spent less than 1% of sales on R&D, the lowest among all games. Innovation efforts are focused on cost reduction rather than product differentiation. But of all MINE participants, these upstream businesses were the least interested in innovation. Their competitive strategies rely more on acquisitions and plant expansions, which are effective at lowering costs through economies of scale.

Downstream businesses compete differently. Their products and services range from packaged goods and personal care products to machinery, financial products, and services such as hospitality. They offer more potential for differentiation and branding in markets whose pace of change is much higher and whose rivalries are much more intense. Among downstream businesses, product innovation matters as much as cost reduction.

Despite their differences, both upstream and downstream groups play the same innovation game, but at a different levels of intensity. Here is what we learned from the MINE survey and case studies about their innovation activities:

The products and services involved in this game stand alone, fulfilling their benefits without a third party. This differentiates them from systems, which require contributions from several parties to deliver their benefits. The iPad, for example, requires inputs from content suppliers to yield its benefits. Producers of stand-alone products and services need no third-party inputs. They fully control their products' features and the benefits they deliver.

The products and services are mature. Customers are experienced and know, often in great detail, about a product's features and benefits. Markets involved in New and Improved games grow at a slow, steady pace. Of all the games, New and Improved was associated with the lowest annual growth in sales.

The products and services evolve slowly. Differentiation comes from incorporation of the latest technological developments, which tend to come from outside the industry. Experienced as they are, customers are not particularly faithful, and price remains an important criterion. As the market evolves, companies enrich the benefits they provide to their customers. Gillette and Schick, for instance, are now both offering lubricated razor blades. Innovation involves a lot of trial and error as producers attempt to track the needs of their customers. In the MINE survey, companies playing the New and Improved game conducted 85% of their innovative activities within pre-established knowledge roadmaps. Only 15% of R&D is oriented toward the renewal of the knowledge base.

In most markets, most companies do not place innovation as the center of their competitive strategy. In the MINE survey, participants in New and Improved games recorded lower sales growth from innovation than participants in any other game. They also attributed a lower proportion of profits to innovation. Marketing muscle and building barriers to entry were more important profit drivers than innovation. Yet, in downstream markets, New and Improved innovations provide continuous product differentiation. The differences may seem trivial, as we have seen in the razor market, but they are still meaningful to customers, and in the long run add up to significant progress. In upstream markets, innovations are more oriented toward continuous improvements in productivity and cost reduction, and play an important role in profit growth.

As a proportion of sales, participants in New and Improved games spend less on R&D than participants in any other game. In the MINE survey, R&D among New and Improved players represented 3.5% of revenues. (Such low percentages can be deceiving. Among companies with billion-dollar sales figures, these R&D investments can add up to immense amounts.)

Businesses involved in New and Improved games cast a wide net to get their ideas for improvements. MINE participants indicated that, in 60% of cases, their innovative ideas come from outside. Businesses exploit their ecosystem of customers and suppliers to find the latest technologies for improving their products or lowering their costs. The most important external sources of ideas mentioned were customers (24%) and suppliers (20%).

The importance of innovation varies greatly in this game. Some firms compete on the basis of innovation, but other are much less concerned by it. The game conditions, namely mature industries and stand-alone products, can create a relatively placid environment. Strong oligopolies, high barriers to entry, and product regulation can insulate such an industry from the need to compete on the basis of innovation. But every market has its own idiosyncrasies, and no competitor can fall too far behind in terms of cost or product performance without risking loss of market share and ultimately its own demise. In such an industry, companies invest in innovation primarily to keep up with the competition. Continuing competitive pressures focus the corporate mind and help product and R&D managers gain access to corporate capital investment.

Innovation Drivers

New and Improved games and their low uncertainty environment allow innovation to be routinized. The game has three basic drivers of innovation.

Enriching the Portfolio

Businesses in mature industries manage a portfolio of products, each targeted at specific segments. Product managers continually seek to improve the performance of individual products in their portfolio. They attempt to develop new segments with variations of their basic products and to give a second life to tired products. Consider Clorox, founded in 1913 to extract bleach, or sodium hypochlorite, from the San Francisco Bay salt ponds. Over the years, it has extended its franchise from this basic commodity into a large family of household cleaning products. It now offers hundreds of cleaning products in all sizes and shapes, relying on innovation to enrich its portfolio. While doing nothing spectacular, Clorox has nevertheless institutionalized innovation, constantly coming up with new products, broadening its franchise and strengthening its personality. To generate new product ideas, it taps many sources. It operates creativity seminars with customers. It calls on experts from other industries. It seeks input from its suppliers. It picks up ideas from its competitors. Continuous product innovation does not require rocket science, but it has kept Clorox going for 100 years. Its annual sales now exceed $5 billion, and its market capitalization is approaching $10 billion. As long as it can keep coming up with new household cleaning products that are as good as or better than those of its competitors, Clorox will continue to thrive in the marketplace.

Bigger and better-known Procter & Gamble follows a similar

approach. With annual sales of $80 billion and a market capitalization of $175 billion, it has routinized product innovation, which year after year maintains its place among the world's most admired companies.[4] Changes in its flagship products occur almost every year. Its ability to differentiate and rejuvenate its products also allows it to maintain a price premium over competitors.

Offsetting Commoditization

Clorox's well-known product Bleach is a solution of sodium hypochorite, a basic chemical. Clorox's strong brand prevents Bleach from being commoditized and allows it to obtain a premium price. Nevertheless, to maintain its differentiation, Clorox has to continually come with a new and improved Clorox Bleach, working on the concentration, adding complements, changing the packaging, and the like. Almost all mature products are vulnerable to commoditization as they standardize and as low-cost competitors enter the market. Unless a company continuously differentiates its version, price becomes the defining factor. As commoditization advances, margins dwindle, pressuring a company to find new uses for its product.

Industrial gases epitomize a commodity product. Apart from their purity, such one-molecule products look much the same, no matter whose label is attached. Oxygen was the first gas to be industrialized at the turn of the twentieth century as it became widely used for welding and cutting metals. Numerous start-ups were set up to produce it, extracting oxygen from the air, purifying it, bottling it and delivering it to machine shops and factories. One such start-up was Air Liquide, founded in France in 1902, and now the world's leading producer of industrial gases. To fight the commoditization of its products, it purposely structured itself around a research-and-development organization dedicated to finding new uses for industrial gases. Since its inception, industrial engineers have dominated its managerial ranks. It gradually expanded into a wide range of industrial gases, all generic, but continually finding new uses. It now has sales of €15 billion and manages a large product portfolio that includes oxygen, nitrogen, helium, carbon monoxide, and rare gases and serves a wide range of industries, from steel-making, petrochemicals, and semi-conductor foundries to hospitals and biotechnology companies. Air Liquide clearly demonstrates the power of innovation to fend off commodization.

The same drive can be observed in the aluminum industry. As steel, plastics, and composite materials have encroached on their traditional markets in the automobile and airplane industries, the global aluminum producers such as Alcoa, Rio Tinto Alcan, and Norsk Hydro have to continually develop new markets for aluminum. They work closely with existing and potential customers, often setting up formal R&D alliances. Their basic strategy has two prongs: lower costs, a common thrust in any commodity industry, and development of new markets through a very intense product-directed innovation program. As a result, they become quite innovative, somewhat of a paradox for commodity-oriented organizations.

Relentless Pursuit of Process Efficiency

Since commoditization usually leads to a loss of control over prices, a company can often increase profits most effectively by working on costs. Continuous improvement of productivity is achievable by integrating knew knowledge and new technologies in production processes. As the environment changes, plants inevitably stray from the optimal level of efficiency. Furthermore, a company that manufactures a range of products in multiple plants can gain productivity simply by optimizing production mandates as output evolves.

In 1996 Raymond Royer, a former manufacturing executive schooled in the transportation equipment industry, became CEO of Domtar, a struggling mid-sized paper manufacturer. During a period of 10 years at the helm of Domtar, Royer propelled Domtar to the top of its industry by pursuing a value-creation strategy centered on continuous improvement of its production processes and their cost bases. The tight financial conditions it faced in 1996 did not allow it to achieve this strategy through capital investment in new machinery and plant modernization, so Royer tapped into his previous transportation equipment industry experience to attack Domtar costs and inefficiencies by using Kaizen techniques.

Developed in Japan in the 1960s, Kaizen is a production philosophy that calls for involving everyone in a company, from the worker on the production line to the CEO, in a process of continuous improvement. In a 'Kaizen project,' managers and employees work together to analyze a specific issue and propose a solution that will yield an improvement in efficiency. At Domtar, Royer encouraged the formation of Kaizen groups throughout the company, from forestry and mill operations to logistics, warehousing, and corporate services, to tackle a wide range of productivity bottlenecks. This approach allowed Domtar to achieve significant productivity gains despite its limited capital resources. By 2006 Domtar had become the leading North American manufacturer of fine paper. It achieved this success primarily by incorporating thousands of improvements into its processes, which increased the company's efficiency, reduced its costs, and bolstered its profitability. Eventually, Domtar acquired less productive mills and turned them around by applying the same Kaizen processes to increase productivity.

A Canadian company, Syncrude, followed a similar process of sustained innovation aimed at lowering the costs of extracting oil from the giant tar sand fields of western Canada. Formed as a joint venture by several oil companies, Syncrude set out to build the first large-scale plant to extract oil from the oil sands. It aimed to produce oil at a cost that was competitive with deep-sea oil wells, the highest-cost alternative source. When operations started in 1978, Syncrude relied on draglines, bucket-wheel reclaimers, and huge conveyors to mine the sand and transport it to a plant, where the bitumen was separated from the sand to be further processed into oil. That initial process turned out to be much too costly, so Syncrude set out on a path to dramatically improve its productivity. Looking throughout the entire operation for ways to save money, the company made numerous improvements in mining methods, materials handling, equipment maintenance, and extraction processes. It also formed an alliance with Caterpillar, the equipment supplier, and decided to replace its billion-dollar investment in draglines and conveyors with mobile equipment, acquiring a fleet of the largest mining shovels and trucks ever built. That change in operation method allowed Syncrude to reduce its costs significantly and become profitable. It opened a second site in 1998, achieving the same low-cost efficiency as in its first operation. Other companies then moved in. New production methods appeared, in particular extraction of the bitumen by injecting steam into wells, which eliminated the open pits and reduced costs while enhancing the industry's environmental performance.

Information technology is also used in mature industries to reduce costs and improve productivity. The Enterprise Resource Planning (ERP) systems that SAP pioneered allow firms to integrate all their databases. By giving universal access to critical data in real time, ERP enables a firm to reduce clerical staff, better control work in process, and more efficiently allocate resources. Companies may also rely on complementary systems such as Supply Chain Management (SCM), Customer Relationship Management (CRM), Product Lifecycle Man-

Table 11.1. New and Improved Innovation Strategies

---

1. Strategic intent
   - A strategy maintained over the long term
   - An organizational structure reflecting the strategy
   - Sustained investment in innovation
2. Innovation culture
   - A key component of the official discourse
   - Employee engagement
   - Rewards
3. Process and tools
   - Corporate process
   - Tools
   - Intellectual property
4. Casting a wide net
   - Bottom-up innovation
   - Fighting the Not Invented Here syndrome
   - Technology brokering
5. Innovation metrics

---

agement (PLM), and Assets Management (AM) to enhance their productivity and drive down costs.

What is common to all these productivity initiatives is their routine character. In mature industries with stand-alone products, the most successful companies pursue continuous marginal improvements of their production processes, constantly raising their level of performance. Current management orthodoxy calls for businesses to become customer focused. This is good advice. But in mature industries, continuous improvement in costs is just as important.

New and Improved Innovation Strategies

New and Improved innovation strategies revolve around five axes, presented in table 11.1. They start with a clear strategic intent, aimed at value creation through continuous innovation of both products and processes. They are supported by a culture of innovation. Each employee is fully aware at all times of the importance of continuous improvement. As well, managing and extracting value from innovation requires specific processes and tools. Moreover, the ideas may not necessarily come from within the company or even the industry. Successful innovators cast a wide net to catch new ideas. Finally, performance is measured with the proper innovation metrics.

Strategic Intent

There are many ways for companies in mature markets to focus on innovation. One company may choose, for example, to become a low-cost producer. Another may choose to reap economies of scale and pricing power through industry consolidation; BHP Billiton, the mining company, is pursuing such a strategy by buying out its rivals. Companies may invest in reducing costs and increasing the scale of their operations. They can also move production to a low-wage country. In the highly commoditized global t-shirt market, for example, Gildan has become the cost and sales leader by moving all of its production from Montreal to Central America. All these options enable a company to fend off commoditization, and they require little or no innovation. But an innovation strategy is always an option.

There are three generic continuous improvement strategies: sustained product differentiation, as Gillette does; developing new markets, à la Air Liquide; or cost reduction, as Domtar has done. Whatever path or combination of paths chosen, the strategy must be pursued for a long period, since the impact of each strategy is cumulative. Such long-term commitment demands that the continuous improvement strategy be well ingrained within a company's culture to survive changing market conditions, short-term market disruptions, and changes in corporate leadership. The strategic intent can be reflected in the structure of a company's operations. For example, P&G operates 26 research centers worldwide where it spends about 2.5% of its $80 billion in annual revenues. Management cannot ignore their ideas. Likewise, L'Oréal, which also pursues a New and Improved innovation strategy in the global cosmetic and perfume market, has 18 research centers around the world where it spends about 4% of its $20 billion revenues.

But integrating continuous incremental innovation into operations is a challenge. Innovations must be given priority within each business unit, close to the product or process to which it applies. Functional experts, and in particular R&D managers, may share responsibility for developing business-unit innovation strategies. But ultimately, accountability for innovation lies with operational managers, who tend to be concerned about efficiency and meeting this year's operating objectives, which often clash with innovation strategies. New products, new markets, and process improvements must form a significant part of these managers' objectives. Their annual plans should reflect the corporate commitment to organic growth through continuous upgrading of products and processes. Capital investment must support innovation as well, taking limited resources away from other growth vectors such as marketing, new plants, or distribution. To win the thousands of corporate skirmishes that such allocation entails, innovation must be strongly championed within an organization.

A Culture of Innovation

In mature markets, the corporate culture must support and reward innovative activities, as they often clash with the 'cash-flow'-generating activities. A culture of innovation facilitates the acceptance of a certain level of uncertainty associated with trials and experimentation. It encourages acceptance of higher margins of error and tolerance of higher risk. In such a culture, failure does not threaten an individual's career. On the contrary, career advancement depends on challenging the status quo.

The official discourse of New and Improved innovative companies such as P&G often singles out innovation as a core purpose. References to innovation appear in their company slogans, mission statement, value statements, and websites. In their organizational development, these companies adopt policies that emphasize the importance of innovation and that foster company-wide conditions friendly to innovative activities and change.

There is an abundance of managerial literature about creating permissive conditions for innovation in mature companies. Common to all approaches are some best practices: strong signals from the top, empowerment, rewards for experimenting, ownership of issues, acceptance of failure, and collaboration between marketing, production, and R&D. In all cases, senior management must be committed to innovation as a business strategy, and they must communicate that commitment constantly to the whole organization.

Process and Tools

In New and Improved innovation games, innovation becomes routine. To achieve this, companies rely on a wide array of tools and processes. An abundant literature on the management of innovation disseminates best practices.

Project management capabilities. This is a pre-requisite. Innovating implies a break with current operations. Yet execution of an innovation initiative is often assigned to ad hoc project teams. Widespread diffusion of project-management best practices is thus useful.

Stage-Gate system. In use for more than 25 years, this managerial tool enable companies to structure the development of new products by breaking that development down into phases, each ending with a GO–NO GO gate. Stage-gating is efficient at eliminating ideas that stand only a small chance of succeeding.[5]

Six Sigma. Invented at Motorola, this management tool improves the quality of processes by identifying and removing causes of low performance.[6] It has been widely adopted in manufacturing industries. The former CEO of General Electric, Jack Welch, became one of its best-known promoters.

Toyota's product development system. Widely copied, this system has revolutionized the design of new products in many industries. The system closely integrates R&D with manufacturing to accelerate the process.[7] It is also a key component of the lean production system.

Voice of the Customer. VOC allows a company to organize the required information about customer expectations to guide the development of a new product and the evolution of its features in comparison with other products available on the market.[8]

Product development software packages. With names like Idea Generation, Product Design, In-Sourcing of Ideas, and Portfolio Analysis, these packages aim to structure the development process of new products.

A good organizational design can also help a company to sustain innovation. In successful mature market innovative organizations, a functional unit has the responsibility for supporting innovative initiatives. Some companies appoint a Chief Innovation Officer on their senior management team to coordinate and foster a culture of innovation.[9] The CIO's responsibilities include seeking out initiatives in the budding stage and encouraging their development. The CIO also promotes the transfer of technologies and experience between business units, attacking the silo mentality. Practices to facilitate technology transfer include cross-functional teams, formal transfer of champions from one unit to another, and collaborative product development with lead internal users. The Internet has also made the market for ideas much more efficient by enabling rapid connection with innovative thinking and thinkers.

Since many good ideas can remain trapped below the radar screen in large organizations, innovative companies install bottom-up innovation processes to facilitate their upward flow. Bottom-up processes allow organizations to tap the resourcefulness of experienced employees as they deal with real issues that affect the company's performance.

To stimulate the adoption of innovation emerging from R&D departments, companies may offer incentives to business units to reduce the risks involved. Companies may also employ other ways of encouraging business units to explore new technologies and new markets. The process typically starts with the exchange of ideas and knowledge during joint exercises involving R&D and marketing. Some companies adopt probing techniques such as mapping exercises, scenario building, and consulting with gurus.

In a mature market, one company very rarely owns a unique discriminating feature. As we've discussed, some mature companies rely to some degree on patents to create value. Patenting can make life more difficult for competitors, forcing them to build around a patented concept. But patent protection is seldom the critical element for capturing value in New and Improved games. The relevant technologies are usually widely available, so companies more often capture value through marketing and optimizing manufacturing. The patents' main contributions are the royalties, especially for production techniques and design features. In this respect, patenting can be a lucrative activity, a business unit by itself. But it has little to do with the incentive to innovate. Innovation is driven above all by the need to remain relevant in the marketplace.

Casting a Wide Net

In 2006 a *Harvard Business Review* article written by two senior Procter & Gamble executives, Larry Huston and Nabil Sakkab, announced a fundamental shift in the innovation strategy of that most innovative organization. Experts noticed. P&G's new innovation strategy, Connect and Develop, relied on a systematic search for ideas beyond the perimeters of the company. It called for P&G to reach out to suppliers, competitors, and scientists for new ideas and technologies that the company could incorporate into its products and processes. If P&G proceeds with an idea, it often works in partnership with the external provider.[10] According to the two managers, more than one-third of P&G innovations in 2006 originated from externally generated ideas, and half of its product development initiatives included key elements that came from outside the company.

With Connect and Develop, P&G set out deliberately to fight the Not Invented Here syndrome that plagues many mature organizations. Most major companies have now espoused open innovation. For instance, since 2010 General Electric has joined with venture capitalists to launch several innovation challenges to researchers all over the world for innovative projects in selected areas, such as breast cancer, clean technologies, and smart electric grid, setting aside several hundred million dollars to fund the best ideas submitted. Generating ideas sufficiently powerful to feed the process of continuous improvements is a major bottleneck in New and Improved games. The open innovation movement (sometimes called technology brokering) has developed to address these bottlenecks. It rests on programs and policies that structure the explicit licensing and sharing of technologies and ideas with suppliers, lead customers, partners, and even competitors. The process requires a company to open its organization to other corporate ecosystems, a task often coordinated centrally by a technology brokerage office.

Open innovation can also orient and shape the innovation efforts of companies.[11] Lead customers have always provided ideas for product improvements. But approaching the external sourcing of new product ideas on a systematic basis is a new phenomenon, making it more democratic and open.[12]

The popularity of open innovation has given birth to a cottage industry that acts as intermediaries with potential sources of ideas. Companies such as InnoCentive, MVS Solutions, and Nine Sigma harness ideas and solutions to problems in organizations around the world. They also act as product development consultants, operating global open-innovation idea networks.[13] On behalf of clients in their fields of specialization, they acquire and sell ideas to develop products and technologies. As consultants, they also advise on best practices to harvest ideas from external sources.

Measuring Innovation in a Company

Measuring the effectiveness of innovation efforts has posed a perennial challenge for management.[14] Innovation and R&D tend to aim for long-term targets, and evaluation of their achievements tends to be more subjective than for sales or manufacturing targets. Nevertheless,

Figure 11.1. The Industrial Research Institute's Technology Value Pyramid

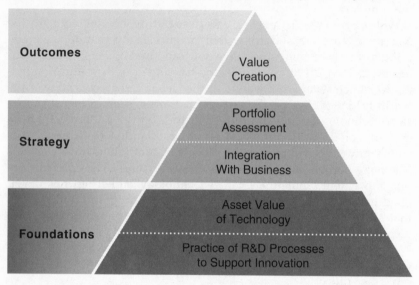

a wide range of metrics have been devised to measure the impact of innovation in a corporate setting. A common measure is the percentage of sales represented by products less than five years old. Other measures include new products launched, cost reductions as percentage of cost, patents obtained, R&D spending as a percentage of sales, and the number of active development projects.

However, no single metric captures the overall innovation performance of an organization. Management also struggles to precisely define a new product and to identify the specific causes of cost reductions. To narrow the scope of interpretation, the Industrial Research Institute has devised the Technology Value Pyramid, presented in figure 11.1, which covers five categories of metrics: outcomes, value of the portfolio, integration with the business strategy, value of the technology, and R&D support process.[15]

Metrics should be developed in each category. Definitions tend to be company specific and somewhat subjective. One company might have a lot of patents and new products in its portfolio but may not exploit them effectively, while a competitor with a smaller portfolio and older products may be much better at capturing their value.

As the management mantra says, what gets measured gets managed. Measuring innovation communicates clearly the importance of the innovation strategy throughout an organization. Monitoring these metrics and communicating the results send a strong message about a company's commitment to innovation.

Winning at New and Improved

In mature markets, a business generates its profits by being efficient at what it does. Optimizing is a fundamental principle. Thus, there is a strong reward to managers that ensure predictable and consistent results. But in the long run, a company generates superior profits by differentiating its products and by reducing its costs beyond the industry standards. These two objectives can be achieved with a specific innovation strategy. The intensity of innovation will vary by industry and market, but what matters is being ahead of competitors. Although laggards may pursue copy-cat strategies, they will end up with product strategies designed by their competitors, and miss out on first-comer's advantages. A company can always choose to compete on terms other than innovation, relying for example on pricing, lower margins, better locations, or a strong brand. But forfeiting innovation as a strategy greatly reduces the options.

Mature markets are characterized by experienced customers and established designs. Businesses compete at the margins, differentiating their offerings and nurturing perceptions of superior value, which allow them to charge a higher price. A product as commoditized as a cola is differentiated through constant improvements in packaging, distribution, and format. Perceptual associations are also developed with advertising and ever-changing slogans ('We are the world ...'). Through innovation, a company's market shares can creep up in a mature market, a few tenths of a percentage point per year in soft-drinks markets. Over the long run, this adds up. In 2009 Coca-Cola outsold Pepsi-Cola in the United States by 41.9% to 29.9%. Moreover, Diet Coke will soon overtake Pepsi as the number two soft drink in the US market.

In New and Improved innovation games, major upheavals are rare and market share changes slowly. Turbulence tends to be found only at the bottom end of the market, where 'discounter' competitors enter with low-cost strategies. But as the airline industry in North America and in Europe indicates, all but a few of these entries fail after a few years.

Necessity is the mother of invention, and often the mother of innovation. In mature markets, innovation is most intense in industries where product differentiation is difficult and copying is easy. We observe it in consumer goods, where thriving innovative companies such as P&G and Coca-Cola bank on next year's new and improved product to maintain their preeminent positions.

12 Mass Customization

In the spring of 1989, 50 senior automobile industry executives converged from all corners of the world on Acapulco, Mexico. They were attending a three-day conference on their industry held by the International Motor Vehicle Program (IMVP), a research consortium set up by a group of MIT professors to provide an independent assessment of the health of the global automobile industry. Accompanying them were about 20 researchers who had spent the previous few years studying the industry. (One of the authors, Roger Miller, was among them.)

At the time, US and European automobile makers felt alarmed by the inroads made by Japanese products into their domestic markets. According to conventional industry wisdom, the Japanese benefited from lower labour costs arising mostly from their network of quasi-captive suppliers clustered around their assembly plants.

But as the 1980s progressed, reality challenged that view. In 1984, for example, General Motors set up a joint venture with Toyota allowing the Japanese company to take over a plant in Fremont, California, that GM intended to close. The joint venture gave GM and the rest of the industry a chance to see first hand how the Japanese organized themselves to build cars.

At the time, the American automobile industry still followed Henry Ford's 1912 approach to mass production and Alfred Sloan's later approach at GM to product strategy. Sloan had adopted the concept of a GM family of models, each targeted at a distinct market. This allowed the auto maker to capture economies of scale, through large plants and basic platforms, while providing a multitude of models covering the wide range of the automobile market. To function properly, such a system required relatively good sales forecasts and good marketing. With these resources, a manufacturer could plan its production activities. The system also required a network of efficient suppliers to deliver parts at the lowest possible price, and mastery of assembly processes used to manufacture the automobile. Inventories acted as a buffer throughout the system. In one of the most famous economic books of the post-war years, *The New Industrial State*, John Kenneth Galbraith celebrated the performance of that system, lauding the automobile industry as the epitome of achievement of the Industrial Revolution.[1]

But the Fremont plant, taken over by Toyota, turned out to be an eye-opener for the American automobile industry. Toyota relied on the same American unionized workers as GM. It operated from the same old assembly plant using most of the same machinery and equipment. Toyota added Japanese training, production methods, and workflow design. The results were startling. Under Toyota's leadership, Fremont, one of the least productive auto assembly plants in the United States, became one of the nation's most productive facilities and, to add insult to injury, met quality standards seldom achieved in other US plants at that time. From that moment on, the 'cheap labour' argument went out the window.

The IMVP researchers fully documented the lean production system developed by the Japanese automobile industry. The system empha- sized dependability, teamwork, cutting waste, and improving quality. Contrary to the myth of fragile supplier relationships, it encouraged strong and dynamic partnerships sealed by mutual commitment. US auto manufacturers gave their suppliers detailed specifications and then dragged them through tough take-it-or-leave-it negotiations on price. By comparison, Japanese auto makers regarded their suppli- ers as full partners with significant responsibilities for the design and improvement of the components they manufactured.

Most revealing was their approach to designing cars. Unlike the US industry, which was schooled by the principles of mass production developed by Henry Ford and Alfred Sloan, the Japanese auto industry had never enjoyed the luxury of a mass market. As the Japanese indus- try took shape in the late 1940s and early 1950s, it had to tailor its prod- ucts to fragmented markets, each with its own specific requirements, from urban cars to farm vehicles to delivery trucks, limousines, and taxis. The US concept of mass production had no place in the Japanese industry.

IMVP researchers showed how Japanese auto makers coped with the diversity of their markets in a number of ways. They emphasized quality and tighter physical standards, allowing much higher inter-operability of components and a higher percentage of common parts. Of equal importance, they became efficient in designing cars for small-volume markets. Reducing the cost and the time required to design a variety of new models became a key competitive competency. By the 1980s, Japanese auto makers were designing a new car in half the time that Americans took and spent one-third as much as Americans on engineering. They could well afford to design distinct models for a wider range of niche markets. Add to this their high quality standards on the production line, and it was clear the Japanese had become the most efficient car makers in the world.[2]

Japanese automakers had become very good at mass customization. They could produce high-volume models such as Toyota's Corolla and Camry and Honda's Civic, achieving economies of scale, while continuing to manufacture low-volume models to address demand from niche markets, competing always on quality. With their lean production and lean design arrangements, they achieved a quasi-craft production approach, manufacturing an automobile based on buyer specifications and delivering it within a few weeks.[3]

Nearly 25 years after the Acapulco meeting, mass customization remains much more advanced in the Japanese automobile market than elsewhere in terms of the range of models offered and the options available on each model. The ability to meet specific demands of buyers with no significant delay remains a key competitive feature of their automobile industry.

The North American auto industry is still trailing. US manufacturers produce far fewer models of automobile for the US market, and rely on options to achieve customization.[4] The Japanese not only also provide options, but they design cars targeted at smaller niches. For the US market, their models are designed to be profitable with one-quarter of the sales required for competitive American models. Accustomed to their fragmented domestic market, they see these smaller US runs as still relatively large, allowing them to reap significant economies of scale. Designing models more rapidly, with fewer engineering hours, gives the Japanese a tremendous competitive advantage, on top of their ability to manufacture cars with fewer defects and greater durability.

Mass customization did not first appear within the automobile industry. One of its earliest manifestations was in retailing, with the development of the department store. Inspired by the pavilions at the Paris International Exhibition of 1855, Aristide Boucicault added departments to his small drapery store, Au Bon Marché, to address the general needs of the middle-class Parisian consumer. In the process, he created the world's first department store. Within a decade, numerous imitations had appeared in Paris, London, and New York. By the end of the century, department stores had become the largest stores in major cities around the world, usually with several hundred thousand feet of retailing area, offering a wide range of ready-made general merchandise, particularly clothing, shoes, and accessories. By keeping an abundance of inventory on hand, organized by department, these stores could target their customers' specific preferences in size, color, and style. More globally, department stores competed on the basis of products, brands, services and, more importantly, shopping experience. Galeries Lafayette, for example, built its landmark store in Paris around 1910 that included a six-storey dome of glass and steel to allow natural lighting throughout the building. One hundred years later, that flagship store on Boulevard Haussmann still dazzles customers.

In the 20th century, several retailing upheavals affected the format. The five-and-dime store emerged as the first discount format in general merchandising. The leading five-and-dime store, Woolworth's, refined the concept of the chain store, becoming the largest retailing company in the world. In 1915 the first self-service store appeared and the concept was even patented by its inventor, Clarence Saunders, from Memphis, Tennessee. According to Saunders's patent,

> the object of the said invention is to provide a store equipment by which the customer will be enabled to serve himself and, in doing so, will be required to review the entire assortment of goods carried in stock, conveniently and attractively displayed, and after selecting the list of goods desired, will be required to pass a checking and paying station at which the goods selected may be billed, packed and settled for.[5]

Shopping has never been the same since.

Similar advances occurred in food retailing. A&P embraced the self-service concept in the mid-1930s, establishing the supermarket as the dominant format for selling food and A&P as the largest food retailer in the world. A few decades later, in France, Carrefour created the hypermarché, expanding the format from food to general merchandising. It too became for a while the largest retail company in the world, and remains to this day the second-largest retail group in the world in terms of revenue.

And then came Wal-Mart. Wal-Mart and its emulators offer a huge array of day-to-day household goods, up to 150,000 different items from all over the world in their larger stores, priced attractively, all located within a short drive of most middle-class consumers in America and western Europe. Behind this simple concept stands a huge and complex system overseeing procurement from thousands of suppliers, logistics, replenishment, merchandising, and store operations. The result is mass customization. Within a few minutes after leaving their homes, customers can pick a basket of goods that fit their own specific needs, drawn from all over the world and offered at incredibly low prices.

Retailing is not often thought as mass customization. Indeed, when we designed the MINE survey, we did not include a retailer in the sample. But the complex systems that support modern retailing share many similarities with the systems used in assembling complex products such as automobiles. Retailers played Mass Customization games of innovation long before the automobile and electronics industries joined in.

What MINE Has Taught Us

Mass customization first appeared in management literature in the late 1980s. It described large-scale mature systems that handled progressively more diversity and that aimed at addressing the specific needs of each customer without incurring a cost penalty.[6] In our MINE survey, we classified 112 respondents as being involved predominantly in a Mass Customization game, as either a system operator or a supplier. All were in mature industries structured by large complex systems. From our analysis of the statistical results and from the case studies, we drew the following conclusions:

1 As more industries structure themselves around complex formal systems of production involving numerous firms, mass customization is becoming widespread in the economy. It dominates automobile and electronics manufacturing, retailing and hospitality, and is increasingly present in financial services. We estimate that close to 20% of GDP is generated in industries in which this game plays a prominent role. There is a common pattern: a complex system designed by a core enterprise integrates a wide array of contributions from numerous suppliers to provide products and services that can be tailored to its customers' specific needs. Companies involved in games of Mass Customization compete to offer most conveniently

to each customer the product and service that he or she specifically wants.

2 The critical contextual characteristic of the game is the high degree of interdependency between the customer, the core enterprise, and its suppliers. This interdependency arises mostly from the high level of modularity involved in providing the product or service, requiring cooperative arrangements between the core enterprise and its suppliers. The core enterprise focuses on the design of the offering and its marketing, assembly, and delivery. Its network of suppliers focuses on the specific elements of the offering, whose modularity adds to the complexity of the system. Their coherent integration and the smooth functioning of the delivery system require a high level of coordination.

3 Mass Customization games take place in mature environments. Dominant architectural choices already prevail. Improvements from technical advances occur mostly at the margin. Technical progress tends to be slow paced. Radical change occurs infrequently, and pursuing it is not a priority. Stability makes it easier to develop the complex industrial arrangements that tie suppliers to core enterprises, making suppliers active participants in the functioning and evolution of the systems.

4 The core enterprise sits at the interface between customers, who seek a customized offering, and the industrial arrangements to provide them. The key asset of the core enterprise is the system within which it can design, assemble, and deliver a basket of products at competitive prices, tailored to the specific needs of each customer, and marketed under a proprietary umbrella brand. Most core enterprises generally occupy substantial market positions. Examples of a core enterprise include auto makers, electronic equipment manufacturers, food chains, mass retailers, large home builders, Internet retailers, and credit card companies.

5 In the MINE survey, which was biased toward manufacturers, research, development, and engineering (RD&E) expenditures represented 7% of sales of core enterprises, and they devoted almost 14% of their staff time to innovative activities. Core companies tend to centralize their RD&E activities. In the automobile industry, new models are developed at RD&E facilities located close to headquarters and to the primary assembly plants. Centralization allows better coordination of engineering and marketing activities. In electronics, core companies such as Hewlett-Packard, Cisco, and Sony

focus on design and engineering, while subcontracting manufacturing to specialized third parties, usually in low-wage regions.

6 Core enterprises manage flexible provisioning systems, allowing high levels of customization and resilience to wide variations in demand. These systems require sophisticated industrial arrangements. A core enterprise may produce key components in house but rely on suppliers for most elements of the finished product. The in-house components, such as the engine of an automobile, often differentiate the brand.

7 Suppliers are not all equal. In manufacturing, tier one suppliers master domains requiring high levels of expertise and are responsible for entire subsystems, such as cockpit instrumentation in an airplane or seats in an automobile. Core enterprises expect them to continually improve the performance and the cost of their products. As a result, tier one suppliers must develop the innovation processes that relate to their domain. The core enterprise also manages an ecosystem of secondary and tertiary suppliers. Some provide unique components or services; others are simply reliable and trusted providers.

The Development of Mass Customization

In mature industries built around complex value chains and systems, mass customization is now the dominant form of competition, involving continuous incremental progress in two key areas: making products or services more responsive to customer needs, and improving the cost and flexibility of the system to allow more efficient and more customized delivery.

Three broad trends in the economy have supported the development of mass customization. First, information technology allows firms within a value chain to interact in much more complex ways. A core company that controls the system, such as an auto maker or a large retailer, can engage in fairly sophisticated industrial arrangements with suppliers and service providers. In retailing, for example, core enterprise and supplier engage in real-time collaboration not only involving store-by-store replenishment ('two dozen men's socks, model xyz, size 8–9, brown color in store 22514') but also merchandising, promotion, and new product development. In manufacturing, core enterprises and suppliers work together to achieve lean-production objectives. In the few Internet systems whose architectures have matured and stabilized, such as Amazon, e-Bay, and Expedia's travel reservation system, similar complex arrangements to facilitate real-time cooperation govern electronic data interchange and common databases. In all sectors, advances in communication allow more cooperative design and greater decentralization of innovation.

The second trend is the rapid progress in logistics, brought by advances in communication, transportation, and storage technologies. Better traceability allows better control, warehousing, and multi-modal cross-docking. Interconnected information systems contribute to efficient just-in-time delivery, not only reducing working capital costs but also facilitating greater customization of final products and tightening the supply chain. Finally, transportation costs have declined steadily while frequency of delivery by air, sea, rail, or road has increased. All these factors have improved the value chain by allowing components of a complex physical network to interact much more efficiently.

The third trend is globalization. Globalization involves much more than trade between knowledge-rich advanced economies and low-cost developing economies. Globalization first and foremost spreads technological know-how among economies with very different cost structures. This creates new opportunities for innovation, as lower-income countries approach problems from a very different perspective. In disseminating know-how, globalization allows companies to tap the comparative advantages of a wide variety of countries.

These three trends, largely interrelated, have led to the emergence of global production systems. Given the maturity of the technology and the markets involved, core companies compete on meeting the specific needs of customers, putting pressure on their system to become flexible and adaptive. Instead of commoditization, the maturing of these systems brings its opposite: increased differentiation and, in parallel, lower cost.

Mass customization has tinted the innovative palette of a wide range of sectors. Retailing embraced the game first, and today's retailers are still refining the concept. In the 1990s, for example, Zara became a global women's clothing chain by honing its supply chain, keeping it highly flexible, and making the best of modern communication capabilities. In each store, the company capitalizes on its intimate understanding of its 20- to 30-year-old customers and on its ability to continually test new products. When a product takes off, Zara relies on its sophisticated system of communication to respond quickly, gearing up production and disseminating the successful product throughout the chain. With excellence in design and replenishment, Zara stays on top of the notoriously fickle fashion industry and maintains a relatively manageable range of hot clothes in each of its stores.

Food retailing has also become increasingly sophisticated, with a significant broadening of the offering, particularly in the 'fresh' departments. At one end of the market, traditional discounters such as Wal-Mart attract customers on the basis of old-fashioned low prices on a limited offering of products. At the other end, highly successful retailers such as Whole Food in the United States, IGA in Quebec, and Monoprix in France target customers with a cornucopia of fresh vegetables, fruits, cheeses, meats, breads, prepared meals, organic versions, ethnic alternatives, and gluten-free varieties. At the back of the store, customers can still find conventional dry groceries packed into dense corridors. Although both models have established themselves, the popularity of customized stores will likely grow at the expense of the price-fixated discount stores as customer affluence continues to rise.

Mass customization is also the driver behind Internet retailers. While big-box retailers with a vast assortment of goods displayed over 100,000-plus square feet of shop floor have displaced the printed catalogue, Internet stores have emerged as new competitors. With an enormous range of products and improved logistics, Internet-based retailing will likely outprice the big-box stores while nearly matching them on convenience. Big-box stores will have to add other benefits to their formula or become marginalized. It will be interesting to see how Wal-Mart, the epitome of the big-box concept, navigates this changing tide. Will bargain-hunting customers remain loyal to a store that offers 142,000 different products in a 185,000-square-foot facility,[7] or will they migrate to the convenience of the Internet retailer who offers the same variety at the same or lower price? Or will Wal-Mart evolve into a big-time Internet retailer?

Mass Customization games have also become common in industries with mature systems for producing complex items. Somewhat like the auto industry, aircraft production involves a wide range of suppliers organized in tiers around a core company that masters the overall design and marketing of a finished product. The industry relies increasingly on customization to produce niche products, along with a large choice of options for each model.

As the information and communication systems mature throughout established industries, mass customization will increasingly become the norm. Indeed, capturing the needs of individual customers and managing a supply chain and production system to deliver the appropriate product or service has emerged as the wave of the future in an increasing number of industries.[8]

Complex Strategies

A Mass Customization strategy reflects broad systemic thinking, taking into account the architecture linking the parties involved: customers, core companies, and their ecosystem of suppliers. Improvements are made by competing systems both at the system level and at the level of suppliers. This is what distinguishes Mass Customization games from other games of innovation. New Tide, for example, is not produced by a system, nor is Viagra, whereas the benefits that Wal-Mart and Amazon provide to their customers are delivered by a system. Innovative activities to improve the product and enhance its value can be widely distributed along the value chain.

Production complexity, much more than demand heterogeneity, determines the extent to which a core company can engage in a game of Mass Customization. Most customers like products and services that recognize their individuality. Whether it involves perfumes, aircraft, or hotels, customizing a product or service is generally a winning proposition. The question is whether it's worth the costs.

The strategy must harmonize the contributions of the core company and that of its suppliers. The core company owns the relationship with the customer and thus controls the product or service. But its suppliers pursue their own strategies, often in a New and Improved game. The challenge of the core company in a Mass Customization game is to harmonize the interest of its suppliers to its own, with special attention paid to its tier one suppliers.

Table 12.1 summarizes the key Mass Customization strategies of core companies and of their key suppliers. At the top of the list are the brand and the positioning of the system, in relation to the offering. Mass Customization games involve battles of brands, which encapsulate the complex benefits of the system's offering. In a single glance, customers recognize brands in all their complexities and choose the ones whose perceived benefits best meet their own needs.

Positioning the Brand

An exhaustive literature exists on brands. From an innovation perspec-

Table 12.1. Mass Customization Strategies

Core Companies

1. Positioning the brand
2. Customizing the offering
3. Managing the ecosystems
4. Improving the platform
5. Coherent evolution and growth

Complementors

1. Managing the integration
2. Building balance of power
3. Product evolution

tive, the critical concern is the maintenance of the brand's coherence as competition blurs its distinctiveness in the eyes of the targeted customers. This is not always easy. Wal-Mart had to address this concern in 2009: its same-store sales had flattened under pressure from deep discounters such as smaller dollar stores. In response, Wal-Mart tried to expand its target market to include more upper-scale customers while at the same time stopping the drift toward dollar store competitors with selective 'price investments' (usually called price cuts outside the retailing universe). It decided to replace its longstanding everyday low-price strategy with a so-called high-low strategy that emphasized weekly specials. It also introduced upscale products such as fashion clothing and organic food to broaden its customer appeal. The combination flopped, failing to attract new customers and annoying loyal core customers. Within a year, Wal-Mart abandoned the strategy. Retreating to its old strategy, it promised to execute better, a business euphemism for 'we're cornered.'

Many auto makers reached similar strategic dead-ends when some of their models lost their lustre and loyal supporters became annoyed by brand incoherence. It can happen in any system. In business competition, there are often more losers than winners. A proper brand strategy is a critical success factor for core enterprises in Mass Customization games. Such a strategy involves the following complementary thrusts:

• Clearly identify the targeted segment of the market
• Develop a strong umbrella brand that ties your offering with the targeted segment's expectations and values

- Use innovation to personalize even more the offering to this loyal customer base, driving its expansion
- Use technology and business arrangements to make the supply chain and its production system more flexible, allowing continuing improvement in both customization and costs
- Marshall the support of suppliers to come up with innovative and, hopefully, exclusive products and features

Customizing the Offering

Database marketing has progressed rapidly with the spread of loyalty programs that allow tracking of customer preferences and facilitate promotion of individual offerings. Personalized marketing is the new frontier in any sales-driven organization. A key concern arises for core companies over the extent to which customer information should be shared in their ecosystem. Since most suppliers deal with several core companies, there is a risk that the information will be useful for competitors. But how can a core company expect a critical supplier to be innovative if it has no information about the ultimate users of its product? (Privacy concerns are taken care of by keeping individual profiles secret.) The dilemma is not easy to resolve. There are great benefits in sharing such information within an ecosystem, but it has to be done within the framework of proper business and contractual arrangements. As techniques advance for learning more from individual customers, brand loyalty strategies will play a growing role in games of Mass Customization. Online buying will only accelerate the trend.

Managing the Production Ecosystem

Complex offerings typically emerge from cooperation within the ecosystem of suppliers coordinated by a core company. The core company owns the relationship with the ultimate customer. In a typical value chain, the value added by a core company is less than 50% of the final product value, and sometimes less than 35%. Suppliers provide the rest, in the form of parts, components, or products and services to be resold. Managing the relationship can be complex.

Indeed, in no other area of business management is the conflict between short-term results and long-term value creation more evident than in these relationships. In the short term, a core company can squeeze more value from its suppliers by demanding price reductions or more services such as replenishment. This is the traditional but short-sighted recipe of all cost-cutting specialists, to boost the bottom line. It can be done without fearing retaliation from competitors, as their response time in luring dissatisfied suppliers is much too long. Many financially troubled companies resort to such tactics. GM and Volkswagen did it in the early 1990s, when both companies hired cost-cutter Ignatius Lopez. The move worked for both of them in the short term, but did little to create sustained value.[9]

In the long run, a core company may cripple itself by squeezing suppliers, especially the better ones that usually have other options. The success of a core company depends on a dynamic, innovative, and flexible ecosystem. Good suppliers innovate, both in reducing costs and in improving product features. A good reputation helps attract the best of them and, more important, helps a core company get first crack at their new products. In a healthy dynamic ecosystem, a core company and its suppliers embrace mutual dependency and highly beneficial relationships.

More importantly, in the long run, a command-and-control approach with suppliers does not allow a Mass Customization system to reach its full potential, as it cripples innovation. This game requires cooperation and creativity, not blind obedience. When a core company needs knowledge and expertise to compete in the realm of innovation, it will get much further with bilateral cooperation and trust in its supplier ecosystem.

Improving Platforms

Competition demands ever-improving platforms. Changes are never as radical as in emerging system games, whose dominant architecture has not jelled yet. Mass Customization platforms are stable, but they have to evolve continually with the progress of technologies. But there are numerous sources of resistance. Many suppliers have a vested interest in the status quo, having integrated their information systems with the platform. When Wal-Mart issues a new release of RetailLinks, it has a tremendous impact on thousand of companies in Wal-Mart's ecosystem, requiring them to change their own systems. Proper management of a platform evolution requires political skills. Japanese auto makers, for example, have mastered this skill through years of dialogue with their suppliers. The American and European automobile industries still have a lot to learn.

Steering the Evolution of a System

The retailing universe is littered with great names such as Woolworth's and A&P that have slowly faded into the sunset of obsolescence. In mature systems, change occurs slowly, but it does occur. If an organization resists change, pressure builds on its existing systems. There's no guarantee that Wal-Mart will survive for 100-plus years as Galeries Lafayette has. The founding family still controls Ford Motor Company. Upstart General Motors, founded nearly 20 years after Ford, went on to become the largest auto maker in the world. But in 2009 General Motors wiped out its shareholder investments, skidding into bankruptcy, while Ford weathered the crisis. In a mature industry, the 'If it is not broken, don't fix it' syndrome can freeze a system. When it comes to change, the question is not 'if' but 'how,' as no environment is immune to change.

Steering the evolution of a system demands a long-term vision, a definite and often idiosyncratic view of the future. Unfortunately, chief executive officers are not often chosen for such views; they tend to lean toward protecting the status quo. But on the other hand, there is no magic formula. The future itself is undefined and highly uncertain, and it has fooled more than one chief executive officer who didn't have the vision and guts to deal with changing times.

Equally important is the ability to convince others to support the vision. A system demands a collaborative ecosystem. The role of the visionary leader is to ensure coherence among the stakeholders who must participate in fulfilling the vision. After all, some of the best ideas may come from them.

Complementor Strategies

In a Mass Customization game, complementors integrate their activities into a system that slowly evolves as it delivers value to the final customer. Integration is a great source of value creation for a supplier, extending beyond the physical production and delivery of a product or service. It allows the optimization of inventory levels and replenishment, two critical activities in a lean production system. Integration can also influence product evolution and facilitate collaboration in product design. Finally, integration allows for coordination of investments as changes in product specification trigger the need for new equipment and machinery.

Nevertheless, managing operational integration is often a challenge, as suppliers have to deal with several competing systems. Although core companies prefer exclusivity, such arrangements are rare, since they seldom provide a supplier the volume to ensure a competitive offering. Moreover, most suppliers do not like to be dependent on solely one buyer of their wares. But dealing with multiple core companies creates problems. Specifications usually vary from one to another, imposing differences both in the product and in the way it's delivered. Most complementors manage such diversity without difficulty. But the more a complementor can integrate its operations with each of the core companies that it serves, the better the deal it can get from each of them.

Building a Balance of Power

Complementors and core companies are involved in a power relationship for several aspects of their cooperative activities, including the complementor's margins, payment terms, new investment facilities, and service levels. The tension is permanent. Core companies seek the best price, along with reliability and exclusivity. They also tend to treat all suppliers in the same way. Suppliers have different priorities, such as better margins, flexibility in service levels, higher market share, and more shelf space.

Large complementors with strong brands can get much better deals than smaller ones. In retailing, for example, Nestlé, Coca Cola, and P&G enjoy the power of their global stature. In electronic products, top suppliers such as Intel can wrest better deals from core companies using their powerful brand that appeals to the ultimate customer. Not surprisingly, a key element of supplier strategy is to develop long-term bargaining power. Suppliers can do this in several ways, such as differentiating design, exclusivity, capitalizing on one dominant product to carry the others, logistics and, when it can matter, a brand. No matter how they do it, suppliers must continually build their bargaining power to offset the similar efforts of core companies as they push private branding, dual sourcing, allocations, and other tactics. The relationship involves a never-ending tug-of-war specific to each industry. But for a complementor, building power in its sales channels is a paramount concern.

Product Evolution

When locked into a customization game, dealing with several competing core companies, a complementor's best defence is to have the best product and the lowest costs. This may appear obvious in any business, but in a mature system, where competition is about customization to the specific needs of customers, it becomes inescapable. Complementors in such markets must innovate in a tightly specified marketplace.

It is a challenge worth taking. Great complementors manage the evolution of their product line with continuous improvement in cost and features. They strive to gain access to final customers so they can incorporate their inputs into their products. Large consumer goods companies conduct extensive market research exercises to remain informed and intimate with the users of their products. These exercises generally bypass retailers. These large suppliers also manage a pipeline of new products, often playing one core company against another by offering exclusive launch windows and other benefits. Component manufacturers in automobile, aerospace, and electronics equipment compete with each other on the basis of the latest technologies integrated into their products. In these industries, cooperation between core companies and complementors on new products is essential, since the systems design must also evolve to integrate new features from complementors.

A complementor ultimately succeeds or fails based on its ability to distance its products from its competitors' while taking full advantage of its core-company relationships to obtain better margins and gain greater share in its categories. Improving the product is one thing. Leveraging the improvements is something else.

A Game with a Great Future

Globalization, the industrialization of information, and progress in logistics are supporting the emergence of complex systems that deliver increasingly customized benefits to customers. This stimulates the multiplication of Mass Customization games. These games rarely involve radical changes. In fact, they are all about controlled evolution. They are driven by a continuing flow of innovations on many fronts, transforming the traditional mass production systems into responsive systems. It is an evolution that bears on more than personalization of modular products. It involves the building of industrial arrangements to deliver increasingly precise responses to evolving and idiosyncratic customers' demands, for which those customers are increasingly ready to pay. Core companies must attract customers and interact with them, while at the same time managing flexible production systems that involve numerous partners all acting coherently in a tight supply chain that can deliver individualized products. The ecosystems around these production systems are generally quite heterogeneous. Much of the continuous improvement of the final product arises from initiatives taken within these ecosystems.

The brand is the identity of a Mass Customization system and the symbol of an offering of goods and services that the customer trusts. Properly managing the brand minimizes the risk perceived by the customer. A core company is responsible for the brand image and for the bundle of goods and services that the brand represents. In parallel, it must manage decentralized innovation in its ecosystem of suppliers. In an integrated modular system, where all pieces must fit together, this duality presents a critical challenge. Not surprisingly, such mature open systems that are successful involve great – and well-managed – companies.

13 Pushing the Envelope

The Millau viaduct over the Tarn Valley in central France is a stunning engineering feat. At 343 meters, it's the tallest bridge in the world, and at 2.5 kilometres it's the longest of its type. It is also a work of art that has become a major tourist attraction. As a functional piece of infrastructure, the viaduct allows a heavily used highway to pass through the Tarn Valley without disrupting the inhabitants below.

The viaduct was built over a three-year period by Eiffage, a large French construction company, and opened in 2004. But its planning started in 1987, and the decision to build it was made in 1994. That year, an international tender was issued for the design of the viaduct. The winning consortium was led by Norman Foster, a British architect, who took several years to develop the technical specifications. In 2001 a second tender was issued for the construction of the bridge and its operation for the next 75 years. That led to the selection of Eiffage as concessionaire, who built and financed the €320-million project and will run it as a toll bridge until 2079.

The Millau viaduct incorporates the best technologies available for large bridges. It is a good example of an infrastructure project conducted as a Pushing the Envelope (PTE) innovation game. In PTE games, a multitude of technical, financial, and social components are assembled into a daring capital investment that pushes the state of the art by combining the best available technologies. PTE games are played mainly in three broad arenas: public infrastructure such as roads and bridges, industrial infrastructure, and large IT systems.

Games of Ambition

In a PTE game, a capital investment innovates by accommodating numerous leading-edge solutions to improve the delivery of a product or the cost of its operation. In the MINE survey, 102 firms were involved in PTE games. Capital investments by governments and companies represent around 20% of GDP in industrialized economies, and this is where most PTE games are played. As a result, a significant portion of innovations in the economy arises from Pushing the Envelope games.

What are the characteristics of PTE games that set them apart from other games?

First, PTE innovations start with a customer, as in Breakthrough games. Faced with the need for a major capital investment, a customer decides to build a competitive advantage by going for the best available technologies instead of a proven off-the-shelf solution. Often motivated by sheer ambition, the customer decides to push the envelope and do what no one else has done before. Most often these customers are governments and major corporations such as banks or retail food chains that are among the leaders in their industries. PTE sponsors are also found among real estate developers seeking bragging rights for the tallest, the deepest, the brightest, or the most remarkable structure in the world. Other PTE sponsors include consortiums assembled to undertake large and unusual projects, like the group of banks and construction companies that built the Chunnel under the English Channel. All these promoters have one thing in common: ambition.

Second, successful PTE innovations require much more time for planning than for building. The planning phase includes developing the design, lining up the financing, getting support from affected communities, getting regulatory approvals, and solidifying the agreement within the sponsoring group on a specific solution. The Millau viaduct took fourteen years of planning and only three years to build. The long planning period is somewhat typical of large infrastructure projects; the rule of thumb is a minimum of two years of planning for each year of construction. This applies to large IT projects, as well.

Third, PTE projects entail a lot of uncertainty at the outset. The state of the art can change significantly over 10 years, requiring ongoing adaptations. Project management is a necessary competency for the successful delivery of these projects. Industrial PTE projects face additional challenges, as they typically extend beyond the delivery of new facilities and require major changes in business processes. Pushing the Envelope projects usually entail new ways of doing things. As a consequence, they demand a major reorganization of work patterns.

Fourth, because of their impact on their physical, social, or organizational environment, PTE projects can trigger resistance and hostility.

The successful execution of a project requires consultation with stake-holders and factoring in of their concerns. When this is badly done, stakeholder opposition can cause projects to fail. Moreover, the long gestation period of these projects and the time needed for reaching con-sensus increase the potential for disruptions.

Fifth, PTE projects can cost hundred of millions and often billions of dollars. Errors can accumulate, and when these are combined with disruptive reactions, losses can become catastrophic, often leading to project abandonment. The Chunnel, an iconic PTE project, was beset by delays and cost overruns and became a financial disaster. In Canada in 1975, the Canadian government with great fanfare opened the 'first airport of the twenty-first century' in Mirabel, just north of Montreal. Twenty-five years later Mirabel was mothballed, as travelers stayed away from the place in droves. White elephants like Mirabel are fre-quent among PTE projects.

Large innovative projects involve high risks. But these are not market risks, which are usually under control, as PTE projects often replace existing facilities. More critical are the risks associated with timely delivery and operating performance. PTE projects can get tripped up by their size, the degree of innovation involved, the design compromis-es forced by stakeholders, and the time it takes from original proposal to launch as economic and technological changes occur.

PTE projects are also often characterized by large irreversible com-mitments. Momentum carries them to their launch, even as their flaws become evident. The shortcomings of Mirabel Airport were known well before it opened, but the project was too advanced to be stopped or even radically reconfigured. In this respect, PTE projects sometimes resemble awful big-budget Hollywood movies, which are doomed before their release. You can see one of these white elephants of PTE innovation as your plane lands in Rio de Janeiro, a big tall white build-ing that was designed as a hospital of the future and that now stands as an unused testimonial to the risks of Pushing the Envelope.

New Approaches to Risk Management

Most civilizations have undertaken large-scale PTE projects. The pyra-mids, the Great Wall of China, the Eiffel tower, and the Empire State Building in New York all testify to ambitious sponsors who pushed the technological envelope of their day. But over the past 50 years the number of large PTE projects has mushroomed, from the massive Three

Gorges dam in China to the manned flight to the moon, as advances in the capacity to manage them have reduced their risk.[1]

The traditional approach to large-scale projects is premised on extensive rational planning at the outset to ascertain costs, identify risk, and raise capital by presenting the best possible picture to investors. Detailed specifications are prepared before tendering for contractors, who bid on costs and are mandated to build according to plan. The rationale is simple: an organization that commits hundreds of millions to a project must ensure that the project is well planned. Bankers who finance these projects want to see every risk covered, and they want detailed cost estimates before they'll commit their funds. Detailed contracts define the obligations of the respective parties. Uncertainty is dealt at the outset, by investing in information.

Unfortunately, this traditional approach is not appropriate for ambitious projects that seek to push the state of the art. In fact, it discourages innovation early in the design phase, as innovation creates too much risk and uncertainty, the exact things that the design phase seeks to reduce. But more importantly, PTE projects are rarely islands of stability. In projects that take 10 to 15 years to complete, surprises inevitably spring up, making even the most detailed advance planning ineffectual. Sponsors often demand that their projects incorporate state-of-the-art technologies, but often, these become available only after the project has begun, defeating the purpose of the detailed design phase. The traditional approach was always ineffective for dealing with innovative large-scale projects. To address its limitations, a new approach has emerged, revolving around innovations that provide more flexibility in project management and greatly improve the success rate of ambitious PTE projects.

Better Governance Framework

The first area of innovation is the governance framework. It starts with all stakeholders being brought into the planning tent during the first phase of the project, before the final plans are agreed upon and financing is closed. This is a major departure from the traditional approach, where only a chosen few were admitted into the tent until the project was more or less structured. From the outset, the new framework requires strong foundational contracts with all stakeholders, since turbulence and challenges will inevitably arise during the project's inception. Well-defined rules must anchor it and ensure its purpose, legitimacy, and funding under most foreseeable circumstances. Under the new framework, a project starts with a vision that has broad appeal, and which the sponsor proposes to all stakeholders who will be affected by it during its construction and operation. In this early stage, the project is only roughly defined, leaving sufficient room for improvements and changes to accommodate stakeholder concerns. Most large-scale public infrastructure projects now involve an extensive approval process, requiring open hearings, expert reports, impact analysis, and similar exercises. Only when these exercises have been conducted does the project proceed, usually with several modifications to accommodate stakeholder concerns. Corporate PTE projects now follow a similar process to ensure the buy-in of all groups affected by the project.

This framework commands a much longer lead time at the front end, typically five to seven years in public projects and two to three years in private projects that do not need public approval. This front-end delay does not necessarily impair the ambitious objectives of a well-considered project. But once the concept is approved, a project rests on much stronger social foundations, allowing it to proceed from the vision to a more detailed design.

Front-end delays can be frustrating for sponsors who are eager to proceed and who do not always take kindly to public criticisms of their still unbuilt projects. But in today's world, sponsors need good political skills to steer their project through the shoals of stakeholders' acceptance. Such skills are as important as financing skills and as the abilities to build and operate.

This governance framework has led to new approaches to project management for large PTE projects. In large infrastructure projects, the traditional design-then-tender-to-build-according-to-spec approach is being phased out. The concession model that gives a broad mandate at the outset to design, build, and operate a PTE project is increasingly encountered. The contractual framework associated with the concession model allows flexibility to innovate as long as performance objectives are met. Working under the concession model, Cofiroute, a French private developer of toll highways, was able to reduce by 30% the capital cost of the Paris-to-Poitiers autoroute by using novel technical solutions.[2] Another model, the more common design-build framework, has the advantage of being simpler to implement. By setting performance objectives within a prenegotiated capital budget, a sponsor creates strong incentives for contractors to incorporate innovative state-of-the-art elements into a project to reduce their own costs.

Public tendering regulations are also evolving. The traditional approach, with its fixation on costs as opposed to risk management, keeps future tenders at arm's length, with strict prohibitions on communication among suppliers to minimize collusion before tendering. Sponsors are now sometimes allowed to conduct extensive collaborative discussions with suppliers before bidding begins. In Britain, under the Private Finance Initiative framework, a public-sector body can now choose to buy services instead of assets. It defines the services it wants and then invites private bidders to present innovative solutions to deliver them, either as concessionaires or under design-build contracts.[3]

PTE as a Competitive Strategy

Pushing the envelope is seldom an obligation. But PTE projects can be game changers, upsetting competition with lower costs and superior performance. Thus they are often key strategic moves, allowing a business to outclass its competitors. Sobeys, a Canadian grocery chain, teamed up with Witron, a German manufacturer of automation equipment, to build a large-scale fully automated distribution center that gave Sobeys significant cost advantages in logistics and in-store replenishment. The company is now building a second one, using the experience acquired from the first project. By locking in the experts at Witron, Sobeys also forces its competitors to use less-proven solutions if they want to build similar warehouses.[4] Like most grocery chains in North America, Sobeys could have chosen a less risky strategy, relying on conventional warehouse technology. Instead it has redefined the state of the art and forced its competitors to adapt. Sobeys was well aware of the losses incurred by some companies with innovative warehouses that did not deliver their promised benefits, but it accepted this risk as part of its innovation-based strategy. The reward was worth the risk. Being the leader gave Sobeys a two-to-three-year cost advantage, a significant achievement in the competitive grocery market.

Stage Management

PTE project sponsors have to live for many years with the consequences of their innovative choice. Making sure that no error creeps in is important. Numerous managerial techniques have been developed to optimize these choices. Breaking the design into stages is one of them, as it allows the incorporation of several innovations into project management. In designing an innovative project, project managers must make numerous decisions, all of which respect the integrity of the project. By breaking down the project into stages and demanding closure at one stage before proceeding to the next, project managers ensure that all parties to the design stay aligned.[5] This measure allows much more flexibility on the financial side, as the financial model is reviewed at each stage, using the latest data about cost and the status of the project. Projects now need at the outset only broad financial parameters that define a corridor. At each stage, the corridor is tightened. Each new stage starts on the basis of the agreements that led to the closure of the previous stage. Then a new hypothesis is thrown in for discussion, eliciting criticisms and creative ideas from experts and stakeholders. The manager then reshapes the project's attributes according to this input. Discussions continue until closure on the new hypothesis is achieved, and then the project proceeds to the next stage.

The new approach entails higher soft costs than the traditional approach. On standard infrastructure projects, the soft costs associated with planning can represent about 2% to 3% of total capital costs. In complex PTE projects, they can represent 15% to 20% of capital costs (and even 35% in an outlier case).[6] Many executives will view these soft costs as outrageous, since they involve mostly planning, consulting, and organizational changes, not the actual building of the project. But that is the cost of the alignment behind a particular solution in any complex situation. It should be assessed in light of the avoided costs of overruns and delays, which can easily be higher than 20%. Herbert Simon once referred to the stage management process as procedural rationality as opposed to substantive rationality in the traditional model.[7] Substantive rationality focuses on selecting the optimal option, which any senior executive likes to do. Unfortunately, it is not always easy to achieve. Procedural rationality recognizes the unfolding of time, the presence of strong uncertainty, and the need for collaboration and legitimacy to arrive at an acceptable solution. It is associated with many fewer surprises and, ultimately, greater efficiency.

The Important Role of Experts

Consultants are major players in PTE projects. Sponsoring organizations have neither the knowledge nor the talent to handle the extraordinary challenges that their ambition fosters. So they rely on experts, consultants, engineers, system integrators, architects, investment bankers, and so on, who put the PTE project into effect, while the sponsor who provided the vision foots the bill.

The sponsor chooses consultants on the basis of their reputation and experience. Their competencies depend largely on prior accumulation of knowledge over many projects and on experience with particular risks or issues. The emphasis on experience has led to a dramatic global concentration of expertise within a few dominant firms. Companies such as IBM, Accenture, and Oracle in the IT sector have become global consulting experts as well as providers of solutions. The same global concentration is found among experts in mining and metallurgical plants, petroleum and chemical plants, pharmaceutical plants, and tall buildings, among others.

Consultants actively promote PTE games of innovation. They do extensive work in-house to develop projects, which they pitch to potential sponsors. According to the MINE survey, which includes a large number of global consulting firms, leading firms allocate 18% of their staff time to innovation and capabilities-building.[8] They also work with networks of university professors, gurus, and vendors to accumulate and strengthen their knowledge.

Most consulting firms have also set up global centers of excellence, where they concentrate the accumulation of their expertise. A common marketing practice is to invite senior management in client firms to planning sessions at these centers, where they sketch out novel configurations and applications. They also organize long-range forums with operators to anticipate future directions for the industry and identify opportunities for innovation.

These practices are widespread in the IT sector. IBM, Oracle, and SAP all have several specialized centers of excellence around the world. So do system integrators such as Accenture, which position themselves as neutral experts, although they, too, have their own proprietary solutions. 'Cisco University,' a key marketing program of Cisco, is positioned as a major source of education for potential customers about capital investments in Internet protocols.[9] Microsoft provides similar information sessions that emphasize web-based services.

The close interaction of experts in defining PTE games of innovation brings significant change to the normal client-supplier relationship and opens new vistas for suppliers.[10] For example, Norsk Hydro Oil and Gas faced a particular challenge in developing the complicated Njord field in the North Sea. Using the traditional methods, development of this low-yield field would have called for a capital expenditure of $2 billion, making it unprofitable. Norsk Hydro decided to abandon the traditional methods and embarked on an experimental approach that relied extensively on innovative solutions to be brought by its key suppliers. It invited these suppliers, who were all competitors, to work together to design a better approach to develop the field. A team of project engineers drawn from Norsk Hydro and its suppliers worked on solutions for a full year. Through numerous innovations, they reduced the required capital cost to less than $1 billion, making the project profitable.[11] Norsk Hydro then met one-to-one with participating suppliers to negotiate business contracts to develop the field.

Allowing sponsors and suppliers to work together prior to bidding required changes in the legal framework that governed competition on conventional projects. This was done both in Norway and in Great Britain. These new industrial frameworks, called CRINE in England and NORSOK in Norway, allowed new forms of contracting with suppliers.[12] They enable sponsors and contractors to do away with the adversarial relationships common in more traditional contracts and to work cooperatively on the basis of shared risk and reward.[13]

Coping with Change

PTE projects have acquired a bad image. They often run over budget, are delayed, and are full of unpleasant surprises and unexpected changes. But that messiness is very much part of PTE games. In fact, best practices in PTE projects focus on managing unwelcome surprises.

These surprises occur for several reasons. First, the original vision must be adapted to address the concerns of stakeholders and get them onside. This is a central part of the game, but the change can have unintended consequences, which pop up later on as 'surprises.' Second, a PTE project must integrate numerous innovations, some of which have never before been applied in an actual project. That fact can create additional surprises, and the contractual and financing arrangements must accommodate such possibilities. Third, major changes in the political and economic environment can occur as the multi-year project unfolds, demanding mid-course corrections. And fourth, many large projects, once in operation, impose unforeseen disruptive changes on nearby communities. Communities may resist these changes, a resistance that requires a managerial response.

As a component of PTE projects, change management is as important as technological expertise and project management. We mentioned above that design changes can best be made in the planning stage of a project. But in certain circumstances, design plans have to be reopened and reconsidered even as a project is underway. Despite a tendency to regard decisions as irreversible after a project reaches a certain point, change is always a possibility. This is what happened to the billion-dollar hydro-electric Tucurui dam in northern Brazil. When it was half-built, a major deposit of iron ore was discovered near the dam. Its potential justified the redesign of the dam to accommodate a shipping canal for transportation of the iron ore. The changes delayed the dam by several years, but the returns from the mine justified the additional time.

The Special Case of IT

Pushing the Envelope projects involving IT typically include ample room for changes. Implementing the large integrated systems developed by SAP, Oracle, and other business software specialists creates significant challenges for businesses that migrated from their largely autonomous legacy systems developed in the 1960s and 1970s. But IT technologies change at an exponential rate, in accordance with Moore's Law.[14] Thus, IT systems have to accommodate major improvements relatively late in a project's delivery, as long as the benefits of change outweigh the costs. The challenge in implementing large IT system is not with the software, but with the adaptation of the business processes and of the organization. Although software problems always arise, resolving them is simply a question of time and people. The major execution problems in IT systems are related to the human and organizational interfaces. Three aspects should be underlined in that regard.

1 *IT projects are mostly about redoing business processes.* IT projects aim to improve an organization's operations, which requires more than changes in the information system. In fact, the benefits emerge first and mostly from the re-engineering of business processes that the new system allows. Thus process reviews should account for 75% to 80% of the cost of an IT project.[15] Successful transformative projects place far more emphasis on business process improvements than on selecting critical IT systems. Most of the delays and budget overruns in large IT projects result from a poor review of business processes affected by the system at the outset, and a resulting weak definition of the functional requirements of the new system.

There is no bigger mistake in IT projects than rushing the execution schedule, before needs are fully documented and new processes are agreed upon. Whenever coding is redone or added late in an IT project, one can usually point at managerial errors at the outset, namely short-changing the front-end reviews.

2 *Understanding the resistances to change.* Transformation of processes triggers internal resistance within an organization, as people and business units are affected, some winning, others losing. The organizational power struggles that arise can thwart the project's development and implementation. Depending on the nature of the resistance, new systems may be distorted to accommodate existing operational processes instead of generating improvements in the processes. Because they fail to overcome this resistance to change, many firms do not extract the full potential of their enterprise system.

There are ways to prepare an organization for changes arising from the installation of large IT systems. When Hydro-Québec acquired a new CRM system, for example, it asked two consulting firms, IBM Global Services and Accenture, to assist in preparing the organization for changes to its operating processes. The two firms created more than 40 working groups within Hydro-Québec and challenged them to identify innovative solutions in business processes that the new system might inspire. Hydro-Québec then paid each consulting firm $1 million for a proposal that embedded employees' suggestions into a broad enterprise system. It next developed a request for proposal to integrate the solutions into the CRM system. All of this took time and added a few years to the project. But it also allowed Hydro-Québec to identify major zones of resistance and find ways to deal with them in advance. When Hydro-Québec finally installed its CRM system, the implementation went smoothly, and employees regarded it as a great success.

3 *Managing change.* Organizations can upgrade software at almost any stage in the life of a project. Changes to the organization and its business processes are another story, triggering resistance. The key challenge is not technological but social. A key set of best practices for successful PTE innovation focus on defusing this resistance to change. In that regard, suppliers can help, as they have extensive experience that allowed them to develop their industry-specific, functional, and cross-functional expertise. Unfortunately, when responding to their customer's criteria, suppliers tend to emphasize

their system expertise and not their change management experience. Customers should do best by being concerned by the latter more than by the former.

For the past 50 years, IT advances have triggered a continuing stream of innovative improvements to business processes.[16] In the service sector in particular, IT projects have generated substantial productivity growth primarily by changing the way organizations operate. Progress in IT has also intensified competition in many industries, as companies differentiate themselves from competitors by investing in IT systems.[17] As a result, PTE games of innovation involving new IT systems have become much more frequent, placing ever-increasing demands on management to address the organizational change issues that these games entail.

14 Transitions

Taking delivery of a new car is simple. You put the key in the starter, turn it on, and off you go. That's because the automobile is now a mature product, easy to handle, with no surprises. This was not always the case. For the first 20 years of the industry, before the invention of the electric starter, starting a car was quite a feat: valves had to be open, then the crank turned rapidly, then valves had to be closed, and then the driver stepped in the car.

The automobile industry started at the end of the nineteenth century. Initially, there were hundreds of craft shops that made cars, but then the industry took shape. In 1910 there were 224 car manufacturers in the United States;[1] by 1920 the count had fallen to 126. Consolidation accelerated in the following years, and a new set of competencies became critical for success. By the time the Great Depression hit the industry, there were fewer than 30 manufacturers. The dominant design, with all the key elements of the modern automobile, was in place.

The Battle of Architecture that defined the automobile lasted about 30 years, from 1900 to 1930. From then on, technological progress slowed down and changes became much more incremental. By 1946 the US industry was down to eight players, and Mass Customization was in full swing. Even with globalization, advances in electronics, and pervasive regulation to stimulate fuel economy, improve safety, and reduce pollution, the dominant design of automobiles has prevailed since 1930 against any radical changes.

How Long Do Games Last?

Innovation games do not last forever; new market games typically give way to mature market games within one generation. Mature market games can last much longer, until radical options upset the industrial order, triggering another round of new market games. But as the automobile market suggests, the transition can take time. The current Mass Customization game in the auto industry has lasted for about three-quarters of a century, and there are no signs that the end is near. But eventually there will be an upset, perhaps with the electric car, perhaps with car sharing or some other movement in the marketplace. Inevitably, a change will hit the industry with a great impact. How can a company protect itself in such a transition?

Simultaneous involvement in several games is one way. In the MINE survey, 43% of respondents were involved in more than one game through diversification. This is not surprising. In the pharmaceutical industry, for example, research-oriented companies are pursuing dozens of Eureka! games in parallel, at different stages of maturity, targeting a wide range of therapeutic indications with their portfolio of drugs. Most of these pharmaceutical companies also manage a portfolio of over-the-counter drugs as they compete in New and Improved games. When a blockbuster drug goes off patent and its Eureka! game suddenly ends, these companies absorb the shock of the transition by turning their attention to other markets, where life goes on.

In ITC industries, most large software companies maintain a portfolio of products at different stages of maturity, enabling them to participate in different games. The Battles of Architecture that led to the dominance of the Microsoft operating system and Microsoft Office have been settled. These markets are now engaged in Mass Customization games. But in other markets, such as video games, tablets, and smart phones, no dominant design has yet emerged, and Microsoft is still competing in these markets, as the Battles of Architecture are far from settled.

A similar pattern applies to the aerospace industry, where manufacturers keep improving their current models while developing new planes. Typically they will compete in an expensive Breakthrough game only in parallel with activities in less risky Pushing the Envelope games involving the continuous upgrading of existing models. Boeing epitomizes the technology-rich company that continually pushes the envelope in proposing enhanced designs for its current models. But in tackling the 787 Dreamliner, facing the double challenges of a composite fuselage and global development and sourcing, Boeing also plunged into a System Breakthrough game with its huge uncertainties. It will ride through the turbulence of developing the radically innovative Dreamliner thanks to the profits generated in its more sedate markets.

Figure 14.1. The Principal Transitions

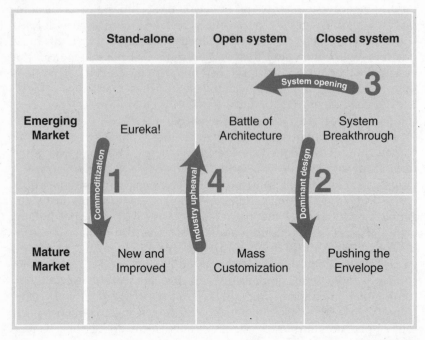

Despite these risk-reducing portfolio strategies, transitions inevitably disrupt the business environment, forcing companies to change their models. Figure 14.1 summarizes the four major transitions that occur when the business environment changes, when conventional strategies become obsolete as a new game emerges. In this chapter, we examine these four transitions.

Commoditization

As a new product developed in a Eureka! Game evolves and improves – that is, it matures – the pace of technological development slows down. Differentiation through innovative product features becomes more difficult, and other competitive factors become more important, such as distribution, accessibility, reliability, the brand, and, last but not least, price. In the drug industry, which relies on the legal protection of intellectual property, patents eventually expire, allowing copycat products competing on price into the market. In general, as products mature, customers become increasingly experienced in their choices and confident in their purchasing decisions. As a result, price and accessibility become more important criteria.

These changes in the marketplace affect the industry's focus. In Eureka! games, companies reap value from the uniqueness of their product, which they renew continually through successive versions. But in a mature market, products become homogeneous. In such a market, maintaining a product's uniqueness becomes more difficult and the risk of commoditization looms. To fight it, a company changes its competitive focus, seeking differentiation through segmentation and marketing, as opposed to technical improvements. It also applies considerable effort to brand differentiation, often by associating the product with customer values. In mature markets like soft drinks, benefits have more to do with the brand than the product itself. Distribution must become critical, so the company can achieve competitive advantages not only with brand differentiation, but with better access and better service.

As markets mature, players must adapt their business models. They will invest less in product development and more in marketing and distribution. Big fat margins are no longer possible, which puts a premium on volume, standardization, and lower costs. To achieve the later, organizational structures are reviewed, leading to centralization of functions and merging of product divisions. Big, bold steps are out, replaced by calculated incremental and continuous improvements.

In the midst of this transition, companies need new skills. Mass marketing and distribution expertise, for example, often replace the visionary skills that prevailed when the company had to launch new product generations every few years or so. Skilled operators, who can trim fat and rationalize product lines and direct costs, are welcome.

Transitions create periods of flux. Since some players adapt faster than others, the industry becomes ripe for consolidation. This is also a period when companies can make strategic and tactical errors, as they are unfamiliar with their new business environment and its rules. Competitors who lag or fail at adapting to the new environment become ripe for takeover. Typically, the weakest performers sell out to eager buyers that want to build scale, strengthen their technological base, and pick up market share. Consolidation can be brutal. The snowmobile industry, for example, contracted from more than 100 manufacturers in the early 1970s to fewer than 10 within a decade.

Transition used to be sharp in patented drug markets, as pharmas were simply quitting it instead of fighting generics when the patents of their blockbusters expired. This is changing. Pharmas are increasingly fighting to protect the franchises built when their patents were running, and join in New and Improved games. They have developed several strategies to stay in post-patent protection markets. Astra-Zeneca, Novartis, and Pfizer, among others, have established generic subsidiaries and assign them their off-patent products to manufacture under a low-cost structure. Other pharmas have developed agreements with generic manufacturers and assist them in delivering the first approved generic version of a drug to the marketplace, a huge first-comer advantage in these markets, in return for a hefty licensing fee.

Pharmas are also capitalizing on the strong brand recognition of some of their blockbuster drugs by continuing their marketing after their patent expires or by introducing milder versions for the over-the-counter (OTC) market. GlaxoSmithKline, for example, still sells a prescription version of Zantac, once the best-selling drug in the world, even though its patent expired several years ago. It also licensed Boehringer Ingelheim, a German pharma, to sell an OTC version of Zantac. This is typical of the market segmentation that occurs in New and Improved games.

A similar strategy was used for Claritin, the most popular antihistamine drug ever, whose patents expired several years ago. It is still available as a proprietary prescription drug in various generic formats, and in the OTC market as Claritin, Clarityne, and Claritin-T. Obviously, pharmaceutical companies have seen the value in playing New and Improved games once they lose the protection of patents on drugs they've developed in Eureka! games.

When a Dominant Design Triumphs

The transition to maturity occurs very differently in open systems, where it revolves around the emergence of a dominant design. Battles of Architecture eventually get settled after competing platforms have fought it out, copying each other's best features along the way, and a dominant design emerges from the convergence of the most popular ones. Four related phenomena characterize transitions to maturity:

1 *Convergence toward a stable architecture.* Stimulated by network effects, customer choice gradually confers dominance on a particular architecture. The effervescence of competing architectural options

eventually dwindles. Moreover, as systems get more complex, prior choices constrain further innovation.

When the dominant architecture emerges from the battle, supported by network effects, other platform owners are faced with a major strategic choice: either emulate the likely winners or risk marginalization. In the smart phone market, for example, hundreds of millions of units sold by Nokia, Ericsson, Motorola, and Panasonic use the Symbian operating system. But in early 2011 its owner, Nokia, abandoned it and switched to the more resilient Windows system. In the auto industry's emerging market phase, cars operated on three different sources of power: steam, electricity, and petrol. When Ford's Model T assumed a dominant role in the industry, running on gasoline, the other modes faded from the market and so did the manufacturers that didn't make the transition.

The emergence of a dominant design brings significant benefits. It enables all players to align themselves with a single choice, lowering uncertainty, simplifying the interface with complementors, and contributing to lower costs.[2]

2 *Development of open networks.* Once the dominant design becomes the standard, companies reconfigure their production systems around stable networks of fairly autonomous suppliers. Seeking the best technologies and lowest costs, platform owners shift away from in-house production of components and modules toward extensive outsourcing. A division of labor emerges. Platform owners assume the market risks of the platform, while their network of suppliers delivers state-of-the-art modules. Platform owners focus on the design and marketing of the platform and the assembly of the final offering. Suppliers are expected to innovate within their areas and advance the state of the art. This division of responsibilities allows the system to minimize costs and maximize flexibility and responsiveness.[3]

3 *Price competition.* As a market matures, some platforms are left behind. This creates ripe conditions for more intense price competition. Not having much to lose, marginalized players fighting for survival adopt low-price strategies, barely covering variable costs. Overall prices come down, further expanding the accessible market

4 *Differentiated demand.* Within the dominant design, market leaders compete with differentiated offerings, segmenting the market and targeting niches. But that segmentation demands more flexibility from their suppliers, which are also pressured to provide a differen-

tiated offering for each niche, without sacrificing their economies of
scale and scope.

What sorts the winners from the losers in the transition toward a
dominant design and maturity? As product configuration and production processes stabilize, new competition drivers emerge. While late-
stage Battles of Architecture emphasize functionalities and reliability,
Mass Customization competition focuses on accessibility, variety, and
low cost.[4] As customers drift toward the dominant design, powerful
forces of consolidation develop. The winners are those that can harvest
economies of scale and of scope, while remaining flexible. As competing architectures converge, the novelty factor disappears and the value
of a platform increasingly resides in its reach. Customers now make
choices on the basis of performance and price.

Platforms that face difficulties in building efficient networks of suppliers fall behind, compounding their competitive challenges. Without
a structural cost advantage, which depends on the scale of their operations and on an efficient network of suppliers, a platform cannot support the growing price pressures. Their best option is to monetize their
most valuable asset, their customer base, and get out of the market by
merging with a stronger competitor.

There are sometimes fundamental changes in open systems that can
profoundly modify their operation, and indeed bring them down. This
is what happened recently to several platforms in the financial investment industry. The changes can be traced back to the diffusion of major
innovations in risk management tools. In our student days in the early
sixties, derivatives were minor products, relegated to suspicious ads
for puts and calls in the back pages of the Wall Street Journal and to the
commodity markets, where forward sales were common. The deriva-
tive markets took off in the seventies, stimulated by advances in the
theory of finance, such as the famous Black – Scholes formula to price
the value of options. That and other risk management advances such as
the swaps and securitization reshaped the whole investment industry,
and indeed, for lack of proper regulations, were a key factor behind the
2008 global financial crisis.

These innovative tools, such as the Black-Scholes model, came out
of Eureka games. But they were rapidly adopted by the mature financial industry, which can be best described as a mature open system,
and profoundly modified the working of the industry platforms. For
instance, the system for financing the housing market in North America

has evolved dramatically since the eighties. It used to be done through simple intermediation between local banks that collected local savings, and which dished out mortgages in its own market, very much a New and Improved game. But new systems emerged around channels that chain-linked borrowers to mortgage originators, then to local banks, which turned around to investment bankers which bundled and securitized the mortgages, got them rated and sold them globally as amazingly complex financial products to sophisticated pension funds and other aggregators of savings. What went on was a Battle of Architecture, with a few New York investment banks controlling the critical securitization platforms competing at the core. These systems unravelled around 2007-2008 as the products they generated turned out to be toxic. The resulting turmoil dramatically changed the banking industry in the United States and in Britain. What happened what not as much a game change as a new open system crashing.

The Opening of Closed Systems

J. Armand Bombardier was a master mechanic who used Model T Ford frames to build propeller-driven passenger vehicles for the snow-bound country roads of Canada in the 1920s. His vehicles were sold to veterinarians, doctors, priests, and taxis in snow-bound rural Quebec communities. Over the years, he developed a relatively simple propulsion technology for traveling over snow and ice. He replaced the back wheels of his vehicle with two sprocket-wheel assemblies that drove two rubber tracks, like a bulldozer's, and he replaced the front wheels with a pair of skis. His 'Autoneige Bombardier' could carry as many as 12 passengers. Over a period of 20 years he sold several thousands of them. But as governments improved snow removal on winter roads, Bombardier's market for its Autoneige started to shrink.

Seeking new markets, J. Armand Bombardier adapted the sprocket-wheel technology to a much smaller vehicle, creating the Ski-doo in 1959. It was the first snowmobile, which he targeted toward the recreational market. Within a few years, under the leadership of his son-in-law who had taken over the company after Bombardier's death, the Skidoo became the company's principal product, and its success inspired the emergence of hundreds of competitors in rural Quebec and in the snow states of Minnesota and Wisconsin. From that base in this emerging market, Bombardier diversified and went on to become the second-largest manufacturer of passenger trains in the world and the third-largest manufacturer of commercial airplanes. It is also still the largest snowmobile manufacturer on the planet.

With the Ski-doo, Bombardier switched its propulsion technology from the Autoneige's closed-system model to an open system of suppliers and distributors. That switch unleashed powerful innovative forces, many coming from the hundreds of emulators that entered the market, but also from suppliers that teamed up with Bombardier to provide critical components for the Skidoo.

Entrepreneurs often adapt closed systems that have demonstrated their marketability, by opening them to third-party complementors to address a variety of needs, or by simplifying them and addressing new needs. The original innovators, if too inflexible to revisit their model, are often left behind in such transformations. Microsoft is a good example of the benefits of flexibility: it turned the closed-system software it had developed for IBM into a basic platform that was used for a wide range of computers and that attracted a very large number of third-party complementors.

The diffusion of breakthrough technologies in other markets is propelled by a different dynamics than in their original closed systems, driving toward simpler markets and simpler applications. Entrepreneurs adapt the basic ideas behind breakthrough innovations and develop new applications. SAP was the breakthrough innovator behind ERP software in the 1970s; but ten years later, a large number of software firms relied on the same relational database technology as SAP to produce lighter business software systems that competed with SAP's versions.

Breakthrough games call for highly specific skills, such as a bold forward-looking vision, good project management abilities, patience, persistence, and a strong partnership between client and innovator. For innovating in mature markets, these competencies become less important than marketing, distribution, logistics, and brand management. Because of these differences in competencies, it is often new entrants and not incumbents that lead in the transition from a System Breakthrough game to mature market games. New entrants may not have the technological depth and vision, the patience, or the partnership skills required to excell in System Breakthrough games. But by the same token, companies that excel at System Breakthrough games do not usually have the interest, culture, or savvy to excel at New and Improved games, the most likely destination for a Breakthrough technology. Furthermore, a company stands a better chance of making the transition when a breakthrough gives rise to a platform, and initiates Battle of Architecture. Microsoft, for example, made this transition with stunning results.

Disruptive Innovations and the Upheaval of Industries

Disruptive innovations that change the way a particular need is addressed in the economy regularly upset the industrial order. Incumbents whose assets reflect the technologies of yesterday and who hesitate to embrace new and still imperfect technologies risk faltering under waves of creative destruction. New entrants, who have no vested interest in technologies of the past, embrace new ones more readily, allowing them to topple the established order and its incumbents.

Schumpeter was the first to draw attention to these upheavals at industry levels, referring to major new technologies such as the steam engine, railroads, electricity, industrial chemicals, the automobile, and airplanes. Computing and biotechnology would surely make the list as well. But as authors such as Richard Foster and James Utterback have pointed out, industrial upheavals can be triggered by much more modest technological changes.[5] The accumulation of knowledge continually gives rise to new technologies that displace less efficient ones and enrich our industrial capabilities. Incumbents with vested interests in the established order, and who lack the required skills and attitudes to switch, tend to hesitate before embracing a disruptive technology, putting themselves at risk of being displaced.

Clayton Christensen's investigation of disruptive innovation has greatly enhanced our understanding of the concept.[6] He distinguishes between disruptive and sustaining innovations: a sustaining innovation improves the existing industrial order, whereas a disruptive innovation challenges the existing order by encouraging customers to switch from old solutions to new ones. Christensen observed in detail the industrial transitions associated with the adoption of disruptive innovations. They are first adopted by marginal groups of customers, at either the low or the high end of the market. The disruptive product is initially deemed inferior by incumbents, even though it better addresses the needs of these neglected segments of the market. After building a beachhead in these segments, new entrants refine their disruptive technologies and deploy them in mainstream markets. Incumbents who remain wedded to old technologies fall by the wayside.

To illustrate his concept, Christensen referred to the disk-drive market, where 8-inch disks gradually replaced the original 14-inch floppy disk of the 1960s, only to be soon replaced by 5.25-inch disks. Each transition allowed new actors to enter the market, initially with a new and still rough-at-the edge technology. Each of them perfected its technology in a neglected market segment that it served well before moving into the mainstream.

Most of Christensen's disruptive innovations occur within the same innovation game, bringing a change of players and technologies but not changing the markets and the customer base. But Christensen also identified more powerful Schumpeterian innovations that brought about the demise of an entire industry. Between 1910 and 1930 the automobile marginalized the horse-drawn carriage. In the 1950s and 1960s the airplane marginalized the North American passenger train and the trans-oceanic passenger liner. These transitions led to a change of game, not merely a change of players.

Today, the digitalization of information and the spread of the Internet constitute a typical Schumpeterian big wave, creating major upheavals in information-based industries such as broadcasting, newspapers, and telecoms. The games of New and Improved and Mass Customization innovations that prevailed in these industries are becoming inconsequential and unproductive. Their traditional markets are becoming fragmented and marginalized by new entrants pursuing Battles of Architecture and building new markets, totally upsetting the incumbent industries. Although we are still 'in the fog of war' concerning these industries, their demise is gradually becoming evident. Let's look at their current status.

TV broadcasting as we know it today dates from the 1950s and is built around networks that assemble programming schedules to be distributed to households either directly or by local affiliates. As an industry, it is likely be pushed aside by the Internet, which distributes programming much more efficiently and conveniently than the broadcasting industry ever imagined. In most industrial countries, three or four broadcasters currently dominate the industry. Each owns one historic flagship franchise and several specialized channels. But they find themselves assailed by an army of Lilliputians that provide a wide range of video programming on the Internet. Already people spend more time on the Internet than they do watching TV. Major players like Google and Apple are developing programming for the Internet that will compete directly with TV broadcasts. The Internet has already become the primary delivery platform for news and is pushing aside dominant broadcasters for the delivery of live sports events. On the Internet, customers can watch a Grand Prix race or a football games from 10 different angles – your choice, buddy – with no unwelcome commercial breaks.

TV broadcasting is challenged by this new technology. Its structure revolves around one-way communications from a central node. Broadcasters derive their competitive advantage from their programming ability, building a schedule around the viewing habits of households. To attract a mass audience they must offer a mix of news, entertainment, and sports, then draw advertisers that want to reach the mass audience. Broadcasters are working hard to adapt to the Internet reality. They already make available on the Internet enriched content and old programming, distributed through alliances and partnerships with Internet heavyweights. They are also fully aware that the future for the delivery of video-based material is the Internet, as TV sets become monitors connected to the Internet, giving them access to standard Internet features such as interactivity, search engines, personalization, and access to a wide range of devices.

But on the Web, the dominant broadcasters of yesterday become just small players, competing with new aggregators such as Google TV, Apple TV, Hulu, and Netflix, who rely on different assets and different business models. The dramatic loss of market share that results destroys their business models, which depend on reaching a wide audience.

Will broadcasters be able to reinvent themselves as Internet players? It's unlikely: the culture gap is too big. Local broadcasters that produce little content will have a particularly difficult time. The networks may hope to retreat to what they do best, producing news, sports, and entertainment. But they will find new competitors in these fields. Sports clubs will produce their own material. User-produced content is already changing the face of news reporting. In the entertainment field they face independent producers of movies, music clips and games, and, more importantly, new entrants with lower-cost approaches, schooled in the subtleties of YouTube.

The virtual world has become a different place. Rupert Murdoch discovered this when he took the helm of MySpace, at the time the most popular social media website. It has been a downhill ride during the six years he owned it. In that regard, it will also be interesting to see whether public broadcasting corporations that have multi-media ambitions, such as the BBC in Britain and the CBC in Canada, will succeed where private broadcasters seem to be failing. Of all traditional media, private and public, BBC is the one with the highest penetration on the Web, ranking number 48 in the July 2011 Google ranking of most visited sites.

Newspapers face an even tougher environment. Still reeling from the arrival of cable news and the 24/7 news cycle, newspapers are now attacked by Internet-based media that grab the attention of consumers and advertisers. The development of Internet-based news reporting in the past 10 years has accelerated the decline of the audience and advertising base of newspapers.[7]

Newspapers are fighting back. They rely on their strong local coverage, capitalizing on their unique position as efficient advertising vehicles for retailing, which TV cannot service well. But retail advertising will gradually migrate to the personalized environment of the Web, undermining a key source of revenue for local papers. Some newspapers have also increased the depth of their content, differentiating themselves from Internet headline news and TV's more superficial coverage of issues and events. But the Web is becoming deeper, as well, with content available to meet any reader's interest in a particular topic.

Newspapers are also available on the web. But they face heavy competition, and despite their powerful brand do not fare well in the Internet marketplace. In Google's July 2011 ranking of websites based on the number of visitors, the *New York Times* was the highest-ranking newspaper site worldwide, in 124th position.[8] It was outranked (number 86) by *The Huffington Post*, a web-based aggregator that relies heavily on user-generated content from individuals who, unlike newspaper reporters, don't get paid for their work, don't form unions, don't demand overtime and benefits, and who provide their own office furniture and laptops. Several portals that offer news were also much ahead of the *New York Times*. The same decline is occurring in all countries. Newspapers are no longer the prime sources of written news: upstart websites are.

Nevertheless, the *New York Times* is probably the news organization from the printed world that has fared the best so far in the transition. Before it began charging for its online content, it was still in the top 10 news sites on the Internet in the United States.[9] But now that it has started to charge for Internet content, it has dropped out of the top 10 and may have entered into a vicious circle of declining advertising support, declining subscription base, and declining resources.

Telcos are doing somewhat better than TV broadcasters and newspapers. But their heyday was in the 1960s and 1970s, when they stood out among the largest employers in most industrial countries. AT&T, British Telecom, France Telecom, Bell Canada – all employed hundreds of thousands of people. Citizens accepted their nation's telecom company as a natural monopoly. As long as their regulated integrated networks generated the lowest costs and ensured universal access, no one complained much about the absence of competition.

Three factors put an end to that situation: the deregulation of the industry; the development of mobile telephony, which allowed numerous scrappy players to enter the industry; and the Internet with its open systems of digital protocols that trumped closed operator-owned networks.

The telephone industry has morphed into the telecom industry, providing backbone and access to a new industry, 'over the top' (OTT), which is still ill defined but delivers a wide range of services using Internet communications. It is where the real money now resides, and where the telcos are absent. Internet platforms now serve as delivery vehicles for an endless range of services, from selling books on Amazon and auctioning collectibles on e-Bay to delivering sports programming on Eurosport and movies on Netflix. Mobile phone platforms enable users to make small payments in stores, get driving directions from their GPS, and save money by using electronic promotional coupons as they browse the aisles of their favorite supermarket. It is a new industry fairly close to the telcos, but that they couldn't crack.

The telecom industry will remain significant, but mostly as a provider of basic infrastructure services. There are still many fundamental questions about its future that remain to be answered. Will it ever be a significant player in OTT? Will it ever share in the revenues of the OTT industries, such as 30% of each transaction conducted on an iPhone or an iPad that Apple currently collects? Can it prevent the web-based service providers, such as Google and Microsoft, from encroaching on its basic telecommunication services? What can it do about Skype, which Microsoft has just bought for $8 billion, and which has a 20% market share of overseas two-way communications? Are the device-based platform owners, such as Apple, trying to profit from what is sold on their overlapping platforms, or are the two partners, selling access to smart phone and tablet users that want to reach the Internet? How can it compete with Google, already a big player in telephony with its Android system, which is developing numerous applications to be accessed over the telcos' mobile telephones?

As an industry unto itself, telephony no longer exists. The telecom industry's future will also remain ill defined until the ongoing Battles of Architecture on the Internet are sorted out. If it is to survive in this new and changing universe, the telecom industry may have to seek out the skills it needs in the start-ups of Silicon Valley, where many have adapted quite well to the thrust and parry of Internet-related Battles of Architecture.

Surviving Game Transitions

Game transitions are critical periods for companies. As a transition occurs, the skills required for innovation to thrive change dramatically. In each game, innovation follows a specific set of rules and patterns, and the assimilation of an innovation can take time. Indeed, by the time an incumbent adopts an innovation, it may be too late for its own survival. Some companies, however, have managed to survive transitions and thrive within each successive game of innovation. Perhaps the most remarkable company in this respect is IBM, which has thrived for more than 100 years in an environment swept by two fundamental Schumpeterian waves of technological change. It has successfully gone through several game changes while maintaining its values and a strong culture.

From its creation in 1911 to the mid-1950s, IBM was a manufacturer of office equipment, like dozens of others in the United States, participating intensely in several Eureka! and New and Improved games. Then, like many of its competitors in the office equipment industry, it entered the emerging market for computers in the early 1950s, a market initially thought to be limited to governments, universities, and the military. But as business applications developed in the late 1950s, IBM became a formidable competitor. With its first business computers (the IBM 1200 and 1400 series) and the development of the FORTRAN language, it became the clear winner of a Breakthrough game of innovation. Then, as computerization started to spread throughout business organizations in the 1960s, IBM engaged in a Battle of Architecture and won this game with its System/360 in 1964 and its System/370 in 1970. For the next two decades, IBM clearly dominated the business computer market, with a market share that attained a stratospheric 80% by the mid 1970s.[10] (Twenty years later, Microsoft would occupy a similar position of dominance in the software industry.)

IBM encountered a major setback with the arrival of the PC. While businesses and consumers flocked to the new technology, IBM remained entrenched in its big-box universe. Despite the success of the IBM PC, the company lost the Battle of Architecture in that market to Microsoft, and it failed to capture the value inherent in its own PC technology. Contrary to IBM's assumptions, software operating systems, not hardware, turned out to be the determining factor for capturing value in the PC universe, and the software was owned by Microsoft.

With distributed processing architecture built around PCs and with servers slowly replacing the centralized big-box architecture, IBM plunged into crisis mode in the early 1990s. Its profits collapsed. But it shook itself out of that funk. Within a few years, its entire senior management team had been replaced; an outsider, Lou Gerstner, took the helm in 1993. Not only had he earned his credentials in a company unrelated to IBM, but he came from a completely different industry, as CEO of RJR Nabisco, a consumer goods company. IBM's board challenged Gerstner to address the woes that had befallen their deeply troubled company. Only five years earlier, IBM was the most admired and most profitable company in the world. Yet a disruptive transition in its industry had almost destroyed it.

Gerstner did the job. Within a few years, he repositioned IBM as a global consulting service company. Instead of selling systems alone, it also sold its expertise to companies and governments around the world. With IBM's support, clients could fully benefit from the information technology revolution that had swept across continents. Hardware remained important, but in Gerstner's vision, IBM's future lay in IT services. To achieve his vision, Gerstner focused on the culture of IBM. In particular, he instilled a strong customer orientation, an essential element in the Pushing the Envelope game of innovation that IBM had started to play. Within six years of Gerstner's arrival, IBM's stock had rebounded from a low of $10.50 in 1993 to more than $120 in 1999. It was one of the greatest comebacks in recent business history.[11]

Entrenched in the business computer market, IBM missed the transition from the innovation game of Mass Customization that it played so well to the Battle of Architecture that began with the arrival of the PC. Under Gerstner's leadership, the company adapted and survived, relying on its expertise in information systems to become a global leader in system integration. Services now represent half of IBM's revenues, more than hardware and software combined. In early 2011 IBM ranked 14th in the world in terms of market capitalization, far below the leading position that it occupied in the mid-1980s, and below its former nemesis, Apple, which it had once regarded with disdain. Still, to regain such prominence after wrenching transitions testifies to the resilience and capacity of a great organization.

PART THREE

Looking Ahead

15 Winning Strategies

Winning at innovation games depends on having the right strategies and executing them well. Prowess can be observed in the long run, as in the case of Procter & Gamble, or at a product launch, as in the case of the iPod and the iPhone. However, another interesting viewpoint is provided by incumbents during game transitions, which are generally tough on them. Of all the world's computer companies, for example, only IBM was able to survive the emergence of personal computers. And even it hit the wall in 1991, 15 years after the PC's introduction. The traditional telephone companies are encountering similar difficulties in the face of the Internet revolution. Their inability to participate in the innovation games spawned by the Internet and to expand beyond the provision of connectivity, a service that is likely to become increasingly commoditized, is a major strategic failure.

When the Internet took off, the telcos' closed systems were still tightly controlled, while the Internet was wide open to all new entrants. The telcos did not really understand the impact of that fundamental difference and did not capitalize on the inventive power of third-party application developers, who turned the Web into the dominant platform of today. Initially, telcos saw the Internet mostly as a new market for connectivity, to sell kilobits of data. As the OTT ('over the top') markets developed, they strategized about investing but missed many opportunities. Skype, Yahoo, e-Bay, Amazon, Apple, RIM, and Nokia could all have been brought, at prices that large telcos could afford. No other industry spent as much on consultants to assist them in understanding the OTT opportunities.[1] Despite their large capital base, huge cash flows, and ambition to profit from the Internet, they made very few investments, hesitating to enter the OTT marketplace.

Why did they remain focused primarily on the connectivity business? As we have argued in Chapter 4, we have to go back to their decision making to get some answers. Connectivity was and still is a business they have always known and felt comfortable with. Within their ranks, the operating units always had the real organizational power, generating the cash flows that supported quarterly earnings. Operators resisted any initiative that might have cannibalized their traditional business. Any Internet service such as Skype that took business away from their basic services was the enemy. OTT businesses, on the other hand, were seen as unprofitable distractions. Their business was connecting customers on networks and routing their kilobits of data to their destination.

Telcos are still today mostly providers of connectivity, competing by offering better access and worrying strategically whether they should charge by the kilobit per month or by the customer, regardless of the kilobits consumed. They subsidize the purchase of smart phones, but only to sell more kilobits to more users. Meanwhile, application providers generate millions of dollars in revenue on smart phone platforms.

With hindsight, it is clear the telcos never anticipated that their historical business, connecting people, would be radically transformed into the infrastructure segment of a much broader industry. They also did not anticipate that their connectivity activity would be commoditized, while the action would move 'over the top' of their connectivity, where a trillion-dollar industry developed, right on their door step. Thanks to the booming Internet traffic, the telco business is larger today than ever before, but it is a much narrower business, providing only kilobit-routing and access to infrastructure. Moreover, new entrants are likely to provide significant competition with their more efficient use of the radio wave spectrum. The telcos may be stuck in a low-margin business, as differentiation between infrastructure services hardly matters to anyone.

Could they have developed a better strategy? This is far from certain. Strategic choices are made in a context of uncertainty and ambiguity. Hindsight generally distorts the perceived risk of the moment. Until recently, telcos did not believe that OTT Internet services would endow their providers with power over the companies that control the infrastructure. OTT services were assessed as new business opportunities, not as strategic threats. Telcos did not realize that a Battle of Architecture was raging and that new Internet-based platforms would emerge to coordinate most of the services provided by the Internet. Since telcos were not venture capitalists, with a diversified portfolio of Internet properties, their aversion to risk may have justified their reluctance to get into OTT services. When a game of innovation changes, incumbents must accommodate disruptive innovations and learn new rules. The telcos surely saw that the Internet was disrupting their traditional market; they simply did not figure out the new rules.

Seven Principles

Could they have responded better if they'd assessed their strategies within a framework of games of innovation? This again is not certain, as they were blind-sighted by the cash flows from their traditional businesses. Moreover, each game of innovation calls for its own set of strategies, and each is quite different from the others. We've described these strategies in some detail in the chapters devoted to each game. But certain strategic principles apply to all of them. The seven principles that we present below merely summarize the concepts and are not meant to be exhaustive. They emphasize the importance of innovation as a strategy. And they demonstrate clearly that some ways of addressing innovation are better than others.

1. *Innovation must be an essential strategic thrust for creating value.* No business can afford not to integrate innovation into its strategic plans. This may sound like a truism. In emerging markets, innovation strategies form the core strategic choices. Indeed, in emerging markets, any business that survives must continually upgrade its products and watch for innovative business models that may upset current market practices. But businesses in mature markets often neglect innovation in their business strategies. In a recent survey of the 1,000 public companies around the world that spend the most on R&D, done by the management consulting firm Booz & Company, about half of the firms, which are mostly in mature markets, 'say that their innovation strategy is inadequately aligned with their overall corporate strategy.'[2] The fact is that many firms choose not to compete on the basis of innovation, adopting other strategies, such as emphasizing service, investing in new facilities, making acquisitions or expanding in new areas and new markets. Their myopic strategic reviews seldom lead them to set up a system for continuous improvements, nor establish objectives such as the percentage of sales represented by new products or services. Growing small and medium-sized businesses, often comfortable in their niche markets, also tend to stick to proven formulas.

Yet in companies of all sizes, a strategic review should map out product portfolio evolution, in terms of features and processes, with the objective of improving market positions and creating additional value. Such multi-year planning of both resources and performance requires that innovation be a pillar of the business strategy. Competition will always change the marketplace, moving in line with evolving customer preferences; companies should prepare themselves to deal with these changes through innovation.

2. *Knowing which innovation game a business is in.* If telcos aspire to be more than just dumb pipe providers, they must engage in Battles of Architecture. Companies engage in these games with open platforms, based on their ability to develop network effects, enlarge the base of customers, and attract third parties to provide modules. Most telcos, however, thought they were involved in games of Mass Customization, continually improving the performance of their network and tailoring their offering even more closely to each customer's needs. Their customers knew better. As users of phones, they take access for granted, and seek – and pay for – the additional benefits provided by their devices, which are increasingly delivered by the software platform powering the device. Telcos have been out of the devices business for several decades, concentrating on networks. But the real platform competition is between devices, and it bears on hosting applications. This is where market power is derived and where margins are highest. Network performance matters less.

Businesses generally know what game they're in, and they learn about the game's best business practices by observing the winners. But game changes can easily fool a business, as they did the telcos. A new game has to be recognized rapidly, as laggards can be severely punished. Even the best-run business can suddenly find that it lacks the critical skills and assets to compete in the new game.

Google's decision to enter the smart-phone market with a powerful open platform, for example, may turn out to be a brilliant strategic move. As the only major open platform available to device makers that do not have their own software platform, Android is able to harvest significant network effects. Google's rival, Microsoft, also runs a smart phone platform. But it is not as open, and to date has attracted only one major device manufacturer, Nokia. Given the powerful network effects that prevail in the industry, Microsoft may have already lost the race.

But knowing which game a firm is in does not mean that the full implications of the game are well understood. In particular, the influence of the product's architecture is sometime neglected. Stand-alone products' dynamics are relatively easy to understand. It gets a little more complex in closed-system games, with their required customer intimacy and their high-risk undertakings. It is a different ball game when the game involves an open modular system: the formation of coalitions is required, conflicting interests must be balanced, and the capturing of network effects is central to success. The dynamics of each architectural state are quite different, particularly in new markets. Management should be aware of the specific competencies and structures required to succeed in a competitive race defined by a particular architecture. Deploying the wrong competencies is a recipe for disaster. Yet it is often done, especially when an entry is achieved through an acquisition and the acquired company is playing in a different game.

3. *Assigning the primary responsibility for innovation to the front line.* The Schumpeter II model assigns that responsibility to a central unit, heavily relying on R&D, an approach that is still frequently encountered in large businesses. Indeed, the proliferation of Chief Technology Officers (CTOs), reporting directly to the CEO, reflects a 'let's take charge of innovation' attitude in the upper echelons of business. But product innovation is best done in close interactions with customers. And if product innovation is to be done on a continuous basis, then it should be the responsibility of those managers who have daily personal contact with customers and who are in position to observe competing products in the real environment of the market place. When the CEO is also the chief product manager for new products, which Steve Jobs was at Apple, no one is surprised to see him closely involved in the development of innovative products. Yet Steve Jobs was an exception. Most CEOs are not product managers, and only exceptionally is product management done at the C-suite level.

Shifting the responsibility for innovation to the front line brings a number of challenges. Product managers are asked to meet ambitious sales objectives, and tinkering with the development of new products can blur the focus demanded from them. As well, good innovations require close interactions with customers, to get their ideas, to sense their reactions to competing innovations, and to get real-time feedback. Effective innovation also calls for the development of metrics and their incorporation in the performance objectives of front-line managers. Finally, it demands that the development groups responsible for the development and evolution of new products be under the overall command of front-line product management executives, as opposed to product development experts. There can be exceptions. Breakthrough products such as the first IBM PC and Apple's first iPod, which were strikingly different from their product portfolio at the time, were developed by task forces, as front-line executives, unfamiliar with the target markets, were deemed to bring little to their development.

The same principle applies to process innovations, aimed at improving costs and reliability. Front-line production executives should be assigned the responsibility of continually improving their processes. That may call for support from R&D experts, but the primary responsibility for innovation should lie with the executives in the front line of the production processes.

Assigning the primary responsibility of innovating to the front line affects the role of the CTO. Centralizing innovation support capacity makes sense. The CTO should also be tasked with monitoring the performance of the front lines on innovation. But more importantly, his or her role is to develop a culture of innovation throughout the organization and to strengthen the competencies of front-line managers. These are critical responsibilities.

4. *Managing a portfolio.* Most companies manage a portfolio of products, each of which is potentially at a different stage of its game, or in different games altogether. The allocation of resources within a portfolio should take into account the specific dynamics of the games. When a company wants to harvest emerging network effects in a Battle of Architecture, for example, capturing new customers and preventing them from going to competing platforms become critical, requiring significant marketing investments if the platform is to stay in the game. Likewise, when an industry starts consolidating during a Eureka! game, a company must invest in strategic acquisitions as competitors drop out. If for some reason senior management blocks all acquisitions during that period, 'because prices are too high,' the company might as well drop out of the game.

The challenge of a portfolio involves more than the application of resources. Some games require specific attitudes toward risk. In their early stages, Eureka! games and Battles of Architecture are fraught with uncertainty, and low-cost providers do not necessarily enjoy significant strategic advantages. How does a mature company, with well-defined processes and tight controls, cope in a game involving products that are still being defined? The standard response is organizational. As IBM did when it entered the PC business, companies set up an autonomous division and leave it alone. That response has become a best practice:

separate games, separate divisions. But to what degree should corporate bodies such as investment committees and new product committees interfere in the operations of autonomous divisions? In diversified companies with products competing in different games, providing the right answer to this question is critical.

The answer has challenged some great companies. Despite making huge investments, why has Microsoft struggled to diversify its aging core of products and come up with a big new winner? How does Google manage to do it more successfully? In the 1980s, as we've all learned, Xerox made astonishing advances at its Palo Alto Research Center (PARC), but no matter how hard it tried, the company failed to commercialize them. As new products emerge from their enormous R&D facilities, pharmaceutical companies fiddle with the structures and processes involved with managing product development, chewing away precious years of patent protection. The challenge of steering the evolution of a diversified portfolio is not one of awareness of opportunities but of the delicate art of management.

5. *Multiple sourcing of ideas.* Open innovation is hot at the moment, and with good reason. Innovation comes from the mixing of ideas. More often than not, innovation involves adding new ideas to existing products, to come up with a Tide Bricket, a once-a-day pill, a sharper video graphic, or a slower-moving rotary kiln. Most of the innovation in our economy occurs in increments like these. Innovations come from the combination of ideas, new and old, into a product. Having a strong pipeline of qualified ideas increases the probability of innovation. This is the advantage of open innovation, which calls for tapping new ideas from the most promising sources, inside or outside. The best source for improving products is a company's customers, while its employees provide the best source for improving processes.[3] Other sources include young inventive minds, scientists in enabling fields of technology, and people who simply feel strongly about an issue.

Regardless of the source of new ideas, management should make sure that it accommodates viewpoints beyond its own narrow scope to fuel the innovation processes. Unfortunately, management often becomes narrow-minded as products mature. Over time, product and production managers become quite good at what they do, and often overconfident. For the sake of coherence and continuity, they follow an orderly and well-controlled innovation process. Yet their views can become locked in: once effective practices can become outdated. In their preoccupation with controls and efficiency, managers often neglect or ignore the best sources of creative ideas for enhancing products and processes. This is what P&G's 'Connect & Develop' strategy is attempting to address.

In emerging markets, where innovation is the strategic imperative, businesses are more open to outside influence. A best practice is to make it mandatory to harvest ideas from external channels, anticipating the inevitable objections against openness: 'We don't have time,' 'These people do not know our business,' 'We already have a strategy,' and so on. In an emerging market, the marketplace clearly determines the winners. And the marketplace, by definition, is open to all new ideas, good and bad.

Open systems tend to be more creative than tightly controlled closed systems. In emerging markets, where products evolve rapidly, openness to outside ideas can turn into a major competitive advantage, as long as the process is well coordinated. The success of open innovation also draws attention to the limits of patents in the innovation process. In the development phase of a product, companies sometimes avoid patents to maintain secrecy. They must also take into account the stifling effect of secrecy on new ideas. A company may derive a competitive advantage by jealously guarding the configuration of a product, as Google does with its search algorithms. But management also has to be aware of the opportunity costs associated with closing projects that require creativity as a fundamental ingredient.

6. *The importance of healthy ecosystems.* Open innovation points to the critical role of ecosystems in innovation. A healthy ecosystem is in symbiosis with a core company. Such two-way exchanges bring two types of pay-off. First, suppliers and distributors, who constitute the key players in most ecosystems, bring additional expertise to the game. Suppliers contribute their technical mastery of a specific area. Distributors contribute their intimate knowledge of customers within a market. A company must ensure that key players within the ecosystem participate fully in the innovation process, by encouraging their constant input. This requires a company to share its game plan, which it may regard as a risk. But the risk brings a much greater reward in the form of enhanced innovation.

Second, a mutually beneficial commercial relationship creates a stronger partnership. Loyal partners will take their own initiatives to further the relationship. Innovation entails risk. In a dynamic ecosystem, risk is shared with partners. This requires mutual trust, which demands time and effort on the part of management. It does not emerge instantly through legal agreements. Instead, a company and its suppliers, distributors, and other partners create a dynamic ecosystem over years of mutually satisfying commercial exchanges.

There are two barriers to the development of healthy ecosystems. First, some firms focus exclusively on price to avoid leaving money on the table. But relationships that depend on obtaining the cheapest component do not bring much more than the cheapest partnerships. Healthy ecosystems seldom emerge from the conventional procurement policies that assume an adversarial relationship between a company and its suppliers.

The second barrier to a healthy ecosystem arises when companies become overly concerned about the leaking of corporate secrets to their competitors. Certainly, most suppliers and distributors deal with competitors within an industry. But there are good ways and bad ways to handle this issue. The bad way is to choke the flow of sensitive information on the basis that it could be leaked. Companies cannot build the trust required for a rich ecosystem by withholding information from their partners. The better way is to manage intelligently the flow of information, ensuring proper control of its diffusion. Far more than maintaining control, good management depends on weighing trade-offs and building trustful relationships.

In the literature of economic development, ecosystems extend to the institutions that deal indirectly with a business. Government agencies, universities, and financial institutions may operate at the periphery of a company's ecosystem. Yet they too can contribute to the conditions required by a company to create a healthy ecosystem. Silicon Valley's venture capitalists, for instance, play a big role in the entrepreneurial effervescence of the region. The region also thrives on cooperation between large businesses and universities over oriented basic research.

7. *Leader or smart follower?* Smart follower strategies are common in business. The concept is simple: wait for the innovative competitors to identify a new product, market, or process; take the time to sort out the winning formulation; and then enter with a copycat, or a better product if possible. Microsoft did this with the spreadsheet, launching Excel after VisiCalc and Lotus 1-2-3. It did it again in the 1990s with Internet Explorer, knocking out Netscape. Much later, Google did it with Chrome, zooming in on the weaknesses of Internet Explorer, and holding 15% of the browser market in 2011.

Smart follower strategies exploit two major advantages. First, a smart follower saves significantly on development costs, entering the market after many of the bugs have been worked out and a sustainable design has been achieved. Second, it avoids investing in dead ends. With a few exceptions, we seldom hear about failed products or processes, because their promoters withdraw from the market before they lose too much money. Smart followers avoid these zero-return investments, by waiting for the market to develop and sustainable designs to emerge.

But smart-follower strategies come with two important drawbacks. First, they forsake the first-mover advantage. A Johnny-come-lately has to compete with well-established rivals, and on their turf. Microsoft, for example, launched MSN Maps and MSN Virtual Earth to compete against well-entrenched rival products from Google, and neither of the Microsoft's offerings took off. Second, the smart follower has to accept market conditions shaped by competitors. These may not conform to their own strengths, attributes, and preferences. In particular, latecomers have to provide the benefits already offered by earlier entrants and that are likely to reflect their strengths. A latecomer may not have these strengths, but they still have to provide the benefits.

The trade-off between advantages and disadvantages is often market specific. It also depends on how much a company wants to invest. A deep-pocket company may prefer to enter when the broad parameters of a new market have been established, especially if the innovators are financially stretched starts-ups; this may explain why late entry and smart follower strategies are common in new markets. However, the difficulties Microsoft and Google had in diversifying their portfolio illustrate the limits of the deep-pocket advantage. Neither company succeeded, for instance, in capturing a major share of the emerging social media market. Mature markets present even bigger challenges, as market shares are much more resilient, and first-mover advantage often trumps all the other advantages that a smart follower tries to reap by waiting a few years to enter.

Specific Game Strategies

The principles that we've just discussed cover aspects of strategies common to all innovation games. But as we have seen, each game entails its own strategic imperatives, whose application can make the difference between success and failure. That calls for specific game strategies, which we will review briefly.

Eureka!

This game starts with a Eureka! discovery, about which we can say little except that they are sporadic and difficult to predict. Moreover, there's a good chance that the inventor of the original Eureka! discovery will be rapidly forgotten. Who remembers Ed Roberts from Albuquerque, New Mexico, who invented the first personal computer? He sold his company, MITS, in 1975, and went on to become a country doctor. The names we remember, such as Apple, Atari, and Compaq, came after him. So let's turn the page on Eureka! moments and look at the early years after the discovery, when the product gains traction and the dynamics of the market set in.

Marketing and product management are the early key competencies, as the game calls for successive launches of versions and variations of the new product, along with development of a customer base. Branding rapidly becomes important for customer awareness and market development. Long before a patent becomes useful, a recognized brand is the most valuable intellectual property of a successful start-up.

Early-stage entrepreneurs often have a technological background, and for them prioritizing marketing over the technical development of the product can be a challenge. Once the product architecture has gelled, technical challenges become less important. The product strategy has more to do with listening to customers and steering the evolution of the product in the proper direction. Most critical is expanding the marketing reach, which bears on distribution, resellers, advertising budgets, and the like. These are key success factors in the early years of a new product.

At this stage, the difference between success and failure is often a good management team. Although management must be nimble and marketing-oriented, it should also develop the systems and controls to sustain the company as it grows rapidly, carefully hoarding its cash. The evolution of the entrepreneurial culture associated with a start-up into the stable culture of a growing organization brings enormous difficulties.

The strategic competencies required evolve as the market grows. When it approaches the consolidation phase, M&A and financing abilities join marketing and product management as key competencies. Acquisitions can drive market share gains, improving market reach and allowing for economies of scale at a time when margin pressures increase. Successful consolidators buy the right companies at the right price, filling holes in their portfolio, and are good at integrating them. An acquisition can derail even the highest-flying company if it has to waste significant time and resources integrating it into its operations.

Large businesses do not have many of the competencies to succeed in early Eureka! games, such as nimbleness and close-to-the-market decision-making. They often have too many second thoughts about too many questions, from the brand and the intellectual property to the liabilities and the costs. Even arm's-length subsidiaries are at a disadvantage, having to cope with the rule book of corporate headquarters. Moreover, the risks of failure are high in early-phase Eureka! games, which also explains the absence of large businesses at the early stage.

They find it easier to enter a Eureka! game through a strategic acquisition in the consolidation phase, when there is much less uncertainty. Depending on their ability to digest the high acquisition price and manage the inevitable culture shock, most large companies that participate successfully in emerging markets choose this path.

Different rules apply to pharmaceutical products, as the regulated environment of the industry and the high costs of developing new drugs shape the growth dynamics of their Eureka! game. Biotech companies are efficient upstream, until the heavy and risky investments in clinical research make it too difficult them to continue alone. Handing off their high-potential products to a big pharma is usually their best strategy.

Battle of Architecture

This game is about developing a platform, attracting both users and application developers, and capturing network effects. In the incubation phase, which often lasts a few years, similar platforms may vie for the right mix of ingredients to stimulate a market to take off. Social media took about six years of incubation, for example, before it took off in 2003. Once the right formula appears, all the incubating platforms copy it, and the race starts.

The immediate challenge is to build a customer base sufficiently large to cross the threshold for network effects. Giving away the product (often done on the Internet) or heavily subsidizing it (e.g., the early smart phones) are common tactics. Marketing is important, especially toward influencers, who can be active in viral marketing. Facebook clearly demonstrated in 2004 and 2005 that brand positioning can matter, as it prioritized students from elite universities, a good strategy for youth-oriented social media. Having a popular application on an exclusive basis, even if it is a three-month fad, can also bring these early customers. The product must meet a technological threshold, as RIM learned when it launched a tablet without an Internet connection. But once this threshold is crossed, technical superiority is seldom a discriminating factor. Most early adopters value blockbuster applications, status of the brand, and the platform's reach much more than technological prowess. These early customers want to be 'wowed.'

Once network effects have kicked in, the game changes. Getting the most out of the ecosystem of suppliers becomes paramount, as the platform's popularity depends as much on its intrinsic attributes as on its modules (e.g., applications for Internet platforms). Orchestrators must stimulate the creativity of their platform's ecosystem. That calls for a combination of a good business model, making it worthwhile for partners to develop and launch new modules, and the proper mobilization of those partners. Star power helps in that regard. Entrepreneurial heroes such as Steve Jobs and Mike Lazaridis commanded the attention of third-party developers and distributors.

Customers are a major source of ideas for open platforms. Being good at listening to them can be a competitive advantage. Zara has developed a sensitive system that track sales and feeds back into their production plans. Continually experimenting with new variants reveals avenues for product and benefits development.

Network effects rapidly turn Battles of Architecture into oligopolistic competition, as three or four platforms usually manage to cover most of the marketplace. Since one platform resembles another, and each platform offers the most popular modules or applications, brand image and customer loyalty now become critical. Investing in brand marketing can make a major difference for a platform orchestrator.

As the market matures, platforms become complex and somewhat unwieldy under the weight of their accumulated modules. Wise orchestrators look over their shoulders at this point to see if a new technology or a new system has started to deliver the same benefits with a different and simpler formula. Microsoft's Operating system is feeling such new competition from free open-source software (FOSS) operating systems, which are now inching toward a combined market share of 50%. In retailing, displacement of aging platforms that do not rejuvenate their offering and their image is common.

System Breakthrough

This game can also be broken down in two phases. The initial breakthrough that gives rise to the game calls for a duo that picks up the

.huge challenge of successfully removing a bottleneck. The client in the duo must bring the vision, the money, and the determination, and must chose a project manager that will be sponsored to achieve the vision. The project manager assembles a team of experts and manages the execution of the project. Not only do both have to meet their own objectives, but they also have to work together harmoniously throughout the project, not an easy feat considering that most System Breakthrough projects end up over budget and over schedule. This last challenge is compounded by the fact that deep-pocket sponsors that attack bottlenecks and experts that are confident that they will achieve a breakthrough usually have strong personalities and can enter easily into conflicts. Carefully choosing who one partners with is probably the first rule to follow for successful System Breakthrough projects.

Proper funding is a critical element behind successful System Breakthrough projects. Shortage of funds can sometimes force compromises that can jeopardize a good project. A primary responsibility of the sponsor is to arrange additional funding when required. Conversely, the primary responsibility of the project manager is to control spending and avoid large overruns.

Turning a breakthrough into a business is the other major challenge of this game. Much depends on the arrangements at the outset between sponsor and project manager. When both are from the same company, as in the Dassault example for Catia, the decision is easy. But more often than not, the two come from different organizations, and the initial partnership contract becomes important. It is normal for sponsors who foot the bill to seek to keep ownership of any intellectual property stemming from breakthrough projects. They are concerned that their own competitors do not get their hands on the technology. Wal-Mart's tight control over its RetailLink technology is quite legitimate. But project managers have a strong interest in commercializing their breakthroughs. Luckily, most of them usually find a way to implement the technology elsewhere. ERP systems are credited to SAP, the original project manager, and not to Imperial Chemical Industry, the original sponsor. Project managers that are careful to keep the technology away from their sponsors' direct competitors usually can implement it elsewhere.

Nevertheless, successful breakthroughs are rapidly copied, as removing a bottleneck gets noticed by competitors of the sponsor. Moreover, experts in the same areas as the successful project managers see a business opportunity and propose similar solutions. A competitive game starts in earnest, and the breakthrough solution gets improved on as it is implemented elsewhere. Accumulation of knowledge, leverage of one's reputation, and marketing reach are the most important competitive assets in a System Breakthrough game. Quite often, the expert team that has engineered a breakthrough will choose to join a larger organization with marketing clout to leverage its capacity and deploy their knowhow rapidly on broader markets.

New and Improved

This game involves, first and foremost, a mindset: *to compete by offering the best products on the market and the best costs in the industry*. This mindset begins with the organization's leadership and its values. It is reflected in the organization's business strategy and annual plan. Innovating typically finds its way into the company's mission statement and signature. Companies that are successful in this game are usually close to their customers, and are recognized as marketing oriented. They organize their product development activities in the most efficient way, tapping the best sources of ideas for product and process improvements, internally and externally. They neither recognize nor accept the 'Not Inventive Here' syndrome.

They also pay attention to the churn in their product portfolio and have developed appropriate metrics to measure it. There is a formal pipeline of products in development, widely shared between divisions and functions. On the cost side, there is a commitment to improve continuously. They have processes such as Kaizen to involve employees in a permanent drive for more efficiency, and use metrics to control quality, waste, down times, and so on. Such a continuous improvement philosophy would not be sustainable without the same attention to corporate costs, controls, and margins. They cannot emblazon their products, decade after decade, with the words 'New and Improved' unless they generate strong commitments across their organization to continuous improvement.

In New and Improved games, ecosystems provide ideas and feedback. To play that role effectively, successful companies keep their ecosystem healthy and dynamic. To this end, they encourage open two-way communications. That requires mutual respect, which is a challenge. Management and business literature generally emphasize cost at the expense of maintaining a healthy ecosystem. Business journals are full of articles about senior executives that have lowered their costs, and in particular their component costs. Articles about CEOs that get creative inputs from their suppliers are much less frequent.

A mere commitment to innovation does not guarantee success: the commitment has to be sustained. CEOs come and go, and each wants to imprint his or her strategic vision onto the company. Circumstances such as a recession or a major unexpected loss may demand a shift in priorities from continuous improvement to a radical reduction in costs or tight controls. This will influence the company's prevailing culture. Even after a company emerges from these circumstances, it may not succeed in rebuilding a culture of continuous improvement; it may not even try. Of the thousands of companies operating around the world over the last century, only a few, such as P&G or Air Liquide, have remained permanently committed to the mantra of continuous improvement. That record alone attests to the challenges involved.

Mass Customization

In this game, 'core' companies operating large systems in mature markets compete to deliver complex bundles of benefits to their customers. Market shares are relatively stable, and customers are experienced. Large retail chains, automobile manufacturers, the airline industry, and the hospitality sector participate in games of Mass Customization. Competition boils down to a better offering for each of their customers, an offering that targets customers' individual needs.

The basic strategy of a core company is deployed on several fronts. On the customer side, it is a classic marketing play. Through its brand and its distribution network, a company targets a specific clientele. Coherence is critical here. But as that client base can be large (think of Wal-Mart), the challenge is to avoid a bland image and stay meaningful to each customer.

On the operations side, customization materializes through a delivery system that is as personalized as it can be, with significant attention paid to customer interfaces. Wal-Mart, Disney, and Club Med are highly effective on that front.

The goods delivered by the platform come mostly from third parties, and a key element of a Mass Customization strategy relates to the management of that complex interface. Both the orchestrator and its suppliers jointly control the benefits received by the ultimate customers. In retailing the interface involves product selection, replenishment, margins, promotion, exclusivity and, more importantly, new products, as the offering must be continually refreshed. The orchestrator strategy is made more complex by the fact that their suppliers are pursuing their own strategies, usually a New and Improved one. From their perspective, the relationship with an orchestrator is delicate, since they also deal with its competitors. To get more power in the channel, and better deals, suppliers seeks to establish strong brand identities. Managing the conflicting interests and the resulting struggle for power in the channels is paramount for an orchestrator. This is done via a combination of detailed business agreements, involving contracts and codes of conduct, and elaborate rituals generically called 'suppliers days,' where the orchestrator's top brass courts their supplier ecosystem, shares their commercial strategies, and strengthens their allegiance. It is, however, clear that some orchestrators are better than other, in developing trustful partnerships with their suppliers. On the single dimension of innovation, such partnerships are definite advantages.

Finally, there is the orchestrator platform, which is industry specific. It links the supplier ecosystem and the distribution network to support the business exchanges underlying the open system. Competition demands continuous improvements in the platform, which is an orchestrator responsibility. The management of that evolution must take into account the previous commitments and contracts of third parties attached to the platform. This tends to exclude disruptive moves from Mass Customization games. The systems are too complex and decentralized to accommodate abrupt changes. An orchestrator is prisoner of the previous investments made throughout the system. Let's recall the 2009 Wal-Mart attempt to move its positioning slightly upscale. The move upset the delicate equilibrium that ensures the coherence of its system. Somehow, customers, store employees, and suppliers lost their traditional synchronicity: sales slumped, surprises erupted, and stakeholders became unhappy. Wal-Mart had to rapidly backtrack and a few senior VPs lost their jobs. A mature open system is not a fertile ground for strategic revolution.

As globalization progresses, Mass Customization games gain in importance. Global brands and global procurement will put more pressure on customization of the benefits offered, allowing more room for innovation as a competitive tool.

Pushing the Envelope

In playing a Pushing the Envelope (PTE) game, a customer strives either to surpass previous achievements, as in the Millau viaduct, or to beat the competition with a competitive advantage that cannot be replicated rapidly, as Sobeys did with its automated warehouses. To address the challenge, the ambitious sponsor assembles a team of experts with the same competencies required by Breakthrough games: a solid partnership, deep pockets, project-management skills, and technical expertise.

The PTE challenge is more modest than a breakthrough: pushing the envelope and going further than anybody else, rather than removing a bottleneck that few people believe can be removed. The game is played over and over by experts, who improve their CV with every new project. Reputation is a critical factor in this game, along with project management skills and the ability to put together a team of experts that work well together and stand at the forefront of their disciplines.

The development, installation, and application of large information systems used by banks, retailers, government agencies, and other information-intensive organizations usually involve PTE games. So do projects involving shipbuilding, defence equipment, large industrial facilities, and infrastructures that provide a customer with a major competitive advantage. Sobeys' automated warehouses are typical projects involving games of PTE innovation. Clients in these games are ambitious. They tend to demand the most bang for their budget dollar, and more.

Risk reduction and risk sharing are important, and much time is spent at the outset to reduce and allocate risk. In information system projects, the reputation of the integrator matters in that regard. In infrastructures projects, governments turn to experienced public–privatepartnership (PPP) concessionaires that have mastered the management and transfer of risk, allowing them to tackle projects lying beyond the capabilities of most organizations. The major risk they assume is completion of the project on schedule and within budget. Once the project is completed and the revenue flows are established, they usually sell it to pension funds seeking long-term annuities.[4]

SME Innovation Strategies

So far, we may have given the impression that most innovation games involve large corporations. What about the rest of a nation's industrial economy, its small and medium-sized enterprises (SMEs)? Don't they get involved in games of innovation?

The answer is yes. SMEs participate in all games, in four different ways.

Entrepreneurial SMEs are important at the birth of new industries. The early years of Eureka! games are populated by small entrepreneurial businesses, as economies of scale do not play a major role. They have significant advantage over large firms at that stage: nimbleness, quick decision making, focus. But a Eureka! game is unforgivable: only a few will make it to the end, and by that time, none is an SME. The same pattern is found in Battles of Architecture, where platforms have been launched by entrepreneurs, one of the most famous being Mark Zucker-berg at Facebook. Moreover, entrepreneurial SMEs dominate the ranks of third-party application providers in these Battles of Architecture. But if successful, the entrepreneurial SMEs in emerging markets do not stay small for long and can grow rapidly into large firms.

Second, SMEs abound in New and Improved games of innovation, in the ecosystems of large firms, where they play a vital role in the inno-vation process, as large firms rely on them as specialized suppliers that master niche technologies to provide them with improvements. SMEs can turn out to be important contributors in New and Improved games.

Third, service-oriented SMEs in local markets pursue 'New and Improved' games, and there are a lot of them, filling yellow page directories. However, in local markets, competing does not necessar-ily demand innovation, as personal relations, location, reputation, and inertia play important role in shaping customer choices. Locally ori-ented SMEs still have to take into account any change in the offering by local competitors. Moreover, many of them innovate by being 'first in their local area' with new offerings: the first medical clinic to employ a robot, for example, the first local supermarket to stock probiotic food, or the only machine shop within a 25-mile radius to use a laser cutter. What may appear as diffusion of new technologies to business economists is perceived as innovating by the local entrepreneurs who bear risks.

Finally, SMEs abound in the expert domains that are critical to Sys-tem Breakthrough and PTE games of innovation. The contribution of their expertise is entirely unrelated to their size.

The Internet as a retail channel has attracted a large number of SMEs, eliminating the geographical road block. But it has not changed their competitive landscape. Internet retailers are still involved in games of innovation that are defined by the maturity of their market and by the architecture of their products. The Internet is simply a new retail chan-nel, albeit a powerful one, as Amazon, Facebook, and Apple are current-ly demonstrating. SMEs that master it are bound to grow, while those that ignore it may be pushed aside by more aggressive competitors.

Innovative SMEs should carefully assess their competencies before choosing to enter into a new market with an innovation. A successful innovation attracts emulators that become competitors. In a new market, first-mover advantage is of limited value, as compared to proficiency in marketing. Not only are most SMEs not good at marketing, but marketing competencies are not easily transplanted into a small or mid-sized entrepreneurial company that has never focused on it. Without such competencies, SMEs can often do better as supporting actors in an ecosystem, relying on core companies to handle competition.

Competing on Innovation

Innovation stems fundamentally from business decisions to break rank. Depending on the game of innovation involved, some businesses have more leeway than others to make these decisions. Businesses committed to establishing themselves in emerging markets have little choice. In an emerging market, competition depends on innovation. The moment a business stops innovating, it becomes history. Businesses in emerging markets must thus learn the most effective ways to innovate and to profit from their innovations.

In the early stage of a Eureka! game, when innovation is unshackled by regulations or conventions, the path is clear: listen closely to the marketplace, create new versions of a product, and build the brand as the customer base grows. In these markets, the players are mostly entrepreneurial firms. Large businesses seldom compete in early-stage Eureka! games. Nimbleness matters, not size. The most dangerous competitors are firms of similar size, skilled at product management and brand building. Winners in this game always build strong management teams. Until the market starts to consolidate, acquisitions are distractions.

In Battles of Architecture, the platform can linger in latency for a few years while all the key elements get assembled. When the market takes off, the race is brutal. Many entrepreneurs may start the game, but within a few years only a handful of them remain. Successful ones capture network effects and build coalitions of developers. It helps if a company has in place a valid business model; such models often call for giving away the service in the first years to build a customer base. Building a simple platform that attracts hot third-party developers is also part of a winning recipe.

In Breakthrough games, success depends above all on the quality of the duo at the helm: a qualified sponsor and a qualified project integrator. Once the technological breakthrough has been achieved, what matters are the contractual arrangements that could allow its diffusion by the system integrators, before competitors emulate it.

Mature markets require different strategies. In mature market games, the primary rule is to be serious about innovation as a competitive weapon. Best practices vary greatly, depending on the type of game being played. In Mass Customization games, Wal-Mart and Toyota and the like must address the complex evolution of their platform and the systems, while managing their brand on the one hand and their network of partners on the other.

The P&Gs of this world, in New and Improved games, operate in a simpler environment. Nevertheless, the challenge of reinventing detergents and razors every five years while maintaining enthusiasm for the products among tens of thousands of employees is not to be underestimated. Finally, in Pushing the Envelope games, the client is the critical cog: the ambitions that drive the project have to be well defined. Once this is achieved, the challenge boils down to good project management, something that successful PTE innovators have learned to do well.

It remains unclear why some businesses in mature markets rely more than others on innovation to create value and compete. But as we will discuss at length in the next chapter, the search for an explanation constitutes an important public policy issue.

16 Public Policies

The Organisation for Economic Co-operation and Development (OECD) in Paris serves as the economic council of the world's industrial countries. With a staff of 2,500, the OECD provides advice and observations about the major economic issues facing its 34 member countries. As expected, it has done extensive work on innovation. As it states on its website, the OECD

> monitors and benchmarks Member country technology and innovation policies and assesses their impact on economic performance. It identifies good policy practices in areas such as support to R&D, public/private partnerships for innovation, and overall management of national innovation systems.[1]

The OECD has also set up a permanent Working Group of Technology and Innovation Policy, made up of high-level policy makers from its member countries. The Working Group meets twice a year to oversee the work done in the area by the OECD staff. The importance of innovation as a driver of economic growth amply justifies that interest:

> [Innovation] accounted for between two-thirds and three-quarters of labour productivity growth in OECD countries such as Austria, Finland, Sweden, the United Kingdom and the United States between 1995 and 2006 ... It is also a key source of future growth for emerging economies.[2]

In 2010 the OECD's Board adopted a policy statement on innovation developed by the Working Group. This document represents the consensual views on the policies pursued by OECD member governments to stimulate innovation. Published as *The OECD Innovation Strategy:*

Getting a Head Start on Tomorrow, this comprehensive policy statement
is structured around a five-point framework:

1 *Empower people to innovate,* through better education, facilitation of
  organizational change, and fostering of an entrepreneurial culture
2 *Unleash innovations,* through well-thought-out competition policies, proper funding of innovation, particularly in new firms, and
  fostering of open markets and a culture of healthy risk-taking and
  creative activity
3 *Create and apply knowledge,* through public support for R&D, proper
  knowledge infrastructures, efficient technology transfers, and innovation in the public sector
4 *Apply innovation to current global and social challenges,* such as the
  environment, new energy sources, international cooperation, and
  assistance to low-income countries
5 *Improve the governance and the measurement of innovation policies,* treating innovation as a central component of government policy, with
  strong leadership

One noticeable element of this strategy is the third point, the creation and application of knowledge. Its inclusion in national innovation
strategies illustrates the lingering influence of the Schumpeter II linear
model, with its emphasis on discoveries at the frontier of knowledge in
large research centers. It also explains why most governments integrate
their science and technology (S&T) policies with innovation policies.
The development of scientific and technological knowledge, the core
of an S&T policy, is achieved primarily by supporting research in universities and government research centers. Indeed, most of the public
funding earmarked for innovation support goes to finance advanced
research in universities and government agencies. In 2009 OECD member governments invested $342 billion (close to $300 per person) to support R&D. Most of it went to universities and public research centers,
which spent $295 billion on R&D activities.[3]

To what extent does this funding influence innovation? Our games-
of-innovation framework tells us that new knowledge underpinning
innovation arises from a far wider range of activities than research conducted at the frontiers of science and technology. Although most innovations can be partially traced back to some new knowledge minted
from a research lab, it is its combination with other knowledge that creates the innovation. Social media, to name one recent major innovation,
provides a good example. It did not emerge from a research lab nor

did it depend on the accumulation by researchers of vast quantities of scientific knowledge. But it would not have been possible without the major progress made in computer technology, which is heavily indebted to lab research in various ways. Most innovations own something to new knowledge and, through that linkage, to R&D, but the linkages are often complex and there are usually more important linkages supporting their emergence.

In this chapter, we examine the way public policies stimulate innovation. We will begin by discussing government S&T policies and the extent to which they influence innovation.

Universities and Innovation

Economists characterize fundamental research as a public good, as it produces knowledge that is available to all at little or no extra cost. Profit-oriented organizations have no financial incentives to fund basic research, since they cannot easily recover their investment by selling the results. Consequently, governments pay for fundamental research on the assumption that it benefits society as a whole. In most countries, universities have become the primary delivery mechanisms for fundamental research, integrating these activities into their mission of delivering advanced education.

Universities see their role as providers of research as an important cog in the system of national innovation. They argue that this critical role in innovation amply justifies the financing of universities' research, particularly in recognized areas of national priority such as advanced medical research, computational techniques, and green energy.

But the premise that universities are engines of innovation is far from accepted by development experts. Richard Florida, an authority on the role of cities in economic growth, is one of the sceptics, as this observation of his clearly indicates:

> A theory of some sort has emerged that assumes that there is a linear pathway from university science and research to commercial innovation to an ever-expanding network of newly formed companies in the region. This is a naïve, partial and mechanistic view of the way universities contribute to economic development.[4]

The games-of-innovation framework provides a more realistic view of the way universities contribute to economic development. It suggests that their most important contribution is made through their educational activities. This in no way belittles the value of research, which makes an important contribution to the advancement of knowledge. But the advancement of knowledge is a global phenomenon. To the extent that innovation is localized, happening at specific places and times as organizations propose better solutions that improve 'the way things are done,' research in local universities has little bearing on whether innovations occur or not.

Nevertheless, most universities place the research mission on par with their educational mission, seeing themselves as institutions devoted to the advancement of human knowledge. This is reflected in broad trends in the conduct of basic research. In the OECD countries, around 17% of total R&D is carried out by universities[5] seeking a better understanding of natural phenomena, life, society, and behavior. Globally, their contribution to technological progress has been fundamental. Advances in scientific knowledge led to the development of antibiotics, semiconductors, laser, and nanotechnologies, to take a few examples. So how can we say that advances in knowledge are not critical to the innovation process?

The links between the advancement of knowledge and the actual innovations that eventually arise from it are most often quite loose. Advances in knowledge from all over the world are continually soaked up by the global commons of knowledge. In parallel, innovators pick ideas from that global commons and use them to develop or improve products that meet human needs. Research results are first reported in scientific publications, where they are scrutinized, leading to further research, further publications, and so on. Slowly, new knowledge accumulates, mostly in the public domain. Ideas circulate freely and widely, with some coming from far away. The global commons of knowledge is continually enriched. Sporadically, an inventor captures an idea that, combined with information he or she already has, leads to an innovative or improved product. Thus, the knowledge behind an innovation comes from multiple sources. There is seldom a straight line path from a local research lab to a local business that innovates.

Some Eureka! moments can be heavily dependent on recent advances in knowledge. Genentech was created on that premise, to develop products from the advance in knowledge resulting from Dr Boyer's fundamental research. But Genentech is the exception that proves the rule. Most fundamental research does not lead directly to the invention of an innovative product. The results get blended with other information in the global commons. Then, somewhere, an inventor, intrigued by some information, combines it with other ideas to invent something.

If the invention catches on, emulators will come in and start improving it as an emerging market game takes off. From then on, fundamental research becomes much less important while innovation thrives. New ideas that are incorporated into the rapidly evolving product come mostly from customers, suppliers, competitors, and a company's internal development, and seldom from basic research. As the innovation process shifts into high gear, driven by entrepreneurs, the university world is generally left behind.

The biggest contribution of basic research is found in the advancement of knowledge that precedes big waves of technological change. Mathematical research in the 1930s and 1940s, for example, led to development of computer logic. Research on basic materials in the 1940s and 1950s allowed the development of semiconductors. Genetic research of the 1970s and 1980s is leading to breakthroughs in disease treatment. These advancements result from the collaboration of thousands of researchers, in a series of small steps, which they share by means of journals and scientific conferences. When a major scientific discovery punctuates this process, the researchers gain professional recognition and may take credit for what is fundamentally an accumulation of new knowledge to which they have contributed only the last step.

This does not preclude fruitful collaboration between university researchers and innovative businesses, as the latter are continually seeking new ideas. Such collaboration is most prominent in life sciences, on multiple fronts. Through research partnerships, pharmaceutical companies keep in touch with leading-edge researchers who are important sources of new ideas, as they are active participants in networks of scientists who pursue advances in knowledge. Research hospitals provide clinical research services, supplying patients for clinical trials while retaining their third-party independence. In an adversarial regulatory process, pharmas often depend on the endorsement of leading researchers to further their development of a product. In the above roles, universities provide mainly support services to pharmas and biotechs. Universities play a more critical role in the innovation process by incubating researchers who will eventually create biotech start-ups.

Collaboration is not as extensive in other industries. It is common for university researchers to provide technological assistance on highly specific problems, where leading-edge science may be of assistance. But such collaborations seldom involve university researchers deeply in any innovation games, except in a system breakthrough, where leading-edge researchers may participate in the expert teams set up to tackle bottlenecks.

Several reasons explain these two solitudes. The basic research conducted in university laboratories does not rely on the same skills as those demanded by the types of development encountered in innovation games. Moreover, business R&D centers operate under purpose-driven, time-sensitive pressures that university researchers are not used to and are generally not ready to accept, as those pressures could impair their scientific discovery process. But the major obstacle to close collaboration on innovation projects is the clash of cultures. In emerging market games, fast responses and quick turnovers are essential. The prevalent university culture does not beat at that rhythm, and their values do not support it.

The Critical Role of University Graduates

Notwithstanding the marginal role that their research plays in innovation games, universities remain critical players in emerging market innovation games, through the contribution of their graduates, especially in leading-edge technological fields. Success in new market games depends on the ability of firms to incorporate cutting-edge knowledge into their rapidly evolving products. Graduate students, especially at the master and PhD levels, are not only rich sources of new knowledge, but they enhance the capacity of a firm to absorb that knowledge. Attracting and developing leading-edge talent is clearly a university's primary contribution to its region and to the national innovation process.[6] Graduates who choose to stay in the region have a major impact on innovation and local economic development.

This is a major competitive advantages of Silicon Valley, where companies draw employees from a rich pool of talent at the leading research-oriented universities in the San Francisco Bay Area. The region also attracts the best and brightest young engineers and scientists from all over the United States and beyond. Graduates of the Bay Area universities were founders or co-founders of a large number of the best-known companies of Silicon Valley, starting with Hewlett Packard, Intel, Advanced Micro-Device, Oracle, and Qualcomm and, more recently, Yahoo, Broadcom, Cadence Design, SanDisk, and Google.

Germany has maintained a healthy manufacturing sector because of its technological leadership and despite its high labor costs. In particular, 60 Frauenhofer Institutes throughout Germany keep the country's businesses well informed about advances in technology. At first glance, these institutes resemble applied research centers specializing in highly specific areas, such as robotics, photonics, and bio-medical engineering. But they also train doctoral students and conduct contract research for

German companies, and as such, they operate as 'brain transfer' facilities. Their graduates become familiar with research projects, and then go to work for the businesses that sponsored those projects. In this way, they disseminate technological know-how, which is one of the institute's major functions.

In the mid-1980s, Sweden decentralized its technical university system, establishing 11 new institutions throughout the country. Over the years, these institutions have had a significant impact on productivity and innovation in the cities where they're located. In the process, they've provided one of the few clear measures of the impact on regional development of higher education facilities that train graduates for local firms.[7]

Training of leading-edge graduates is not independent of the research conducted in universities. But what matters most as a contribution to local economic development is not the research itself, but the young researchers that work on these projects, and who eventually migrate to local firms, bringing their avant-garde knowledge, their network of experts in academia, and their ability to tap new knowledge. This highlights the usefulness of regional clusters that encompass both leading-edge research-oriented universities and a strong ecosystem of industrial firms that can hire their graduates. Clusters act as magnets to attract entrepreneurially motivated talent to a region, first as students, then as employees of local businesses, and then as entrepreneurs.

Universities are generally concerned by the lack of connections between professorial research and economic development in the surrounding region. They should not be. Their most important role in local development is not generation of new knowledge, but their ability to attract talent and, through that talent, to disseminate leading-edge knowledge in the local economy. But to attract the best and brightest and properly train them, they need to conduct leading-edge research. So universities should continue to orient their research toward the pursuit of Nobel prizes and peer-review publishing and in the process expose their students to leading-edge ideas. This is what they're good at. The development of new products should be left to tinkerers and managers in the competitive realm of locally based companies engaged in games of innovation.

Encouraging Business R&D

A fundamental tenet in the Schumpeter II linear model is the critical role of business R&D in the innovation process. The OECD keeps a mountain of statistics on the level and nature of business R&D in its member countries. One of its key indicators of a country's innovation climate is the BERD ratio, which measures the value of business expenditures on R&D as a percentage of GDP. Embracing the Schumpeter II model, most OECD countries have made the encouragement of business R&D a central tenet of their strategy on innovation. But does it work?

Let's look at Canada's experience, as this country provides one of the highest rates of financial support for business R&D as a percentage of GDP among all OECD countries. More than 80% of that financial support takes the form of tax credits, the most generous among all OECD countries. A company in Canada can fully deduct all R&D expenditures from its taxable income. Small and medium-size companies have an even more generous regime: if they are unprofitable or have insufficient taxable income, they can claim a subsidy (euphemistically called a refundable tax credit) to provide them with the full tax reduction to which they are entitled. The policy rationale is simple: government estimates that the spill-over effects of the additional R&D induced by the tax credits are worth more than their costs.[8]

But does it work? Canada does not seem to get much in return. Among OECD countries, Canada has one of the lowest BERD ratios, despite its generous tax credits. Surprised by this poor performance, the Canadian government appointed a Blue Ribbon panel to find out why this strong tax support did not translate into higher levels of industrial R&D. The panel concluded that factors such as Canada's industrial structure and foreign ownership could not explain the gap. The main reason, according to the panel, was Canada's too comfortable competitive context, which does not pressure businesses to rely on innovation as a business strategy, despite the much lower cost of subsidized business R&D in Canada.[9] The innovation game framework leads to a similar conclusion. Innovation depends first and foremost on the competitive environment of businesses and on how businesses respond to that environment. The cost of business R&D is secondary, especially in emerging markets. Simply reducing its cost through an R&D-friendly tax structure will not necessarily translate into more innovation.[10]

This does not mean that the cost of business R&D is irrelevant. But cost is not as important a driving factor as the demand for R&D. Fortunately, most countries have understood this and have designed their R&D support policies accordingly, by channeling their financial support for R&D through project subsidies, an approach that belongs to what is called 'Demand Side' innovation policies.[11] (Canada, Belgium, Korea, and Japan are the exceptions.) The OECD data suggest that countries that channel their financial support for R&D through demand-side policies are more successful, in term of BERD and innovation, than countries that relied mostly on tax credits, such as Canada.[12]

A typical demand-side innovation policy is a program that subsidizes a consortium of firms supporting an innovative project, such as the development of a high-speed rail system, a new electric automobile, an alternative energy project, or a new approach to health care. The subsidies are only one aspect of these demand-side innovative programs, the carrot that glues the coalition together behind the project. More important is selectivity: projects are selected on the basis of the strengths of a country and the industrial policies of the government, going much beyond the specific interests of a single firm, which is what is targeted by the traditional R&D tax credits. Moreover, a consortium pools the complementary strengths and assets of the partners, a great source of productivity gains. Finally, demand-side programs are concentrated on high-impact projects, whereas R&D tax credits are sprinkled on a large number of projects of various degrees of importance.

The game-of-innovation framework builds on the drivers of innovation specific to each game. R&D costs are not critical drivers in four of the six games, the exceptions being Eureka! and Breakthrough. Competition and the ambition that goes with it are much more important. Talent that can soak up leading-edge knowledge is also more important in emerging-market games. It is with these considerations in mind that one should assess the subsidization of industrial R&D as a driver of innovation.

The sharp differences in the innovation processes encountered in each game also suggest that one-size-fits-all policies, beyond competition and talents, are not likely to be efficient. With this in mind, let's review each game and see how government policies can affect their unfolding.

Eureka!: Building New Industries

A Eureka! game is characterized by a rapid multiplication of firms, generally concentrated in a few regions, followed by a consolidation phase. A small number of winners eventually emerge as the product enters into maturity. Within a period of 20 years a new industry develops, typically around a few regional clusters, a common feature in emerging technological industries and a result that most government would characterize as highly beneficial.[13]

The clusters generated by Eureka! games are shaped by the incubation process of start-ups, where proximity plays a central role. Entrepreneurs who start new firms in the early stage of a Eureka! game already work either in the fledging industry or in a related field. They generally assemble their financing from local investors who are familiar with other local start-ups. Proximity also helps to attract experienced workers and suppliers. Clustering is both a cause and the result of development, as self-reinforcing support effects take hold.

Where a Eureka! game is unfolding through the presence of pioneering firms, the creation of additional start-ups, both as competitors and as suppliers, should be encouraged, generally over the objections of the pioneering firms. Competition is good! What is required is not so much a cluster policy as a policy to help start-ups and the attendant spin-offs of suppliers and competitors, capitalizing on a region's comparative advantage of proximity to nurture their development. These additional start-ups will both benefit from and contribute to the emerging cluster.

Financing is one of the major issues confronting start-ups and rapidly growing firms, as information market failures bring about significant deficiencies.[14] The issue is more pronounced in Eureka! games, as emerging markets are by definition mostly unfamiliar to investors. In such situation, good venture capitalists can make a difference. Policies that encourage venture capital financing will not work unless high-quality venture capitalists participate. We have seen many examples of well-intentioned initiatives to set up community-based venture capital institutions that ultimately have floundered. It takes uncommon investing skills to pick the winners in an emerging and unfamiliar industry. The presence of such skilled venture capitalists in the San Francisco Bay area is one of its great advantages in developing new industries.

Rapid growth also creates significant human resource issues. In this area, public policies probably work more effectively than they do in financing. Governments can expand the pool of qualified labor by supporting industry-wide training programs. Local universities can develop research programs related to the emerging industry, ensuring the development of highly specialized graduates, a major advantage in Eureka! games. In Montreal, the video-game industry has worked closely with local universities to develop undergraduate and research programs specific to the industry's requirements. As a result (and helped by generous training subsidies), the region has gained a significant edge and now ranks among the top five global centers for video-game development, clearly demonstrating the potential of talent-oriented development policies.

We cannot ignore intellectual property issues when discussing Eureka! games. Let's first deal with patents. Although there is a broadly based trend toward more extensive patenting, it seems clear to us that patents do not have a significant impact on Eureka! innovations except in the life sciences. In most industries in the budding stage, patent claims are mostly annoyances to be circumscribed or cross-licensed. In the long run, a strong patent portfolio has the potential to generate significant royalties, but in the future, while weaker patents can generate legal disputes. But in the early years of Eureka! games, myopia reigns. Given the high risk of innovation, innovators *de facto* use very high discount rates to assess the future, marginalizing the impact of uncertain future royalties or patent disputes. Although patents can represent significant income in the long run, as we have seen for IBM, they have little impact on the rate of innovation in a Eureka! game, except as a cross-licensing currency. Patent trolls, who are not interested in cross-licensing, can become a major nuisance. But they also show up several years after the innovation occurs.

Companies can protect intellectual property more effectively through secrecy and branding. From an innovation perspective, the world could be better off if, in most sectors of the economy, patents disappeared altogether. A notable exception is the pharmaceutical sector, discussed below. (In the next section, we will tackle the patent issues in Battles of Architecture, a very different situation.)

With the relatively simple chemical structure of the new molecules that are the active agents in new drugs, and their long and expensive regulatory approval process, strong patent protection plays an effective role in pharmaceutical innovations, as it justifies a five-to-ten-year investment in innovation, ensuring research-oriented pharmaceutical companies that they can recoup costs with a temporary monopoly. Patent protection has recently been strengthened in the pharmaceutical industry worldwide, lengthening the effective period of protection. Shortening, as generic manufacturers wish, would have dysfunctional effects: marginal candidates for research would be dropped from the R&D pipelines, the pharmaceutical industry would spend more on marketing, and it would be more aggressive on prices of new drugs (e.g., raising them) with a shorter effective commercial life.

But in the pharmaceutical industry, patent protection is just part of the story. Despite improvements in the protection regimes and despite significant increases in R&D budgets, the rate of innovation over the last 10 years has fallen significantly in the industry, the consequence of a dearth of fundamental discoveries that can be translated into effective and safe therapeutic products.[15] Given the already high level of public support in the life sciences, it is not clear how more public support can accelerate innovations in this sector. Regulatory reforms would be more fruitful.

Battles of Architecture

To a large extent, public policies that make sense in Eureka! games also make sense in Battles of Architecture. But the latter are more complex and involve many more players. Moreover, in Eureka! games, innovations mostly add up through improvements of a well-defined product that simply gets better – a vertical addition. In Battles of Architecture, platforms get more complex and extend their reach, adding modules and thus offering benefits to more people in more situations – it is a lateral expansion. That fact has an impact on patents, as we will see.

In Battles of Architecture, proximity also plays an important role in the development of an industry, even if Internet-based platforms can manage transactions over distance. As in Eureka games, public policies that facilitate the emergence of capable venture capitalists and that broaden the pool of qualified talent for the emerging industry contribute to a region's comparative advantages in stimulating new industries built around platforms.

Competition policies have a different impact in Battles of Architecture, where they are dealing with network effects, which bring about market concentration. Unlike Eureka! games, where a cluster of dominant firms may take 10 to 15 years to emerge, one or two platforms may assume a dominant role within a few years in a Battle of Architecture, leading to extremely high market share for the leading platforms, as we have seen with Microsoft's operating system and Google's search engine. Table 16.1 illustrates the rapid rise of Google's Android market share in the US smart phone platform market. Since its inception around 2005, this emerging market has been growing by about 50% per year. The Android's rapid ascent started in late 2009, and within 24 months it became the dominant platform, with a 45% market share, still growing as we write this book. The top four software platforms now hold 97% of the US market.

Table 16.1. US Smart Phone Platform Market Share

	Sept 2009	Jan 2010	July 2010	Nov 2010	April 2011	Sept 2011
Google	2.5	7.1	17.0	26.0	36.4	44.8
Research in Motion	42.6	43.0	39.3	33.5	25.7	18.9
Apple	24.1	25.1	23.8	25.0	26.0	27.4
Microsoft	19.0	15.7	11.8	9.0	6.7	5.6
Total top 4	87.2	90.9	91.9	93.5	94.8	96.7
Subscribers (M)	<40.0	42.7	53.2	61.5	74.6	87.4

Source. Selected Comscore Press releases, 2009–2011

Rapid concentration is a demand-side phenomenon, brought by users who find benefits in teaming up with other users of the same platform. To capture these high market shares, network effects easily trump any supply-side anti-competitive maneuver by the firms. Competition authorities are challenged by the rapidly building market power of the winners. Should users be denied the benefits of concentration? IBM in the 1970s, Microsoft in the 1980s, Google in the search market, all had difficulties with US and European antitrust authorities that tend to ascribe rapid concentration in Battles of Architecture to anti-competitive strategies. But the higher costs supposedly borne by users as a result of these high market shares are likely compensated by the benefits derived from the network effects. In other words, consumers tell us that concentration is good in open system markets.

A second public policy issue is the national origin of most of the orchestrators of these platforms; their being American has become an issue in most countries. The Chinese government is using various tactics to limit the penetration of Google and other major Western platforms into the Chinese market. As we write this, there are rumours of a takeover of Research in Motion, the only major global platform not from the US West Coast; we would expect the Canadian government to voice serious concerns if a non-Canadian company were to attempt to buy it. The United States would respond the same way if a Chinese company targeted a major US-owned platform. Open-system platform markets globalize easily. As global open-system platforms multiply, national concerns are bound to increase.

There is some legitimacy in these concerns. Conflicts can arise between national policies and the design of a platform. RIM faces major problems in several countries where Blackberry's confidentiality standards conflict with domestic policies on privacy and access to information. China, as well, frowns on the uncensored searches accommodated by Google. In Germany, fierce opposition has led Google to withdraw Street View. Such conflicts will certainly multiply as more platforms globalize, while their own domestic governments come to their defence.

Standard setting also generates concerns among policy makers. Most countries accommodate international standards. But in large markets such as the United States, China, and Japan domestic standards prevail, and these standards may conflict with global versions. In the cellular phone industry, for example, the United States adopted the CDMA standard, which was not compatible with the GSM standards followed by the rest of the world. Furthermore, CDMA is owned by a private company, Qualcomm, whereas GSM is owned by an international agency. Small-market countries rely for standard setting on international organizations established and monitored by national governments. By contrast, large markets such as the United States and China can develop their own standards set largely by domestic players. The United States follows its own standards in many areas, from the Imperial system of weights and measures to Generally Accepted Accounting Principles, while the rest of the world follows the metric system of weights and measures and uses International Financial Reporting Standards. The Japanese, who often face the same problem, invented the word 'Galapagosization' to describe this adaptation of standards to local conditions, a situation they deplore. Galapagosization hinders the diffusion of innovative products developed according to distinct domestic standards (often higher ones), as Japanese electronic equipment makers have discovered.[16]

There are good reasons for governments and global agencies to get involved in global standard setting and for businesses to demand that their national governments abide by these standards. As global platforms multiply, global standard setting will become commonplace. Even Internet standards, originally set by two private, non-profit US organizations, ICANN (for domain names) and IETF (for technical protocols), have evolved over time into more global standards. The US government influence, still significant, is bound to diminish as other governments and user groups demand a bigger say.

One type of public policy that does little to encourage winners in a Battle of Architecture involves public demonstration projects such as the Minitel in France. Although national demonstration projects may work for closed systems, they tend to fall flat in Battles of Architecture for three reasons. First, to evolve into a winning platform, a new open system must count on a large number of users. Most national markets are too small for that, the exception being the United States, China, and maybe Japan. With only one-fifth of the population of the United States, France accounts for roughly 15% of the population of the European Union. It could not win a Battle of Architecture with a purely domestic entry. Second, demonstration projects tend to be closed systems, not easily accessible to third-party suppliers and application providers. That cuts them off from the rich contributions of third parties. Minitel was somewhat open to application providers, but it remained heavily controlled by its consortium, and it evolved very slowly. Finally, national demonstration projects tend to be heavily subsidized. This not only eliminates competitors and their highly productive emulation, but it leads to one-of-a-kind technology. With no competition, the technology evolves less rapidly and becomes uncompetitive. Not surprisingly, even in France the Minitel was brushed aside by the Internet.

In fact, new platforms do not necessarily need subsidies to make it to the marketplace. They need customers. To woo them, new platforms have to respond to real needs with solutions that customers and advertisers will pay for. A public policy that opens a global market by herding industry participants into a common global standard will prove much more productive than any subsidized local demonstration project.

That brings us back, finally, to patents, which create bigger issues in Battles of Architecture than in Eureka! games, where early innovators really do not care too much about patents' threats. It is a different story in Battles of Architecture, as competitors can threaten litigation and scare away critical third-party developers. The issue is particularly serious in the United States, where the patent system is not kind to open systems on two counts. First, it is highly vulnerable to litigation, a major issue in rapidly evolving industries, where a new product launch can be held hostage by threats of patent litigation and where the threat of injunctions can interrupt the sale of a product. Open-system products are complex, as they include not only the platform but hundred and even thousands of modules, some of which can be critical to the success of the platform; this complexity creates almost unlimited opportunities for patent litigations.

The other weakness is the patenting of business methods, which is recognized uniquely in the United States and which greatly expands the universe of patentable innovations. Businesses are often able to circumvent these claims, with slight modifications. But they create additional opportunities for litigation and blackmailing.

One solution is to promote so-called standard patents, which are automatically licensed against royalties set at a fair level. They are common in software. Proprietary patents, on the other hand, are licensed on a piecemeal basis and can also be kept off the market, thus preventing a competitor from using them. It is the multiplication of these proprietary patents that is creating an increasing problem. Until recently, platform orchestrators protected against each other by assembling a portfolio of proprietary patents, which they cross-licensed. But patent trolls are not interested in cross-licensing and, having nothing to lose, can create significant nuisance in a market by acquiring broadly defined business method proprietary patents and threatening legal action against platform orchestrators that, either directly or through applications they host, are alleged to infringe on these claims.[17] Furthermore, to the surprise of the industry, major players, and Apple in particular, have started to use litigation against competing platforms claiming infringement on their patents, a policy that naturally brought retaliation and can slow down the overall evolution of platforms.

The threat of litigation over patent claims increasingly hinders the development of platforms and their applications. Because of their potential nuisance, patent trolls are extracting unjustified settlement. A reform of the patent system in the software area could reduce the threat of litigation and contribute to a healthier environment for innovation in Battles of Architecture. At first, the reform could do away with injunctions that can interrupt the sale of a product, replacing them with double or triple damage penalties if a firm is found guilty of infringement. Such a policy would not hurt genuine claims, but would remove the primary weapon by which dubious ones, unleashed by patent trolls, hold other firms hostage. Broadening the use of standard patents with their automatic licensing provision or, conversely, restricting the issuance of proprietary patents to genuine breakthrough discoveries could also greatly improve the situation. Finally, eliminating the business process patent, an American idiosyncrasy, would stimulate innovation rather than impair it by encouraging emulators to improve business processes.

Closed-Systems Games

Demand-side policies, where governments, acting as pioneering customers, challenge innovators to come up with breakthrough solutions, are frequently encountered in System Breakthrough and Pushing the Envelope games. These games often bear on areas associated with infrastructures and military systems that are of great interest to governments. These demand-side policies are particularly appropriate for closed systems, where the development of innovations is sponsored by a customer at the outset. (In games involving open systems, players compete to attract customers.) Governments intervene in closed-systems games, either as sponsors or to lower the risks or financing gaps in large privately financed projects such as the Chunnel between France and England. Consequently, governments are often associated with major innovations that stem from such closed systems. Their scorecard is nothing to be ashamed of.

The Internet is probably the best example of a major government-sponsored breakthrough. The Internet emerged from an initiative sponsored by the US Department of Defence in the late 1960s and early 1970s to connect electronically leading research centers and universities. Gradually, a language developed within the rules and protocols of the Internet and was internationalized through links between major research centers in Europe and America. In 1989 Tim Berners-Lee, a researcher in a European research center, adopted the HyperText Mark Up language for document sharing on the Internet, thus laying the foundations for the World Wide Web.

Big innovations can come from closed systems, and governments are often key actors in such developments. Though they seldom initiate these projects, they frequently provide financial support. Perhaps the most successful government agency dedicated to the promotion and funding of breakthrough innovations was the Defence Advanced Research Projects Agency (DARPA).[18] Created by the US government in the wake of the Sputnik, launched by the Russians, DARPA was set up explicitly to prevent strategic surprises. 'Throughout history, technical challenges have inspired generations,' DARPA's motto proclaims, and it set out to tackle critical challenges of its age.

Having a fail-safe communication system between scientists in the era of the Cold War was one such challenge. This is what triggered the funding of what eventually became the Internet. Other jewels in DARPA's portfolio include GPS technology, computerized protein design, holograms, advanced robotics, artificial limbs, and sensor technology. With a $2-million prize for the winner, DARPA has sponsored a 240-kilometre obstacle race in the Mojave desert between driverless vehicles built by hundred of teams from the United States and abroad.

DARPA's success has inspired numerous imitators. For instance, the European Union has developed a wide range of programs to fund innovative projects in sectors such as aerospace, information and communications technologies, and energy, in partnership with businesses, public research centers, and universities.

Challenges are more frequent in System Breakthrough games, as these games are triggered at the outset by 'big problems.' Deep-pocket philanthropists such as Bill and Melinda Gates are likely to be increasingly encountered tackling global societal issues. The challenges of space seem to be a relatively fertile ground, attracting enthusiastic supporters such as Peter Diamandis (X-Prizes) and Jeff Bezos, the billionaire founder of Amazon, who has taken up NASA's challenge of developing a reusable space vehicle. NASA's reliance on the challenge approach to stimulate breakthrough in space exploration could potentially be emulated by governments and applied to other sectors.

To stimulate a Breakthrough game, the contractual arrangements between the project manager and the funder, whether agency or foundation, have to foresee the commercial diffusion of innovations that could emerge from subsidized projects. That means an innovation must have a life of its own beyond the initial project and must be incorporated into commercial products. Investing in the diffusion of a breakthrough innovation takes precedence over issues about ownership of intellectual property.

In the United States, intellectual property stemming from research projects financed by the federal government is assigned by law to the project's sponsors, but the assignment is conditional on licensing the property for commercial development in the public interest.[19] North American universities generally follow the same practice. There is a growing criticism in the United States about the policy, said to hinder the commercial development of inventions stemming from these projects by allowing owners of the patents to hoard them. The alternative would be to license these technologies to all comers. Similar criticisms are directed at the technology-transfer policies of universities. Commentators such as Richard Florida claim that the mere assignment of intellectual property rights to universities hinders the flow of inventions into the marketplace and impedes their transformation into commercial innovations. If they are financed by government, he argues, they should be in the public domain.[20]

Governments are also involved in large infrastructure projects leading to innovations that push the envelope, with widespread economic benefits. By pushing the envelope, innovative projects have enriched the qualifications of experts who worked on them. Incorporating the lessons learned into their expertise will help them attract new commissions and acquire even more innovative skills.

Whether a government plays a key role in closed-system games of innovation depends on its commitment to 'progress.' In short, it boils down to attitude. In financing a major infrastructure project, governments can play it safe and insist on proven technology, which they usually do. Worse, they also impose detailed specifications to minimize cost, practically eliminating any chance of innovation. Alternatively, governments can take a broader view. With imaginative contractual arrangements, they can encourage the development of innovative approaches to the projects they finance. In fact, with only a minor shift in attitude, governments throughout the world could potentially unleash waves of closed-system innovations.

With an innovative attitude, governments can trigger extensive creativity and stimulate business investments by sponsoring projects to develop high-speed rail systems, the electric automobile, alternative energies, or fuel-saving aircraft. Reassured by government funding, business partners commit to projects that go far beyond the specific interests of one firm. Not only do such projects contribute to the strength of a region or country, but the participants disseminate their expertise throughout the commercial economy, leading to further innovation and gains in productivity.

Mass Customization and New and Improved Games

Games of New and Improved innovation and Mass Customization generate the majority of innovations in an industrialized economy. Can they be influenced by public policies? More specifically, can government entice mature businesses to rely more on innovation to compete? This is the issue that preoccupied the Canadian panel on business productivity in 2009, when it concluded that Canada's poor performance on business productivity – lagging 20% behind the United States – was caused by the Canadian business community's reluctance to rely on innovation in order to compete.[21] The Canadian business environment does not seem to induce Canadian businesses to be more innovative. But there is no magic bullet that will change such a situation. What is required is more competitive pressure throughout the economy, and that can be achieved over time, through a wide range of policies, such as:

- facilitating entry into concentrated markets, notably by foreign competitors (for instance, letting Wal-Mart buy a local retailer)
- breaking up monopolies (usually state-owned corporations) in staid industries and marketing boards, mostly in agricultural sectors
- opening markets to imports through trade pacts and tariff reduction
- privatizing government service activities
- encouraging the automatic licensing of standard technologies
- softening regulations that restrict competition, like zoning laws and retailers' opening hours
- loosening labor restrictions that hinder changes in the workplace

Given the wide range of policies that affect competition in a modern economy, what is required above all is a state of mind at government level, a strong belief that competitive pressures will stimulate businesses to be more innovative.

But there will be resistance to governments' attempts to accelerate innovation in Mass Customization and New and Improved games. In many countries and regions of countries, conservative business oligarchies supporting anti-competitive policies still dominate the economy, although few will admit it. Businesses prefer to push for lower taxes and subsidization of initiatives than to support broad measures that upset cosseted market environments. Changing the dynamics of New and Improved and of Mass Customization games takes time. But their importance in the economy, more than 50% of GDP, amply justifies raising questions about the state of competition in the mature sectors of an economy. (In emerging markets, that question is moot.)

Other innovation policies are often promoted in mature markets.

- Local procurement policies can be useful in areas where innovation is required, and can stimulate the important mechanism of pioneering customers.
- Incubators, early-stage financing support, and financial support programs for innovative product development projects can be important for SMEs that are part of ecosystems. They are less effective in emerging markets, where the rate of change is often much too fast to accommodate such artificial support.
- Interface institutions such as the Frauenhofer Institutes and similar organizations can bring leading-edge knowledge to mature-market firms that want to be best-in-class, in both products and processes, as long as they promote the transfer of talent.

These policies are all effective to a degree, but their application is highly localized, one firm at a time. They can never aspire to be alternatives to the tonic influence of competitive pressures on the will to innovate and to win at mature market games.

Effective Public Policies

If we were to rewrite the OECD's innovation policy within the framework of games of innovation, we would specify six broad public policy considerations:

1 New industries are built by emerging market games. A region or a country that wants to participate in the industries of tomorrow and attract some of their activities should create a positive environment for local entrepreneurs to succeed in emerging market games. To this end, public policies should:
   • support the multiplication of start-ups in budding markets, betting on many horses, and ensuring that fast-growing firms in these markets have access to financing as they develop in Eureka! and Battle of Architecture games;
   • encourage the formation of rich and creative ecosystems in emerging markets to support the rapid growth of local firms;
   • protect intellectual property rights in the industries where they matter while encouraging in other areas automatic licensing and other measures stimulating the transfer of new ideas to businesses that could turn them into commercial innovations.
2 Develop a rich pool of technical and managerial talents accessible to fast-growing firms in new markets. By coordinating science and technology policies with innovation policies targeted at new industries, government can ensure that high-potential firms in new markets tap superior talent. Research-oriented universities should develop exchange programs with these firms and develop training programs that respond to their needs.
3 Battles of Architecture require the deft management of complex coalitions that participate in the rapid evolution of platforms.
   • The legal framework of a country should not only support strong coalitions but also facilitate their evolution.
   • Competition laws must accommodate the significant market concentration that arises rapidly in Battles of Architecture, as users benefit from such concentration.

4 Governments are often called upon as financial sponsors of System Breakthrough projects. Properly structured, successful System Breakthrough projects can trigger games that generate significant industrial innovation. DARPA is a model of best practices for a government agency sponsoring breakthrough projects.
5 As major investors in infrastructure programs, governments can push the envelope, contributing to major advancements among local experts and suppliers involved in such projects. For this to happen, government must assume the risk inherent in PTE projects.
6 Businesses in mature markets can follow value-creation strategies based on continuous improvements to their products and processes. To this end, public policies should aim at creating a competitive business environment that values continuous innovation as a strategic thrust.
7 Competition is the driver of innovation in all games. But the diffusion of an innovation, as assessed by the development of its customer base, can vary significantly depending on how much competitive intensity accompanies that diffusion. Stimulating diffusion through a proper competitive environment can accelerate the contribution innovation makes to economic growth. In some games, regulatory policies and standard setting can also do so, as well as the education of new customers about the benefits of the innovation.

These policies complement the OECD's S&T strategy outlined at the beginning of this chapter. But they express more explicitly priorities that focus on the actual process of innovation.

None of our six points refers to the sacred cow of subsidizing industrial R&D outside of mobilization projects. We have seen no credible empirical studies that show a significant impact on innovation from reducing the cost of R&D. Currently, no other business function except employee training receives such extensive subsidies as industrial R&D. In most games of innovation, such subsidies are of limited value. To survive in emerging market games, companies have to focus their resources not on R&D but on product development. They also have to spend heavily on marketing, typically far more than they spend on R&D. Yet no country subsidizes marketing expenditures. In mature markets, subsidies can reduce a company's R&D expenditures. But it is far from certain that a subsidy will affect the firm's overall competitive strategy. In most cases, the firm will simply reallocate the freed capital to other uses.

The public policy environment that best supports successful innovation strategies is far from being fully understood. But as a first step toward understanding such an environment, we recommend focusing on the contributions that generate the most success in any innovation game. In this way, we can distinguish between the nice-to-have – typically more money and more protected markets – and the must-haves or the imperatives. The imperatives will vary from game to game, but they usually include talent, marketing, equity, and the willingness to change.

17 Rethinking Innovation

Andrew Grove is one of the three engineers who left Fairchild Semiconductors in 1968 to found Intel, where he was successively the COO, CEO, and then Chairman until to 2004, when he retired. An immigrant from Hungary who came to the United States in the late 1950s, he became 'a leading figure in the birth of the information society.'[1] *Time Magazine* chose him as its Man of the Year in 1993. He is still recognized today as one of the most authoritative observers of the information technology revolution. In 2010 he was invited to write an article for a special issue of *Bloomberg Business Week* on job creation. The article he wrote startled more than a few readers, as Grove unexpectedly suggested that innovation, and more specifically start-ups, were not the driver of job creation they are commonly thought to be. He argued that it was 'what comes after that mythical moment of creation in the garage, as technology goes from prototype to mass production,' that is important for job creation: 'This is the phase where companies scale up, a period of hard work necessary to make innovation matter.'[2] He concluded that Americans preoccupied with job creation should be concerned much more with the overall health of manufacturing in the United States and less about start-ups.

Grove makes the important point that although they play an important role, start-ups do not tell the whole story about innovation. Limiting innovation to the launch of new products stemming from radical discoveries misses much of the story. Innovations are distributed along the paths of development of products and markets. The start-up phase is evidently important for any path. But from the viewpoint of economic development, investing mostly in the multiplication of start-ups would cover only a small part of the broad process of innovation.

First in the World ...

Economic growth results from the greater and better use of labour, capital, and knowledge in the economy. The game-of-innovation framework focuses on one element of the growth process, the integration of new knowledge into the production realm of the economy, which not only improves the productivity of labour and capital but is the essence of innovation. The processes leading to this integration are not the random heroic actions of inspired entrepreneurs out to unleash the forces of creative destruction. Rather, they are structured into six games, following coherent pathways largely influenced by market conditions and by product architectures as entrepreneurs and managers respond to competitive challenges.

Innovation is best understood as a series of moves occurring on a pathway, with each event being a competitive response that translates into an improvement over what existed previously. Each of these events is an innovation, and their accumulation defines the evolution of a market. The pathway starts at the point in time when somebody shouts Eureka!, having come up with a 'First in the world' invention that fulfills a need in a way that nobody had thought of before. The event is generally barely noticed when it occurs, except by a first ring of pioneering customers and emulators, who see its full potential. The Altair microcomputer on the front page of the 1974 Christmas issue of *Popular Electronics* barely created a ripple in the boardrooms of the computer industry of the time.

However, the entrepreneurial brew that fermented in the San Francisco Bay area, where the personal computer really took off 30 months later and thousands of kilometres from the Altair office, turned out to be much more important. In a similar way, the origin of the social media journey is lost among obscure start-ups in the late 1990s, well before Friendster, MySpace, Linked-in, and Facebook structured the industry. Many inventions that give birth to major markets were first perfected by tinkerers, relying on feedback by pioneering users, until all elements were in position for the market to take off.

The Eureka! moment is thus the beginning of a long journey full of innovations. Emulators improve the product with new 'First in the world' features, some significant, others barely noticeable by customers, but sufficient to fuel competition. The early years of the journey are marked by rapid evolution of the product and enlargement of the customer base. But the economic footprint of these initial innovations is still small. As new markets scale up, successful companies are built and significant job creation starts to be observed. The diffusion process can vary greatly, as can the competitive races that support the diffusion process. But good products eventually reach their full potential. Then the market enters maturity, relying on replacement as opposed to new users. The rate of innovation slows down, although it never stops, and the industry consolidates. Sporadically, a major innovation rocks it, often allowing new entrants to come in.

The initial 'First in the world' inventions are generally responses to advances in knowledge, as they get integrated into the economic fabric. Advances in information and communications technologies are currently fuelling a long wave of innovations, and have created a large number of distinct markets, from communication devices to business software and Internet platforms. But there is more than advances in knowledge. In particular, rising affluence creates new needs that are addressed by innovators. Combining with new knowledge, this ever-changing demand supports the development of a diversity of new products and new services that our forebears never imagined, from artificial hearts to GPS-based store locators.

The diffusion process that characterizes the development of markets for new products is driven by entrepreneurial ambitions and by competition. The diffusion process is how an innovation spreads its economic contribution throughout the economy. Peter Nicholson has coined the initialism 'I&D' to emphasize that both innovation and diffusion processes are intertwined, although they are very different.[3] The innovation process deals with the emergence of superior solutions whereas the diffusion process deals with their adoption. As we have already mentioned, the diffusion process is as critical as the innovation process in harvesting the full benefits of innovation.

The diffusion process is not as uniform as is commonly assumed. A key factor is the intensity with which an innovation is promoted, which depends on both the economic incentives associated with its adoption and the level of competition in the new market. Innovations that are in the public domain take more time to spread than innovations whose commercialization translates into profits for entrepreneurs. In the same vein, intense competition between emulators is likely to result in a faster growing customer base. There can also be cultural and regulatory barriers that affect the rate of diffusion. For instance, making small payments by waving a mobile phone over a reader, although it is seen as a major innovation, is barely starting to catch on in Europe and North America, yet mobile wallets have been used in Korea since 2001 and are also extensively used to make payments in Japan's transportation system.[4]

First in a Market ...

The pathways traced by the diffusion of new products generally wind through a succession of geographically defined markets. This creates many opportunities for emulators to be 'First in a market' innovators, replicating the same phenomena of innovation and development of customers in locally defined markets. This is part of the diffusion process of 'First in the world' innovations through 'First in a market' emulations.

'First in a market' games are thus subsets of 'First in the world' games, and their dynamics are variants of the bigger game. In particular, product development consists in adapting concepts proven elsewhere to local market conditions. But the challenge of developing a customer base is unchanged. Although participants cannot claim to be inventors, they definitely can wear the mantle of innovators, as they face inexperienced customers and indeed must build their customers base. They also encounter the nemesis of all innovators, local emulators, who will bring small improvements to products, positioning and delivering them in a slightly different fashion. The entrepreneurs that succeed in 'First in a market' games tend to have strong marketing and financing competencies. As their local markets develop, they often gradually merge with adjacent local markets, which favors entrepreneurs most skilled at acquiring and combining businesses. From an economic perspective, 'First in a market' entrepreneurs are equal in importance to 'First in the world' ones. They are key players in the diffusion process, basically acting as emulators that adapt new products to new markets. They can also play an important role in having regulatory barriers removed, allowing an innovation to become diffused in a market. Out of their ranks also come great innovators, as some of them tinker significantly with the product to improve it to the point of making them global competitors.

Innovation in Tiger Economies

The 'First in the market' model is particularly powerful in developing countries with large domestic markets, such as China, India, and Brazil. Their economies already benefit from business conditions that support rapid economic growth. This creates unique opportunities for entrepreneurs to enter emerging local markets as 'First in a market' innovators, and build great companies somewhat protected from the competition that has developed in the original First-in-the-world' markets. Baidu, the dominant Chinese Internet search company, was founded in 2000 by Robin Li, a young Chinese software engineer returning from the United States, where he had worked for Infoseek, an early Internet search company. In its early years, Baidu greatly benefited from a somewhat protected market, with its strong idiosyncrasies such as the Chinese alphabet, to develop a strong revenue base. It has now moved beyond China and is competing head-on with Google and other Internet search engines in many countries. But it still owes much to its strong 'First in a market' position in China.

There are thousands of companies in China, India, and Brazil, that started as 'First in a market' emulators, adapting products and technologies developed elsewhere to the specificities of their home markets. Local conditions are strong barriers to competitors' entry, allowing these companies to develop a robust domestic base. As a global market emerges through the merging of these national markets, they find themselves in a strong competitive position, benefiting not only from their domestic customer base, but also from low cost structures that facilitate their global expansion. We have seen this phenomenon in the personal computer market, which is now dominated by Asian firms.

The patterns of innovation in these countries are characterized by the adaptation of products and technologies first developed in advanced countries. We still find the same games as in advanced economies, but the barriers to the entry of foreign firms skew the competition in favor of local firms, while the same local firms benefit from all product improvements developed elsewhere. Why reinvent an Internet search engine or a 911 emergency service, for example, when companies in OECD countries have already developed solutions that can be adapted to local markets? Tiger country entrepreneurs have the luxury of skipping many of the development phases of a product, having only to adapt the dominant design to the specificities of their local market. This appetite for innovative product ideas explains the openness of these countries to foreign investors and to joint ventures.

The adaption of technologies and products used in the more advanced economies to the specifics of these lower-income markets can lead to major innovations. The medical tourism industry that has sprung up in Southeast Asia is not based only on lower labour costs. Rather, Indian and Thai health entrepreneurs have developed major innovations in surgery, resulting in significant gains in efficiency, which are likely to be adopted in the West. The low-cost people car that Tata Motors has developed for the Indian market will eventually make its way to richer markets. A General Electric Indian subsidiary has developed a $1,000 electrocardiogram unit that we will soon see in North America and Europe, competing with the $15,000 machines used in OECD countries. Indeed, General Electric has developed specific strategies to encourage product innovation in China and India, with the ultimate purpose of exporting to Europe and North America lower-cost versions of products currently used in these markets.[5] Developing new solutions to known problems, based on a different trade-off between features and cost, could turn out to be a major source of innovations in developing economies.

Japan went through such a phase in the 1950s and 1960s, resulting in the development of strong industries, particularly in electronics and automobiles, that produced goods reflecting the trade-offs of Japanese consumers. The resulting products were more than low-cost solutions: by also integrating Japanese concerns over quality and reliability, these Japanese innovators developed significant comparative advantages that allowed them to export their electronic products and their automobiles throughout the world. A similar path of evolution may be observed for today's tiger economies.

Innovation in Mature Markets

Mature markets, which account for 90% of the GDP in advanced economies, are characterized by saturated primary demand, repeated purchasing by experienced customers, and relatively stable products. But competition fuels a continuous need for differentiation. Innovating thus becomes a strategic investment. Three reasons push firms in mature markets to innovate, regardless of the game they play.

First, they try to differentiate their products through such tactics as new features, better design, market segmentation, and brand identification, dampening the impact of price competition. Whether they are manufacturers of bolts or car rental services or Proctor & Gamble, businesses tinker constantly with their offerings and continually launch 'New and Improved' products and services. Even the most mature markets provide opportunities for differentiation and improvements.

Second, ambitious entrepreneurs, CEOs, or managers innovate in the pursuit of a vision. Although innovation may involve a business rationale, its main driver is ambition. The competitive spirit drives most innovations, from the five-blade razor to the tallest building in the world or the safest car on the road.

Third, businesses innovate to boost profits. They strive to increase the returns on existing activities. Productivity-enhancing innovations are common in any business where shareholders demand superior performance. For most senior executives, compensation packages depend on the alignment of their interests with those of the shareholders. 'Sweating the assets' through continuous improvements in processes and business methods has become incorporated within the operational practices of businesses. Such pressures generate a lot of small-scale innovations, widely dispersed throughout the economy.

Major technological waves also generate continuous opportunities for innovation in mature markets. Currently, advances in information and communication technologies support widespread innovation. ICT-related improvements are being incorporated into the production systems of all advanced economies, allowing better controls, tighter specification, better fit, superior monitoring, and reduced administrative costs. A classic example is Wal-Mart's RetailLinks, which not only improves Wal-Mart's offerings by reducing the frequency of out-of-stock items, but also significantly reduces replenishment costs, a key requirement to support its low price strategy. These improvements show up in national productivity statistics.

Inert Markets

But innovation is not pursued with the same intensity throughout the economy. Some mature markets, such as salt mines and blueberry farms, may be thought of as being technology somnolent. But even such markets have made major productivity gains in the past 50 years through innovation in process and in the quality of the product.

There are, however, inert markets, where little innovation occurs. We find them in markets with monopolies and organizations shielded from customer or shareholder pressures or both. Government bureaucracies often fit that description. Government regulations even extend such conditions to several sectors at their periphery where para-governmental organizations dominate. In Canada, about 25% of the GDP is produced by government bureaucracies and by para-governmental organizations that get most of their funding from governments and are subjected to Treasury Board rules. Most of them are shielded from competition and thus immunized against customers' discontent. In a government's mindset, competition is duplication.

Governmental organizations lag on innovation because they operate in environments that do not have as a priority the constant search for a better way of doing things. They are governed by rules that reflect the dual concern of efficiency and fair treatment of everyone they deal with. Tinkering with these rules to experiment with improvements is frowned upon. Moreover, the consequences of failure are very different within the public sector and the private sector. In the later case, the entrepreneurs just fade away, licking their wounds in private. In the public sector, the media and the political opposition will seize on any sign that suggests a failure or even a hiccup and use it to generate political gain. Given that the innovation process is full of trial and error, it is a high-risk route for governments. As a result, the incentive to innovate in government is mostly defensive, targeting innovations that can reduce the risk of criticism. This risk-adverse attitude affects an increasingly large portion of modern economies.[6]

Luckily for them, government bureaucracies and para-governmental organizations benefit from the innovations of others, as those innovations get diffused. Innovative capital goods are continually integrated in government activities as part of their normal procurement. The same applies to government agencies and state-owned monopolies. Most of their innovations come from the outside: governed-by-rules monopolistic bureaucracies have difficulties in initiating changes in their own processes. The conditions that create a dynamics of innovation are seldom present in their environment. As monopolies, they do not face competitors, who would try to pry their customers away with a better product or service. They also do not answer to shareholders, who would demand constantly increasing returns as a condition of their support. The inertness of monopolistic state and state-controlled organizations probably explains the failure of socialist economies to match the performance of market economies. But we see the same failure in any government-run organization.

What Is Measured Gets Done

There are no simple ways of measuring innovation. But innovative companies have found ways to focus their organization on innovating, to make it a priority. Various statistics are compiled: percentage of sales represented by new products, annual reduction in costs, and so on. Attention is given to the product development pipeline, which is carefully planned and regularly reviewed. New products are splashed about in annual reports and celebrated on home pages on the Internet. All these indicators are partial, as innovation is much more complex.

As indicators, they are not sufficient to align an organization behind the imperatives of innovation: leadership is also required.

In the long run, a strong innovation performance allows an organization not only to stay competitive regarding product and cost, but also to deliver superior products and superior profits while growing in market share. In an emerging market, successful innovation puts a business in a position to be a consolidator. In a mature market, it allows a business to slowly climb to the top in the markets where it chooses to compete.

At the national level, the extent of innovation can be measured by what economists call multi-factor productivity.[7] Productivity can be roughly defined as the quantity of inputs used to produce an output, the inputs being capital and labor. Multi-factor productivity – innovation – is the added productivity that results from a better combination of capital and labor. It is measured by subtracting the components attributed to labor and to capital from total productivity.

For various reasons, measuring multi-factor productivity accurately is quite a challenge. It relies on an objective measure of the value of specific outputs, in a way that is comparable with past measures and with the value of other goods and services. In new markets, where products are not yet standardized, the data do not exist. It can take decades before a new product is sufficiently standardized to be measured by statistical agencies. In the meantime, new products are lumped with older products. But these new products are the ones we want to measure to assess the benefits of innovation. Product improvements are also difficult to isolate, such as the real change in value brought by an improvement such as the five-blade razor. Yet the accumulation of these improvements over time can add up to significant increases in benefits and hence in real value.

Statistical agencies also do not take into account the value of free services, since these have no market value. For example, the only contribution of Google search to GDP is assumed to be the value of the advertising it sells, an arbitrary value that vastly underestimates its impact on productivity. Likewise, for statistical agencies, Wikipedia does not exist. Free services are assumed to be of no value. Moreover, based on conventional measures of productivity, the contribution to productivity of the multitude of two-sided markets that have emerged with the Internet, Facebook being the best example, is significantly underestimated.

Productivity gains associated with cost reduction or increased output of fixed assets are better measured. Yet, they give a distorted view of the contribution of innovation to economic growth, over-representing their importance compared to innovations involving product improvements or new products. These measurement difficulties lead to an underesti-mation of the contribution innovation makes to productivity. Given all these limitations, multi-factor productivity remains mostly a research tool for economists. We should be very cautious in using any multi-factor productivity statistics to diagnose the level of innovation in an economy.

Fortunately, there are other indicators of the impact of innovations. Chronicling the growth of new industries that emerge from new mar-kets is fodder for business magazines. As Andrew Grove points out, the job count does not matter much in the early years. What are more significant are the number of growing firms, the venture capital invest-ments, the IPOs and, more globally, the rags-to-riches stories.

Industrial development is a major outcome associated with innova-tion. Emerging markets lead to a flurry of new start-ups, most clustered in specific regions. Some will turn into large firms, altering the indus-trial landscape in the process. Over time, these new industries consoli-date through a series of mergers and acquisitions. The number of actual companies falls, but most of the production units of the merged entities stay in place.

Regional economies can greatly benefit from the clustering process in emerging markets. As new industrial clusters mature, the geography of industrialization changes. The economic landscape of the United States reflects this phenomenon: Silicon Valley and the computer industries in the past 30 years, Houston's petrochemical industry in the 1950s, Detroit's automobile industry in the 1920s, Pittsburgh's steel industry at the turn of the 20th century, and New England's textile industry in the early 19th century.[8] Over time, new markets remain the principal drivers of the evolution of the industrial landscape and, regionally, a major channel of the benefits of innovation.

As Andrew Grove noted, the link between job creation and innova-tion is complex, and definitely not direct. Significant job creation occurs in only one phase of the development of a market, the fast-growth phase as the industry emerges. Prior to that phase, the new industry is small and job creation is limited. Once companies have scaled up and the market has matured, the production capacity is set up. From then on, there will likely be more job losses through productivity gains than job creation through expansion of production, although job displace-ments and consolidations are possible. In a mature industry, innovation is directed primarily at improving productivity and does not contribute much to job creation.

The scale-up phase, a period of five to ten years, generates a significant number of jobs, both directly and indirectly, when production is ramped up to meet rapidly growing demand. The most visible jobs are in manufacturing, and increasingly these tend to be outsourced to low-cost countries, a trend that Grove deplores. Manufacturing employment in the US computer industry, for example, has actually declined since the introduction of the personal computer in the mid-1970s. But the scale-up phase has a lot more impact on the job market than just direct manufacturing employment. The hardware outsourced to Asian manufacturers, for example, represents only 33% of the price of an iPhone.[9] The rest of the value added occurs mostly in North America in the form of design, management, distribution, and service activities, all job related. Profits must also be taken into account, as they accrue to shareholders in the form of wealth, which is spent or reinvested. Two-thirds of the value of the product thus translates into domestic income, which seeps through the economy in the form of salaries and profits. Silicon Valley may not have created as many fabrication jobs for the computer industry as Andy Grove would like, but it has created a significant amount of wealth in the form of higher income. It is also associated with wealth creation throughout the rest of the world, where ever-improving computers at ever-lower prices create further value for millions of users.

As a rule of thumb, industries that outsource their manufacturing activities still generate between half and two-thirds of the sale value of their products in their domestic market in the form of salaries, taxes, and income on the capital used. Naturally, that percentage becomes much higher when companies do not outsource their production. Most open systems involved in Battles of Architecture fall into this category, sharing their revenues between the platform orchestrators, the third-party developers, and the telcos that distribute these platforms on their infrastructures. On the whole, the industries that support emerging markets are contributing their share to the economy. But in the overall scheme of things, emerging industries represent only a small share of GDP, and their impact is somewhat highly diluted in the overall economy.

In the Long Run ...

The path-breaking analysis of Edward Denison some 50 years ago pointed to the major contribution of technical progress to economic growth in advanced economies, roughly in the same proportion as labor and as capital. His broad conclusion has held up since then. Assuming a long-term growth rate of OECD economies of 3%, then labor can account for 1%, capital for 1%, and innovation the other 1%.[10] Although we can quibble about the exact value – it will vary from one country to another – this 1% estimate is a good baseline for the contribution of innovation to annual growth of output in advanced economies on a long-term basis – capturing the ability of modern economies to absorb new knowledge in the production realm.

The games-of-innovation framework tells us about where the 1% originates. About one-third of it comes from emerging markets, where innovations are bountiful and products evolve rapidly. Successful business strategies in these emerging markets are structured around bringing a constant stream of innovations to the marketplace. The other two-thirds of economic growth due to innovation comes from mature markets, in the form of improved products, improved production processes, and improved business models. The sheer size of their footprint in the economy, about 90% of GDP, explains the significant aggregate contribution they make to innovation and GDP growth. This should be food for thought for public policy makers, as most 'national innovation strategies' focus on the growth sectors of the economy and on the 'new' economy. Attention to new sectors can be justified on numerous grounds. But the fact of the matter is that two-thirds of innovation-induced growth of GDP occurs in mature sectors. These sectors deserve more attention, as they will always provide the primary sources of productivity growth in an advanced economy. The public policy challenge in mature markets is to make innovation a central element of business strategies, as many other imperatives vie for consideration.

It should also be pointed out that the 1% annual growth attributed to innovation is not contributed solely by innovators at the vanguard of change. As we mentioned, the actual contribution of an innovation to economic growth is achieved through its diffusion. The game-of-innovation framework focuses on businesses that drive innovation by being first with improved products, improved costs, and better business models. They create the competitive pressures that force laggards to join the fray. So it is fair to attribute the whole impact of innovation to these innovative firms, as they are responsible for getting their entire industry to move ahead.

In rapidly developing countries such as China, India, and Brazil, where demand conditions are quite supportive of market expansion, technological progress represents a lot more than 1% per year. The 6% to 10% annual growth rates observed in these countries is evidently supported by a significant increase in labor and by major investments in productive capacities. But it is driven largely by massive 'First in the market' games of innovation, as local emulators adapt product and process ideas from more advanced markets to the economic conditions of their own region. Competition between innovators drives growth, although these races are constrained more by the management of growth and the expansion of markets than by the development of superior solutions, as those are available from the more advanced economies.

The Paradox of Innovation

Governments are routinely presented with two contrasting views of the 'innovation economy,' each with its own set of demands for government support. On the one hand, there is the Schumpeter I model, structured around great discoveries, technological breakthroughs, entrepreneurs, and a multiplication of start-ups. This model has enormous political appeal. It is associated with the rapid development of great businesses such as Apple, Microsoft, Google, Research in Motion, and Nokia, which have succeeded in marshalling the powerful capabilities of the rapidly developing information and computer technologies, and are now among the most valued businesses in the world. Inspired by their example, governments are asked to support basic research, provide tax breaks for R&D and for venture capital, and award exclusive bidding rights on government contracts to local champions. They are also assailed with proposals built around cluster strategies, university–business partnerships, and demonstration projects.

Such proposals do not show the other side of the Schumpeter I story, which is difficult to toss aside. A lot of effort is focused on the first years of emerging markets, before the industry grows rapidly and becomes structured. Emerging markets built around ICT may grow rapidly, but they still represent a very small share of the economy. Moreover, as many governments have found out, investing billions of dollars in basic research does not guarantee results in the country, in terms of job creation and new companies. Finally, governments should be reminded that no country has ever duplicated Silicon Valley, where many of these fast-growing ICT-based markets began.

The other view presented to governments is the Schumpeter II vision, promoted mostly by large businesses and universities. These organizations argue that they can generate the innovations that will shape the future of the country. They demand tax breaks for their large R&D programs, form consortiums with universities to develop multi-million-dollar partnership proposals to be funded by government to address national priorities, and ask that large-scale defence and public infrastructure contracts be reserved to domestic companies. They also support limiting spectrum auctions for mobile radio on national security grounds. They demand more generous export financing programs, and in return they commit to supporting domestic suppliers with generous subcontracts. They demand a stronger patent regime, with less litigation, and they want fewer regulations and lower taxes.

This classic Schumpeter II vision of economic growth and innovation is structured around large businesses with sufficient means and market clout. Their innovative activities are routinized, as part of their day-to-day conduct of business. Rigorous financial analysis guides innovation investments. They argue that real innovation demands proper structures, well-defined R&D programs, and international marketing alliances. Because they have these competencies, they should be recognized as the natural drivers of a national system of innovation.

The paradox is that both the Schumpeter I and the Schumpeter II vision are somewhat correct, although there is still much missing. They both describe important aspects of innovation. The Schumpeter II vision applies to mature industries and to businesses that are in the consolidation phase of emerging markets after finally achieving significant growth. Such businesses are important innovators, mostly because of their sheer size, but also because they have to innovate on a continuous basis to grow. One problem with their vision is the nature of the demands they make on public policy, typically subsidization of R&D and protection of their markets. But from a public policy perspective, the best way to get businesses in mature markets to innovate more is to ensure that they have a lot of innovation-based competition. All the rest is secondary.

The entrepreneurs who promote the Schumpeter I model are also correct in their vision. The economy of tomorrow must pass through the funnel of discovery. In their first years, new markets are dominated by nimble innovators who start their own firms and shoot for the moon. They need all the assistance they can get in the rough-and-tumble environment of new markets. In the budding stage, there is no such thing as too much money. Any financial assistance will be of great help to most start-ups. But what they need most is smart people, young graduates well trained in leading-edge technology and marketing wizards with extended networks of contacts. Venture-capital investors who can act as good mentors also are of great help.

The challenge of governments is to harmonize both views coherently, add what is missing, and develop effective public policies that take into account the strengths and weakness of a country, as opposed to clientelist responses. They can lean toward the Schumpeter I view, which emphasizes new markets at their budding stages. The United States is quite good in dealing with emerging markets. California is still the mecca for the new economy, and its dynamism still outclasses any other high-tech region in the world. Yet as we write this book in the summer of 2011, California's unemployment rate stands at 11%, higher than all but one of the 50 states of the American union. Succeeding in the 'new economy' does not ensure an overall good economic performance.

Others countries do quite well economically without being particularly proficient in emerging markets. Industrious Germany and well-planned Norway are not known for their start-ups or for their strong presence in new industries. Neither is Switzerland nor France. But these countries are doing quite well with their mature industries. They have to be solid innovators to get the performance they obtain. On a per capita basis, Switzerland, Netherlands, France, and Britain are all better represented than the United States on a per capita basis among the Fortune Global 500 companies.[11] How does 'Old Europe' manage to keep up with North America while doing so poorly in the new economy?

Could it be that Old Europe is better at innovation in mature industries? Have you noticed how good their telephone systems are, for example, compared to ours? And their trains? And their cars? They are clearly less proficient at nurturing start-ups in emerging markets. We presume that European companies get into these markets later on, when winners and losers are sorted out in the consolidation phase, either through M&A activities or through the licensing of technologies. Whatever route they are taking, they do manage to find ways to get into these new industries, or they would not stand out so prominently among the Fortune Global 500.

A division of labor between Schumpeter I and Schumpeter II innovation approaches may exist between countries and regions within countries, reflecting their comparative advantages and business cultures. More globally, North America seems to do better in the chaotic and effervescent emerging markets, at least in the early years, whereas the business culture of Europe and Japan seems more attuned to the management of innovation in mature industries.

But regardless of a country's ability to develop a presence in new markets, governments must ensure that the mature sectors of their economy, which generate the bulk of GDP, operate in an environment conducive to innovation. The games-of-innovation framework provides a clear view of what can be done in that regard and what is likely to be inefficient. The different conditions brought by the maturity of the market and by product architecture are an important consideration to take into account.

The efficiency of public policies will vary according to which game is being played. Businesses are good at lobbying for breaks of all sorts to make their lives easier. But such clientelist policies will not necessarily make them more innovative. Furthermore, the inert sectors of any economy are more or less forgotten, although they represent a significant burden for a country's innovative capacity. The size and innovative performance of the inert sectors should be a concern. For instance, no other OECD country has a firmer grip on their health sector than Canada. As you would expect for a system run by government, it is low cost and egalitarian. But it is also one of the least innovative among OECD countries, and Canadians pay for this fact with poor service and long waiting times. The same can be said for primary and secondary education in many countries. Transforming inert sectors into more responsive ones can have a significant impact on the level of innovation in an country.

Homo innovaticus

Economics as a science bears on the allocation of scarce resources. It is still structured around a paradigm proposed by Adam Smith in the 18th century and gradually improved since then. The question it addresses is how a society can best deal with the scarcity of resources that results from needs that are never fully satisfied. A key concept is *Homo economicus*, the rational person who continually optimizes satisfaction of his or her own interest by making sound market choices. As a consequence, markets ensure an efficient allocation of resources (assuming they are properly functioning). Although members of the species *Homo economicus* always want more, they know what is best for them and act accordingly. The entrepreneurs among *Homo economicus* get more by taking risks, defying the status quo to introduce new goods and services to the marketplace. These entrepreneurs are the agents to whom economists, or at least the canon of economics assigns the challenge of bringing innovation to our society. They seem to be failing the task.

Edmund Phelps, the Nobel Laureate in Economics in 2006, suggested recently that *Homo economicus* be replaced by *Homo innovaticus*, also a rational person but one who has, to borrow from Augustine, a 'restlessness of heart,' an impulse to tinker and to do things in a different way. After all, humankind is unique among living creatures, endowed with curiosity and creativity, and 'capable of original ideas, concepts that have not been conceived before.'[12] *Homo innovaticus* believes that scarcities are bottlenecks waiting to be removed by the use of our imagination.

Homo innovaticus encompasses more than entrepreneurs. Every person has an adventurous side, leading him or her to look for better solutions and to invent some. *Homo innovaticus* could help us understand the innovation process, which materializes not only when an entrepreneur shouts Eureka!, but also throughout the economy, all along the value chain, as people and businesses seek to improve what is being offered.

The games-of-innovation approach relies on the widespread presence of *Homo innovaticus* in the economy, allowing innovation to occur in all kinds of settings, but along predictable paths determined by certain specific elements. The six-games framework identifies these patterns. It also suggests avenues that business strategies and public policies can be used to accelerate innovation and to eliminate bottlenecks.

In mature markets, innovation is a response to the pressures on organizations that choose to master their destiny by continually improving their products and reducing their costs to keep their customers and shareholders loyal and happy. High-performing organizations mobilize all their employees around the necessity of innovation. *Homo innovaticus* is also found in their ecosystem, where people have the opportunity to create better products and better services.

The ride is wilder in budding markets, where products, new and still far from optimized, can be easily improved by entrepreneurs with few resources but a lot of guts. This explains the high number of start-ups in these markets. The main challenge is not to keep existing customers happy; it is to attract new customers, who have never tried a product and are somewhat intimidated by it. Great marketers with some tinkering ability do well in these circumstances.

Homo innovaticus is also found in laboratories and research centers, alongside the Terry Chows of this world. Restless researchers are driven to find out more about the way the world works. They are discoverers of new knowledge, which is important for society. They fully deserve their Nobel prizes, as they are preparing the raw material on which the innovators will feed.

Innovation is a state of mind. There is a lot of knowledge 'out there,' offering great potential for innovations. Roger Martin, the dean of the

Rotman School of Management at the University of Toronto, and a noted scholar on innovation, makes that point in a recent column about
Steve Jobs's genius as an innovator:

> For Steve Jobs, it is difficult to find much related to Apple Inc.'s success
> that was about invention. Certainly none of the mouse, the touch screen,
> the MP3 player, the smartphone or the extra-big smartphone (i.e. tablet)
> qualifies. It is hard even to argue that Apple invented the personal com-
> puter, unless the massive parallel simultaneous invention by numerous
> hackers in the nascent Silicon Valley counts.
>
> Innovation on the other hand entails starting with users, obsessing
> about their experience, and being dedicated to creating unique improve-
> ments to it that delight them, even if they never asked for or expect them.
> Xerox PARC invented the mouse, Bill Buxton and others invented the
> touch screen, and Research In Motion Ltd. invented the smartphone; all
> inventions that Mr. Jobs cobbled together to make the Macintosh, iPod,
> iPhone and iPad. But they were cobbled together in the most magical
> ways with the user, rather than the scientist, at the centre of the picture.
>
> ... successful innovation actually means trying things that are unprov-
> en ... Apple's biggest successes derived from doing positively unprov-
> en things – like controlling a PC with a mouse, like twinning iPod with
> iTunes, like twinning iPhone with the App Store, like creating the tablet
> ... Apple had no chance of knowing that they were going to have absolute
> smash hits on their hands. That is what is required for innovation.[13]

Innovation is a pervasive process. It occurs in all sectors of the economy as new knowledge is incorporated into products, allowing them
to better satisfy needs. In emerging markets the process is intensive, as
innovators race against each other to make the most out of a discovery,
rapidly and significantly improving their products while expanding
their reach to all potential users. Innovation is less intense in the mature
sectors of the economy, but still ever-present, as competition supports
forces of change that continually improve products and processes.

The games-of-innovation framework illustrates these competitive
responses, both in emerging markets and in mature markets. This
book has attempted to convey how to be in a position to profit from the
dynamics these patterns generate.

Notes

1 The Diversity of Innovation

1 In 2004 the estimate was 14 billion euros. We projected this total to 2012. See S. Eckhouse, G. Lewison, and R. Sullivan, 'Trends in the Global Funding and Activity of Cancer Research,' *Molecular Oncology* 2 (2008): 20–32.
2 Davis Dyer, Frederick Dalzell, and Rowena Olegario, *Rising Tide: 165 Years of Brand Building at Procter & Gamble* (Boston: Harvard Business Press, 2004).
3 From an interview of Claude Jablon, Chief Innovation Officer of Total S.A., by Roger Miller in June 2004, as part of the MINE project. The archives of the project can be accessed by writing to the author at rmiller@secorgroup.com.

2 Peering into the Black Box

1 Schumpeter's original oeuvre was written in German. It was translated into English in the 1930s, with additions by Schumpeter. However, his original theory of entrepreneurship remains central in the English editions. See Schumpeter, *The Theory of Economic Development: An Inquiry into Profits, Capital, Credit, Interest, and the Business Cycle* (Cambridge, MA: Harvard University Press, 1934).
2 Adolf A. Berle and Gardiner Means, *The Modern Corporation and Private Property* (New York: Macmillan, 1932).
3 Joseph A. Schumpeter , *Capitalism, Socialism and Democracy* (New York: Harper & Brothers, 1942).
4 Robert M. Solow, 'A Contribution to the Theory of Economic Growth,' *Quarterly Journal of Economics* 70, no. 1 (1956): 65–94,DOI 10.2307/1884513.
5 Edward F. Denison, *The Sources of Economic Growth in the United States and*

the Alternatives Before Us (New York: Committee for Economic Development, 1962).

6 Alfred Chandler, *The Visible Hand: The Managerial Revolution in American Business* (Boston: Harvard University Press, 1977).

7 Roger Miller and Marcel Côté, *Growing the Next Silicon Valley* (Boston: Lexington Books, 1987). See also Peter Geoffrey Hall, *Cities in Civilization: Culture, Technology, and Urban Order* (New York: Pantheon, 1998).

8 AnnaLee Saxenian, *Regional Advantage: Culture and Competition in Silicon Valley and Route 128* (Cambridge, MA: Harvard University Press, 1994).

9 David Birch, *Job Creation in America* (New York: Free Press, 1987).

10 Clayton M. Christensen, *The Innovator's Dilemma* (New York: Harvard Business School Press, 1997).

11 Ibid., xiii.

12 The term 'radical innovation' is not used once in *The Innovator's Dilemma*.

13 Bengt-Ake Lundvall, *National Systems of Innovation: Toward a Theory of Innovation and Interactive Learning* (London: Printer Press, 1998).

14 David J. Teece, 'Profiting from Technological Innovation: Implications for Integration, Collaboration Licensing and Public Policy,' *Research Policy* 15, no. 6 (1986): 285–305.

15 Xavier Olleros, 'The Power of Non-contractual Innovation,' *International Journal of Innovation Management* 11, no. 1 (2007): 93–113.

16 Raghu Garud et al., *Managing in the Modular Age: Architectures, Networks and Organizations* (Oxford: Blackwell, 2002).

17 The pioneering work on the modularity concept was done by Richard Langlois. See Langlois and P.L. Robertson. 'Networks and Innovation in a Modular System: Lessons from the Microcomputer and Stereo Components Industries,' *Research Policy* 21, no. 4 (1992): 297–313.

18 Saxenian, *Regional Advantage*.

19 W.B. Arthur, 'Competing Technologies, Increasing Returns and Lock-In by Historical Events,' *Economic Journal* 99, no. 394 (1983): 116–31.

20 W.H. Chesbrough, *Open Innovation: Researching a New Paradigm* (Oxford: Oxford University Press, 2006).

21 Keith Pavitt, *Technology, Management and Systems of Innovation* (Cheltenham: Edward Elgar, 1999).

22 M. Porter, K. Schwab, and A. Lopez-Claros, *The Global Competitiveness Report 2007–2008* (London: Palgrave Macmillan, 2008).

23 Neelie Kroes, 'European Union Commissioner of Competition,' *New York Times*, 1 December 2009.

24 Roger Miller and Xavier Olleros. 'To Manage Innovation, Learn the Architecture,' *Research Technology Management* 51, no. 3 (2008): 17–27.

25 Christensen, *The Innovator's Dilemma*.

26 Stephen J. Kline and Nathan Rosenberg, 'An Overview of Innovation,' In *The Positive Sum Strategy: Harnessing Technology for Economic Growth*, ed. R. Landau and N. Rosenberg, 275–305 (Washington, DC: National Academy Press, 1986).

27 See for instance Barry Jaruzelski, Kevin Dehoff, and Rakesh Bordia, 'Money Isn't Everything,' *Strategy + Business* 41 (Winter 2005).

28 David Mowery and Nathan Rosenberg, *Paths of Innovation: Technological Change in 20th Century America* (Cambridge: Cambridge University Press, 1998).

29 R. Nelson and S. Winter, *An Evolutionary Theory of Economic Change* (Cambridge, MA: Harvard University Press, 1982).

30 Giovanni Dosi, 'Technological Paradigms and Technological Trajectories,' *Research Policy* 11, no. 3 (1982): 147–62.

31 Franco Malerba, 'Sectoral Systems of Innovations,' *Research Policy* 31 (2002): 247–66.

32 Michael Best, *The New Competitive Advantage: The Renewal of American Industry* (Oxford: Oxford University Press, 2001).

33 William Abernathy, *Foundational Thinking about Innovation: Selected Papers of William J. Abernathy*, ed. James M. Utterback (London: World Scientific, 2008).

34 James M. Utterback, *Mastering the Dynamics of Innnovation* (Boston: Harvard Business School Press, 1996).

35 See for instance R.M. Henderson and K.B. Clark, 'Architectural Innovation: The Reconfiguration of Existing Product Technologies and the Failure of Established Firms,' *Administrative Science Quarterly* 35 (2003): 9–30.

36 Other empirical research dealt with much smaller samples. For instance, one well-known study, by Andrew Van de Ven and his colleagues, focused on 14 innovations (Andrew Van de Ven et al., *The Innovation Journey* [Oxford: Oxford University Press, 1999]).

3 Searching for Patterns

1 Roger Miller and Serghei Floriel, 'Value Creation and Innovation Games,' *Research-Technology Management* 47 (November/December 2004): 25–37.

2 W. Chan Kim and Renée Mauborgne, *Blue Ocean Strategy* (Boston: Havard Business School Press, 2005).

3 These games are quite different from those found in game theory, which are tactical options with probabilities of success, possible reactions by adversaries, and outcome-related pay-offs.

4 Roger Miller and Donald R. Lessard, *The Strategic Management of Large Engineering Projects* (Cambridge: MIT Press, 2000).

5 A full description of the MINE project, including the list of the 50 companies on which case studies were done, can be obtained from the author at
rmiller@secorgroup.com.
6 Significance was measured at the $p = 0.01$ level.

4 The Games of Innovation

1 Gagnon, M.A., and J. Lexclin. 'The Cost of Pushing Pills: A New Estimate
of Promotion Expenditures in the US.' *Journal of Public Library of Science
Medicine*, January, 2008.
2 Annabelle Gawer and Michael A. Cusumano, *Platform Leadership* (Boston:
Harvard Business School Press, 2002).
3 'Auto Channel,' 2007, http://www.theautochannel.com.
4 http://money.cnn.com/magazines/fortune/mostadmired/2011/index.
html. P&G was fifth in 2011 and has been in the top ten since the survey
began in 2006.
5 McKinsey Global Institute, *U.S. Productivity Growth 1995–2000: Understanding the Contribution of Information Technology Relative to Other Factors*
(Washington, DC: McKinsey and Company, October 2001).
6 James P. Womack, Daniel T. Jones, and Daniel Roos, *The Machine That
Changed the World* (Boston: Rawson, 1990).
7 National Venture Capital Association, *2011 NVCA Yearbook* (Arlington:
NVCA, 2011), 23–5.
8 The Bureau of Economic Analysis, Industry Economic Accounts Data,
defines the 'information-communications-technology-producing industries' as comprising the following sectors: computer and electronic
products, publishing industries (includes software), information and data
processing services, and computer systems design and related services. In
its annual *Information Technology Outlook*, the OECD uses a broader definition, which, atop the BEA definition, adds telecommunication services,
computer wholesaling, and rental of office machinery. In 2008 this sector
as more broadly defined represented 8% of the value added by the business sector, or around 7% of the GDPs of OECD member countries, and
two-third of it were in services. However, a large percentage of this sector
as defined by the OECD consists of mature markets, such as equipment
leasing and telecommunications.
9 Matthew M. Donahoe et al., *Annual Industry Accounts: Advance Statistics on
GDP by Industry for 2009 and Revised Statistics for 1998–2008, Comprehensive
Revision* (Washington: Bureau of Economic Analysis, June 2010). The 11.3%
could underestimate the actual contribution of ICTP markets to economic

growth, as the newest markets are generally under-reported in official statistics.

10 For instance, the McKinsey Global Institute has recently done a similar estimate for the 'Internet economy.' As defined by them, the Internet economy had significant overlaps with the ICTP sector defined by the BEA, but excluded ICT activities that were not Internet related. On the other hand, they included Internet-based services, such as online shopping (Amazon, Netflix, airline tickets, etc.), which they valued at the retail price of what was purchased. That broadly defined 'Internet sector' accounted for 3.8% of the GDP of the United States. See Matthieu Pelissié du Rausas et al., *Internet Matters: The Net's Sweeping Impact on Growth, Jobs and Prosperity* (New York : McKinsey Global Institute, May 2011).

11 The 35% is obtained through the following formula: $g = [a \times 5b] + [(1 - a) \times b]$, where g is the rate of growth of the economy attributable to technological progress, a the share of GDP accounted for by the emerging sector, and b the rate of growth of the mature sectors of the economy. As we defined the emerging sectors, their growth rate is five times the growth rate of the mature ones ($5b$ in the formula). As a result, their contribution to total economic growth is equal to their share of the economy (a) multiplied by their growth rate ($= a \times 5b$). We also did some sensitivity analysis, with different growth rates and different shares of GDP for the emerging sectors, with results shown in the following table. The horizontal axis lists three assumptions for the share of GDP accounted for by emerging markets (a), namely 7%, 10%, and 15%. The left column lists assumed ratios for the rates of growth of emerging markets and mature markets, which we assume to be five times the mature growth rate in the base case, and which were varied from two times if emerging markets are broadly defined and seven times if they are narrowly defined. The percentages in the table are the share of GDP *growth* contributed by emerging markets under these various assumptions; these vary between 27.3% and 35.7%.

Share of GDP growth attributable to emerging markets

Rate of growth: Emerging/mature markets	Share of GDP contributed by emerging markets		
	7%	10%	15%
7 X	34.5%	na	na
6 X	31.0%	na	na
5 X	na	35.7%	na
4 X	na	30.0%	na
3 X	na	na	31.0%
2 X	na	na	27.3%

5 Emerging and Mature Markets

1 Marcel Côté, Yvan Allaire, and Roger Émile Miller, *IBM Canada Ltd.: A Case Study*, vol. 14 of Study: Royal Commission on Corporate Concentration (Ottawa: Royal Commission of Corporate Concentration, 1976).
2 William Abernathy and James Utterback, 'Patterns of Innovation in Industry,' *Technology Review* 80, no. 6 (1978): 40–7.
3 S.A. Alvarez and J.B. Barney, 'The Entrepreneurial Theory of the Firm,' *Journal of Management Studies* 44, no. 7 (1998): 1057–63.
4 S.A. Alvarez and J.B. Barney, 'Discovery and Creation: Alternative Theories of Entrepreneurial Actions,' *Strategic Entrepreneuship Journal* 1, nos. 1–2 (2007): 11–26.
5 George S. Day, *The Market-Driven Organization: Understanding, Attracting and Keeping Valuable Customers* (New York: Free Press, 2000);George S. Day and Paul J.H. Schoemaker, *Wharton on Managing Emerging Technologies* (New York: Wiley & Sons, 2000).
6 David J. Teece, *Dynamic Capabilities and Strategic Management: Organizing for Innovation and Growth* (New York: Oxford University Press, 2009).
7 For a framework to structure the decision to go alone, see Avinash K. Dixit and Barry J. Nalebuff, *The Art of Strategy: A Game Theorists's Guide to Success in Business and Life* (New York: W.W. Norton, 2008).
8 Michael Cusumano, *Staying Power: Six Enduring Principles for Managing Strategy and Innovation in an Uncertain World* (New York: Oxford University Press, 2010).
9 The critical step between an invention and its successful commercial introduction, which is the innovation, should not be underestimated, a point that Roger Martin, dean of the Rotman Business School at University of Toronto, has made in numerous articles and speeches.

6 Product Architecture

1 The idea that product architecture influences innovation processes is discussed in Roger Miller and al., 'Innovation in Complex Systems Industries: The Case of Flight Simulation,' *Industry Industrial and Corporate Change*, Vol. 4, no. 2 (1995): 363–400. See also C.C. Mondragon et al., 'Managing Technology for Highly Complex Critical Modular Systems: The Case of Automotive by-Wire Systems,' *International Journal of Production Economics* 118, no. 2 (2009): 473–85.
2 Some of the seminal work in that regard was done by two MIT professors, G.L. Urban and J.R. Hauser, in their *Design and Marketing of New Products*, 2d ed. (Upper Saddle River, NJ: Prentice Hall, 1993).

3 Roger Miller and Xavier Olleros, 'To Manage Innovation, Learn the Architecture,' *Research-Technology Management* 51, no. 3 (2008): 17–27; Daniel Whitney, *Mechanical Assemblies: Their Design, Manufacture and Role in Product Development* (New York: Oxford University Press, 2004).

4 See the relentless forms of innovation in Roger Miller and Xavier Olleros, 'The Dynamics of Innovation Games,' *International Journal of Innovation Management* 11, no. 1 (2007): 37–64.

5 The concept of multi-sided markets has been developed by two French economists, Jean-Charles Rochet and Jean Tirole, who have written extensively about it. See Jean-Charles Rochet and Jean Tirole, 'Platform Competition in Two-Sided Markets,' *Journal of the European Economic Association* 1 (2003): 990–1029.

6 Marco Iansiti and Roy Levien, *The Keystone Advantage* (Boston: Harvard Business School Press, 2004).

7 Andrea Prencipe, Andrew Davis, and Michael Hobday, *The Business of Systems Integration* (New York: Oxford University Press, 2003).

8 'Toyota, IBM and Dassault Establish Global Cooperation,' *The Auto Channel*, 26 March 2002, http://www.theautochannel.com.

9 Jianfeng Wang, 'Economies of IT Systems at Wal-Mart – An Historical Perspective,' *Academy of Information and Management Sciences Journal* 9, no. 1 (2006): 45–66.

10 Roger Miller and Serghei Floricel, 'Games of Innovation: A New Theoretical Perspective,' *International Journal of Innovation Management* 11, no. 1 (2007): 1–35.

7 Eureka!

1 For the history of 3M, see the book 3M published for its 100th anniversary, *A Century of Innovation: The 3M Story* (St. Paul: 3M, 2002).

2 Eureka! participants scored 5.0 on a seven-point scale whereas participants in other games scored 4.2.

3 Zoltan J. Acs and David B. Audretsch, 'Innovation in Small and Large Firms,' *American Economic Review* 78 (1988): 678–90.

4 Eureka! games received a score of 5.05 out of 7 on the pace-of-change dimension, compared with an average of less than 4.0 for the other games.

5 Roger Miller and Marcel Côté, *Growing the Next Silicon Valley* (Boston: Lexington Books, 1987).

6 Roger Miller and Marcel Côté, 'Growing the Next Silicon Valley,' *Harvard Business Review* 63, no. 4 (1985): 114–23.

7 Annalee Saxenian, *Regional Advantage: Culture and Competition in Silicon Valley and Route 128* (Cambridge: Harvard University Press, 1994).

8 The Special Case of the Pharmaceutical Sector

1 The cost of developing new drugs is the object of significant disagreement, with estimates for average cost ranging from a few hundred millions dollars to several billions. A number of methodological disputes about assumptions underly these divergences. For instance, some estimates take into account the cost of capital locked in for over ten years. There are also disagreements on the marketing investment required to launch a new drugs. For the two sides of the controversy, see J. DiMasi, R. Hansen, and H. Grabowski, 'The Price of Innovation: New Estimates of Drug Development Costs,' *Journal of Health Economics* 22, no. 2 (2003): 151–85, and C.P. Adams and V.V. Brantner, 'Spending on New Drug Development,' *Journal of Health Economics* 19, no. 2 (2010): 130–41.

2 Gary P. Pisano, *Science Business: The Promise, The Reality and The Future* (Boston: Harvard Business School Press, 2006).

3 Ben Hirschler and Kate Kelland, *Big Pharma, Small R&D* (A Reuters Special Report), Reuters News, 2010, reuters.com/resources/media/editorial/20100621/Big_Pharma.pdf.

4 *Biotech 2011 Life Sciences: Looking Back to See Ahead* (San Francisco: Burrill & Company, 2011), 343.

5 Bruce L. Booth and Bryan Salehezadeh, 'In Defense of Life Science Venture Investing,' *Nature Biotechnology* 29, no. 7 (July 2011): 579–84.

9 Battles of Architecture

1 Danah M. Boyd and Nicole B. Ellison, 'Social Network Sites: Definition, History, and Scholarship,' *Journal of Computer-Mediated Communication* 13, no. 1 (2007), article 11, doi: 10.1111/j.1083-6101.2007.00393.x, http://jcmc.indiana.edu/vol13/issue1/boyd.ellison.html.

2 Spencer Reiss, 'His Space,' *Wired* 14, no. 7 (July 2006), http: wired.com/wired/archive/14.07/murdoch.html. See also Felix Gillette, 'The Rise and Inglorious Fall of Myspace,' *Bloomberg Business Week*, 22 June 2011.

3 See, for instance, a December 2007 article on Stanford students' success in developing third-party applications, in All Facebook, a site that specializes in Facebook news: www.allfacebook.com/stanford-facebook-class-produces-impressive-results-2007-12.

4 *Wall Street Journal*, 30 June 2011, http://online.wsj.com.

5 David S. Evans, Andrei Haigu, and Richard Schmalenses, *Invisible Engines: How Software Platforms Drive Innovation and Transform Industries* (Cambridge, MA: MIT Press, 2006).

6 Walter Isaacson, *Steve Jobs: A Biography* (New York: Simon & Schuster, 2011), chaps. 29, 30.

7 Thomas Ricker, 'Jobs: App Store Launching with 500 iPhone Applications, 5% free,' *Endgadget*, posted 10 July 2008, http://www.engadget.com/2008/07/10/jobs-app-store-launching-with-500-iphone-applications-25-free/. For financial results, see Apple 10-Q, Quarterly Financial Statements, First Quarter 2011.

8 Xavier Olleros, 'The Lean Core in Digital Platforms,' paper presented at the Druid Summer Conference, Copenhagen, 2006.

9 Brian Arthur, *The Nature of Technology; What It Is and How It Evolves* (New York: Free Press, 2009).

10 Dominique Foray, *Economics of Innovation* (Lausanne: Ecole Polytechnique Fédérale de Lausanne, 2010–2011).

11 Paul David, *A Contribution to the Theory of Diffusion*, Research Center in Economic Growth Memorandum no. 71, Stanford University, Palo Alto, 1969.

12 Robert Grant, *Contemporary Strategic Analysis*, 7th ed. (New York, John Wiley, 2009).

13 Joseph Farrell and Paul Klemperer, 'Coordination and Lock-In: Competition with Switching Costs and Network Effects, in Handbook of Industrial Organizations,' ed. M. Armstrong and R. Porter, vol. 3 (London: Elsevier, 2007), 1970–94.

14 H.W. Chesbrough, *Open Innovation: The New Imperative for Creating and Profiting from Technology* (Boston: Harvard Business School Press, 2003).

15 Eric S. Raymond, *The Cathedral and the Bazaar: Musings on Linux and Open Source by an Accidental Revolutionary* (Sebastopol, CA: O'Reilly Media, 2001).

16 US Patent 59660411, issued in September 1999.

17 Pascal Corbel and Christian LeBas, 'The Evolution of Patent Functions: New Trends, Main Challenges and Implications for Firm Strategy,' Groupe d'analyse et de théorie économique Lyon - St Étienne, working paper, February 2011 (www.gate.cnrs.fr); See also Adam B. Jaffe and Josh Lerner, *Innovation and Its Discontents: How Our Broken Patent System is Endangering Innovation and Progress, and What to Do About It* (Princeton: Princeton University Press, 2006).

18 *The Wall Street Journal*, 8 August 2011, http://online.wsj.com/itp.

19 William J. Mitchell, Christopher E. Borroni-Bird, and Lawrence D. Burns, *Reinventing the Automobile: Personal Urban Mobility for the 21st Century* (Cambridge, MA: MIT Press, 2010).

10 System Breakthrough Games: High-Technology Craft

1 There are numerous references to this meeting in the business literature, but also a lot of scepticism over whether it actually happened. What is known for sure was that in 1957, IBM proposed to American Airlines a

reservation technology based on the SAGE system developed for the US Air Force.

2 Students of large technical systems will recognize the influence of Thomas P. Hughes. See W.E. Bijker, T.P. Hughes, and T.J. Pinch, *The Social Construction of Technological Systems* (Cambridge, MA: MIT Press, 1987).

3 See www.xprize.org.

4 The Deutsch de la Meurthe prize, which is documented in Wipipedia, was worth 100,000 francs, about $300,000 in today's money, for the first person who piloted a flying machine on an 11-kilometer pre-set course within 30 minutes. It was awarded in 1902. See also www.flightglobal.com/pdfarchive/view/1909/1909%20-%200021.html for reports on the prizes awarded in 1908–9.

5 See www.grandchallenges.org.

6 For the latest estimates, see Dominic Gates, 'Boeing Celebrates 787 Delivery as Program's Costs Top 32 Billion,' *Seattle Times*, 24 Sept 2011. The initial estimate of $8 billion was never formally acknowledged by Boeing, but was frequently mentioned in magazines and blogs at the time of the program launch in 2005–6.

7 The importance of customers scores highest in the MINE survey, with 5.7 out of 7. On *t*-test, this score is not only statistically significant, but also statistically different from the scores of other games on that question.

8 For a review of the field of systems integration, see Benjamin S. Blanchard and Wolter J. Fabrycky, *Systems Engineering and Analysis* (Upper Saddle River, NJ: Prentice Hall, 1998).

9 For an in-depth study of the industry adoption of computerized flight simulation, see Roger Miller and Xavier Olleros, 'An Enduring System of Innovation: The Case of Flight Simulation,' paper presented at the Annual Conference of the American Institute of Aeronautics and Astronautics, Monterey, CA, 1993.

10 For additional analysis, see Roger Miller and Michael Hobday, 'Innovation in Complex System Industries: The Case of Flight Simulation,' *Industrial and Corporate Change* 4 (1995): 363–400; and Michael Kamel, 'Training Pilots,' doctoral diss., École Polytechnique, Montreal, 2009.

11 See, for instance, Michael Hobday, Andrew Davies, and Andrea Prencipe, 'Systems Integration: A Core Capability of the Modern Corporation,' *Industrial and Corporate Change* 14, no. 6 (2005): 1109–43.

11 New and Improved

1 'Fuck Everything, We're Doing Five Blades,' *The Onion* 40, no. 7 (18 Febru-

ary 2007), http://www.theonion.com/articles/fuck-everything-were-doing-five-blades,11056/.. issue 40-07.

2 The market estimate comes from a circular to shareholders the Gillette Company sent in 2005, when it was taken over by Procter & Gamble.

3 *Consumer Reports* 76, no. 6 (June 2011): 8.

4 *Fortune* website, ranking the most admired corporations on innovation. P&G was ranked seventh in 2007 and fourth in 2006. See http://money.cnn.com/magazines/fortune/rankings/?iid=F_Sub.

5 For an extension of the Stage-Gate model to new products, see Robert G. Cooper, *Winning at New Product Development* (Reading, MA: Addison Wesley, 1993). See also Glen Urban and John Hauser, *Design and Marketing of New Products*, 2nd ed. (Upper Saddle River, NJ: Prentice Hall, 1993).

6 Thomas Pyzdek and Paul A. Keller, *The Six Sigma Handbook* (New York: McGraw-Hill, 2009).

7 James M. Morgan and Jeffrey K. Liker, *The Toyota Product Development Systems: Integrating People, Process, and Technology* (New York: Productivity Press, 2006).

8 Nigel Bradley. *Marketing Research: Tools and Techniques* (Oxford: Oxford University Press, 2007).

9 Mark W. Johnson, 'The Role of the Chief Innovation Officer,' *Bloomberg Business Week*, 10 November 2010.

10 Larry Huston and Nabil Sakkab, 'Connect and Develop: Inside Procter & Gamble's New Model for Innovation,' *Harvard Business Review* 84, no. 3 (2006): 58–66.

11 Henry Chesbrough, *Open Innovation: The New Imperative for Creating and Profiting from Technology* (Boston: Harvard Business School Press, 2006).

12 Eric Von Hippel, *Democratizing Innovation* (Cambridge, Mass.MIT Press, 2005).

13 For more information see Mvsolutions.com, innocentive.com, and Ninesigma.com.

14 James P. Andrew et al., *Measuring Innovation 2008: Squandered Opportunities* (Boston: Boston Consulting Group, August 2008), 44–50. The topic remains on the list of biggest problems cited annually by R&D leaders; see R.R. Cosner, 'Industrial Research Institute's R&D Trends Forecast for 2009,' *Research-Technology Management* 52, no. 1 (2009): 19–26.

15 J.W. Tipping, E. Zeffren, and A.R. Fusfeld, 'Assessing the Value of Your Technology,' *Research-Technology Management* 38, no. 5 (1995): 22–39. See also Lawrence Schwartz et al., 'Measuring the Effectiveness of R&D,' *Research-Technology Management* 54, no. 5 (2011): 29–36.

12 Mass Customization

1 John Kenneth Galbraith, *The New Industrial State* (Boston: Houghton Mifflin, 1967).
2 A surprising discovery that GM made in Fremont was that Toyota did away with the defect and repair areas usually set up in American plants to inspect and correct minor flaws in cars coming off the production line. Japanese cars were expected to be defect free as they came off the production line.
3 James P. Womack, Daniel T. Jones, and Daniel Roos, *The Machine That Changed the World:The Story of Lean Production* (New York: Maxwell MacMillan International, 1990).
4 Davis Stanley, *Future Perfect* (Reading MA: Addison Wesly, 1996).
5 US Patent no. 1,242,872 (1917).
6 Ian P. McCarthy, 'Special Issue Editorial: The What, Why and How of Mass Customization,' *Production Planning & Control* 15, no. 4 (June 2004): 347–51.
7 The number of products varies by type of store. See www.walmartstores.com/pressroom/statebystate.
8 J. Wind and A. Ramaswamy, 'Customerization: The Next Revolution in Mass Customization,' *Journal of Interactive Marketing* 15, no. 1 (2001): 13–32.
9 Michael H. Moffett and William Youngdahl, 'Jose Ignacio Lopez de Arriortua,' Thunderbird case study A02-98-0003, Thunderbird School of Global Business, Glendale, AZ, 1998.

13 Pushing the Envelope

1 For an analysis of large-scale projects, see Roger Miller and Donald Lessard, *The Strategic Management of Large Engineering Projects* (Cambridge, MA: MIT Press, 2000). Although this work does not focus on innovative projects, the authors review best practices thoroughly.
2 *L'autoroute Paris-Poitier*, case study in the International Program in the Management of Engineering and Construction, École des Sciences de la gestion, Université du Québec à Montreal, 2001.
3 See www.hm-treasury.gov.uk.
4 Kroger did the same, in another area of the industry, by teaming up with Dunnhumby, a British consulting firm, to design a leading-edge customer relationship management system. Indeed, when Sobeys wanted to hire a CRM expert to help them set up a similar system, they did not have access to Dunnhumby, the clear leader in the field.
5 Roger Miller and Brian Hobbs, 'The Complexity of Decision-Making in Large Projects.' In *Making Essential Choices with Scant Information: Front-End*

Decision-Making in Major Projects, ed. Terry M. Williams, Knut Samset, and Kjell Sunnevåg (Basingstoke, UK: Palgrave, 2009).

6 Miller and Lessard, *Strategic Management of Large Engineering Projects* (Cambridge, MA: MIT Press, 2001).

7 Herbert A. Simon, 'From Substantive to Procedural Rationality,' Carnegie Mellon University Library, Pittsburgh, 24 September 1973, http://octopus.library.cmu.edu/cgi-bin/tiff2pdf/simon/box00081/fld06519/bdl0004/doc0002/simon.pdf.

8 Eighteen per cent of consultants' time is allocated to keeping abreast, participating in innovative activities, or building capabilities: Roger Miller and Marcel Côté, MINE Survey, École Polytechnique, Montreal, 2008.

9 Michel Langlois, Senior VP Engineering, Cisco, Mountain View, California, interview with Roger Miller, September 2009.

10 For a review, see Andreas Engen Ole, 'The Development of the Norwegian Petroleum Innovation System: A Historical Review,' TIK Working Papers on Innovation Studies, University of Oslo, 2007, no. 20070605.

11 'The Development of the Njord Field by Norsk Hydro: A Case Study,' IMEC Research Program, Université du Québec à Montréal, 2001.

12 NORSOK is a collaborative project linking government, oil companies, and suppliers to replace the old regime of contracting with cost-efficient routines and procedure. See Ole Andreas Engen, 'Rhetoric and Realities: The NORSOK Program,' unpublished paper, University of Bergen, Norway, 1997.

13 Roger Miller, 'Clients as Innovation Drivers in Large Engineering Projects,' in Peter S. Brandon and Shu-Ling Lu, eds., *Clients Driving Innovation* (London: Wiley-Blackwell, 2008), 278.

14 First proposed in the 1960s by Gordon E. Moore, a co-founder of Intel, Moore's Law states that transistor densities in integrated circuit chips double every two years. The 'law' has held for over forty years.

15 William H. Dutton et al., ed., *Transforming Enterprise: The Economic and Social Implications of Information* (Cambridge, MA: MIT Press, 2004).

16 John Zysman et al., 'The Digital Transformation of Services: From Economic Sinkholes to Productivity Drivers,' Berkeley Roundtable on International Economy, Working Paper 187, 6 April 2010.

17 Andrew McAfee and Erik Brynjolfsson, 'Investing in the IT That Makes a Competitive Difference,' *Harvard Business Review* 86 (July/August 2008).

14 Transitions

1 Daniel M.G. Raff and Manuel Trajtenberg, 'Quality-Adjusted Prices for the American Automobile Industry: 1906–1940,' in *The Economics of New Goods,*

ed.Timothy F. Bresnahan and Robert J. Gordon, 71–108 (Chicago: University of Chicago Press, 1996). See also James J. Flink *The Automobile Age* (Cambridge, MA: MIT Press, 1988).

2 William Abernathy and James P. Utterback, 'Patterns of Industrial Innovation,' *Technology Review* 80, no. 7 (June–July 1978): 40–7.

3 The notion of Modular Production Network was developed by Timothy J. Sturgeon at the MIT Center for Industrial Performance: see his 'Modular Production Network: A New American Mode of Industrial Organisation,' *Industrial and Corporate Change* 11, no. 3 (June 2002): 451–96.

4 Clayton M. Christensen, *The Innovator's Dilemma: When New Technologies Cause Great Firms to Fail* (Boston: Harvard Business School Press, 1997).

5 Richard Foster, *Innovation: The Attacker's Advantage* (New York: Summit Book, 1986); James M. Utterback, *Mastering the Dynamics of Innovation* (Boston: Harvard Business School Press, 1994).

6 Clayton M. Christensen and Michael E. Raynor, *The Innovator's Solution: Creating and Sustaining Successful Growth* (Boston: Harvard Business School Press, 2003). In this book, written with management consultant Michael Raynor, Christensen points out that approaching the issues from the standpoint of a disruptive innovation rather than from that of a disruptive technology provides a much better explanation of what occurs in markets.

7 Pew Research Center, 'The State of News Media 2011,' 2011, www.pewresearch.org.

8 http://www.google.com/adplanner/static/top100countries/cn.html, March 2011.

9 http://www.ebizmba.com/articles/news-websites, March 2011.

10 Marcel Côté, Yvan Allaire, and Roger-Émile Miller, *IBM Canada Ltd: A Case Study, Study no. 14* (Ottawa: Royal Commission on Corporate Concentration, 1978).

11 Louis V. Gerstner, *Who Says Elephants Can't Dance?: Inside IBM's Historic Turnaround* (New York: Harper Business Press, 2002).

15 Winning Strategies

1 Our consulting firm, Secor, was involved with the telcos and cable companies in Canada. All large consulting firms had telecom practices, easily collectively raking in a few hundred million a years in consulting fees, mostly about what to do to profit from the Internet boom. There were also numerous consulting firms specializing in the telecom industry, also doing mostly Internet-related work.

2 Barry Jaruzelski, John Loehr, and Richard Holman, 'The Global Innovation 1000: Why Culture Is Key,' *Strategy + Business* 65 (Winter 2011), 2.

3 There is an abundant literature on open innovation, which has now become as much a movement as an approach. For the book that started it, see Henry Chesbrough, *Open Innovation: The New Imperative for Creating and Profiting from Technology* (Boston: Harvard Business School Press, 2003).

4 Secor has worked extensively with SNC-Lavalin, a large Canadian engineering-and-construction firm that is a principal in several multi-billion dollars PPP projects. French and Spanish construction companies are also very active in this market.

16 Public Policies

1 This statement introduces the OECD's Innovation and Technology policy on its website (www.oecd.org/topic/0,3699,en_2649_34273_1_1_1_1_37417,00. html).

2 OECD, *The OECD Innovation Strategy: Getting a Head Start on Tomorrow* (Paris: OECD Publishing, 2010).

3 OECD, *Main Science and Technology Indicators (MSTI)*, vol. 2010/2, Summary Table (Paris: OECD, 2010).

4 Richard Florida, *The Role of the University: Leveraging Talent, not Technology* (Dallas: Science and Technology Policy Research, Summer 1999), 67–73.

5 OECD, *Main Science and Technology Indicators*, vol. 2010/2 (Paris: OECD, 2011).

6 Peter Nicholson, a Canadian authority on innovation and the former president of the Canada's Council of Academies, a leading think-tank at the nexus of science, technology, and economics, has also been closely associated with this position for several years, arguing that universities' main contribution to innovation is through their educational mission.The point is also made repeatedly by Richard Florida. See in particular Florida, *The Role of the University*.

7 Roland Andersson, John M. Quigley, and Mats Wilhelmsson, 'Urbanization, Productivity, and Innovation: Evidence from Investment in Higher Education,' *Journal of Urban Economics* 66, no. 1 (July 2009): 2–15, DOI 10.1016/j.jue.2009.02.004. Surprisingly, the impact of graduate students taking jobs in the local economy is a phenomenon that has been scantily researched by economists and urban specialists.

8 This rationale is presented in a 2007 study by the Canadian government's Department of Finance, which concluded that the social return in terms of additional GDP exceeded the program costs. This internal study is reported in *Innovation Canada: A Call to Action*, Report of the Independent Panel on Federal Support to Research and Development (Ottawa: Government of Canada, 2011), 6–7.

9 That led the government to appoint another panel, to look at all programs supporting R&D in Canada, and which recommended not only major changes in the tax credit program but a redirection of some of its funding to demand driven-type programs. See *Innovation Canada*, chap. 6.

10 This point was also demonstrated statistically by Booz & Company in their 2005 report: see Barry Jaruzelski, Kevin Dahoff, and Rakesh Bordia, 'Money Isn't Everything,' *Strategy + Business* 41 (Winter 2006).

11 OECD, *Demand Side Innovation Policies* (Paris: OECD, May 2011).

12 OECD, *The OECD Innovation Strategy: Getting a Head Start on Tomorrow* (Paris: OECD, 2010), 15.

13 Michael Porter is probably the best-known economist associated with clustering as an economic phenomenon. For recent views of his positions, see Mercedes Delgado, Michael E. Porter, and Scott Stern, *Clusters, Convergence, and Economic Performance*, US Census Bureau Center for Economic Studies Paper No. CES-WP- 10-34, SSRN, 2011; andMercedes Delgado, Michael E. Porter, and Scott Stern, *Clusters and Entrepreneurship*, US Census Bureau Center for Economic Studies Paper No. CES-WP-10-31, SSRN, 2011.

14 David J. Denis, 'Entrepreneurial Finance: An Overview of the Issues and Evidence,' *Journal of Corporate Finance* 10, no. 2 (March 2004): 301–26.

15 Iain M. Cockburn, 'Is the Pharmaceutical Industry in a Productivity Crisis?' in *Innovation Policy and the Economy*, ed. Josh Lerner and Scott Stern, vol. 7 in NBER series Innovation Policy and the Economy, 1–32 (Cambridge, MA: MIT Press, 2007).

16 Fumikazu Kitagawa, *Growing beyond Galapagosization: A Strategy for Approaching Markets Utilizing Japanese Business Expertise*, Nomura Research Institute, NRI Paper no. 146, September 2009.

17 Adam B. Jaffe and Josh Lerner, *Innovation and Its Discontents: How Our Broken Patent System is Endangering Innovation and Progress, and What to Do About It* (Princeton: Princeton University Press, 2006).

18 The agency was created as ARPA (Advanced Research Projects Agency) but a year later added the initial 'Defence' to its name, creating DARPA. Over the years its name has shifted between DARPA and ARPA; currently, it DARPA. More information about the agency is available from www.darpa.mil.

19 The Bayh-Dole Act, passed by Congress in 1980.

20 Richard Florida, *The Breakthrough Illusion: Corporate America's Failure to Move from Innovation to Mass Production* (New York: Basic Books, 1990).

21 The Expert Panel on Innovation, *Innovation and Business Strategy: Why Canada Falls Short* (Ottawa: Council of Canadian Academies, 2009), 201–10.

17 Rethinking Innovation

1 Said of him when he was presented with the first Heinz Award in Technology, the Economy and Employment by the Heinz Family Foundation in 1993; see www.heinzawards.net/recipients/andrew-grove.

2 Andy Grove, 'How America Can Create Jobs,' *Bloomberg Businessweek*, 5 July 2010.

3 Peter Nicholson, 'Quadrants Of Innovation: A Conceptual Framework For Policy,' presentation to How Next Happens: Building Our Economy through Incremental Innovation, Toronto, 25 May 2011.

4 Nancy Feig, 'Mobile Payments: Look to Korea,' *Bank System & Technology*, 25 June 2007, www.banktech.com/blog/archives/2007/06/mobile_payments.html.

5 Jeffrey R. Immelt, Vijkay Govindaragan, and Chris Trimble, 'How GE Is Disrupting Itself,' *Havard Business Review* (October 2009).

6 Lawson Huter and Peter Nicholson, 'An Innovation Agenda for the Public Sector,' in *The Canada We Want in 2020: Towards a Strategic Policy Roadmap for the Federal Government* (Ottawa: Canada 2020, November 2011), 10–19.

7 The Expert Panel on Business Innovation, *Innovation and Business Strategy: Why Canada Falls Short* (Ottawa: Council of Canadian Academies, 2010).

8 For a good analysis of the impact of these Schumpeterian waves on urban development, see Peter Geoffrey Hall, *Cities in Civilization: Culture, Technology, and Urban Order* (New York: Pantheon, 1998).

9 Assuming a US iPhone price of $500 FOB, Xing and Detert estimate that Apple's gross margin is $321, which is almost all US expenditures. On the other hand, of the $179 cost of goods, only $11 is a US cost. This implies a US share of total price of about $332, or two-thirds of the FOB price. An additional US cost not included is the distributor margins, paid to the resellers of the iPhone. See Yuqing Xing and Neal C. Detert, *How the iPhone Widens the United States Trade Deficit with the People's Republic of China* (Manila: Asian Development Bank Institute, December 2010).

10 During the 1999–2007 period, the average annual growth rate for the OECD countries was 2.6% (OECD.StatExtracts, OECD total, PPP, constant US dollars, 1999–2007: OECD Library, 2011). The years 2008 and 2009 are excluded from the calculation, as abnormal years. During the same period, the OECD labor force grew at an average of 0.8% per year. Assuming a 0.2% annual improvement in labor quality would yield an actual 1% annual growth in labor force.

11 Switzerland has the highest number of companies per capita, at 19 per 10

million inhabitants, followed by Netherlands (7.7), France and Japan (5.3 each), the UK (4.8), the United States (4.2), and Germany (3.6): *Fortune* 164, no. 2 (25 July 2011), 161–73

12 Edmund Phelps, 'Economic Justice and the Spirit of Innovation,' *First Things* no. 196 (October 2009): 27–31.

13 Roger Martin, 'Canada, like Steve Jobs, Should Zero In on Innovation,' *Globe & Mail* (Toronto ed.), 20 November 2011.

Subject Index

system integrator 140, 148

Tata Motors 263
tax credits 243
Teece, D.J. 278, 282
telcos 42, 133, 209
3M 55, 95, 98, 105, 283
Tide 8–9
Tipping, J.W. 287
Tirole, J. 283
Total 9–10
Toyota 52, 55, 89, 161, 167
Trajtenberg, M. 289
transitions 199
trolls, patent 104, 128
TV broadcasting 206
Twitter 85

universities 238; graduates of 241–2
Urban, G.L. 282, 287
Utterback, J.M. 29, 205, 282, 279, 290

Van de Ven, A. 279
Vélib' 119
venture capital 57, 102, 113–14, 245
VHS 25
Visa 118
Von Hippel, E. 287

Walkman 77–9
Wal-Mart 24, 52, 55, 84, 87, 90, 171, 175, 177, 179, 231
Wang, J. 283
Whole Food 175
Wikipedia 26
Wilhelmsson, M. 291
Wind, J. 288
Winter, S. 29, 279
Witron 189
Womack, J.P. 280, 288
Woolworth 170

Xerox 65, 221

Youngdahl, W. 288
YouTube 121

Zantac 200
Zara 174, 227
Zeffren, E. 287
ZFT 144–8
Zinga 132
Zipcar 119
Zuckerberg, M. 117, 132, 233
Zysman, J. 289